The Art of Educational Evaluation
A Personal View

The Art of Educational Evaluation
A Personal View

Elliot W. Eisner

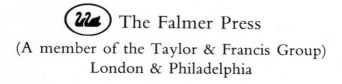

The Falmer Press

(A member of the Taylor & Francis Group)
London & Philadelphia

UK	The Falmer Press, Falmer House, Barcombe, Lewes, East Sussex, BN8 5DL
USA	The Falmer Press, Taylor & Francis Inc., 242 Cherry Street, Philadelphia, PA 19106-1906

First published 1985

W 29910 /14 95. 2·86

Library of Congress Cataloging in Publication Data

Eisner, Elliot W.
   The art of educational evaluation.

   Includes bibliographical references and index.
   1. Educational tests and measurements—United States.
2. Educational surveys—United States.   3. Curriculum
planning—United States.   4 Arts—Study and teaching—
United States.   I. Title.
LB3051.E45   1984° 371.2′6   84-8008
ISBN 0-905273-62-1
ISBN 0-905273-61-3 (pbk.)

Typeset in 11/13 Bembo by
Imago Publishing Ltd, Thame, Oxon

Jacket design by Leonard Williams

*Printed in Great Britain by Taylor & Francis (Printers) Ltd,
Basingstoke*

Contents

Acknowledgements

The Publishers are grateful to the following for permission to reproduce copyright material:

School Review   Vol. 75, No. 1, 1967, Franklin Bobbitt and the Science of Curriculum Construction
Vol. 75, No. 4, 1967, Educational Objectives: Help or Hindrance
Vol. 80, No. 4, 1972, Emerging Models for Educational Evaluation

Rand McNally and Company 'Instructional and Expressive Objectives: Their Formulation and Use in Curriculum' in *Instructional Objectives* Popham J. et al) AERA Monograph Series on Curriculum Evaluation, 1969.

Journal of Aesthetic Education Bicentennial Issue 1976, Education and Connoisseurship and Educational Criticism.

Teachers' College Record Vol. 78, No. 3, 1977, On the use of Educational Connoisseurship and Educational Criticism for Evaluating Classroom Life

Educational Leadership Vol. 35, No. 6, 1978, The Impoverished Mind

Journal of Curriculum Studies Vol. 10, No. 3, Humanistic Trends in Curriculum

Journal of Educational Evaluation and Policy Analysis Vol. 1, No. 6, 1979, The Use of Qualitative Forms of Evaluation for Improving Educational Practice

California Journal of Teacher Education Vol. 8, No. 1, 1981, The 'Methodology' of Educational Connoisseurship and Educational Criticism

Educational Researcher Vol. 10, No. 4, 1981, On the Difference Between Artistic and Scientific Approaches to Qualitative Research

Phi Delta Kappan Vol. 63, No. 1, 1981, The Role of the Arts in Cognition and Curriculum. Vol. 65, No. 7, 1984, Can Educational Research Inform Educational Practice?

Paper and Reports, Series No. 53, Northwest Regional Educational Laboratory, Portland Oregon, 1981 Conceiving and Representing: Their Implications for Educational Evaluation

Foreword

At the turn of the century William James published his classic *Talks to Teachers on Psychology* and in it wrote:

> I say moreover that you make a great, a very great mistake, if you think that psychology, being the science of the mind's laws, is something from which you can deduce definite programmes and schedules and methods of instruction for immediate schoolroom use. Psychology is a science, and teaching is an art: and sciences never generate arts directly out of themselves. An intermediary inventive mind must make the application, by using its originality.

It is with inventiveness and originality that Elliot Eisner in more than a quarter of a century of dedicated teaching and lucid writing has shown how raw has been much educational psychology, how much in need of tempering it has been. With wit and sensitivity, and drawing on an encyclopaedic knowledge in art and poetry and literature he has given educational psychology and educational measurement a human face.

But this has been only part of his remarkable academic career. The other part has been in Art Education, researching its nature, purpose and content. His writings have become standard texts wherever the education of teachers of art is to be found, in Europe as well as in the United States.

These two sides of Elliot Eisner's work combine in this personal collection of his papers on educational evaluation to produce a blend of imaginative challenges to the view of education *as a science* and lucid expositions of education *as a human endeavour*. It is educational qualities that Eisner argues should be revealed through the processes of evaluation not simply performance against objective standards as if no issues of value, human and moral, were entailed.

These papers will not be Elliot Eisner's last words. His openness to experience will see to this as will his restless explorations of the nature and meaning of man's aesthetic experience.

It will, I know, not be seen amiss by him, that his work echoes the early insight of a considerable American psychologist and philosopher, William James. It should be a source of pride to him that his work has kept open a window on an ideal: that of ensuring that education remains an endless quest not a foregone conclusion.

Philip Taylor
University of Birmingham
England
June 1984

Introduction

The articles that constitute this book reflect a personal, autobiographical view of educational evaluation. The ideas I have developed over the years about curriculum, teaching, and especially educational evaluation are rooted in my interest in the role of the arts in human expression and in the contributions they make to human understanding. What you will find in these articles is, in a sense, iconoclastic. It regards teaching at its best as an art and educational evaluation as a process that can profitably employ the methods and perspectives of those who appraise the work of artists. I make no apology for my iconoclasticism. On the contrary, to my mind the field of education in the United States and in those nations that try to emulate it, has not searched widely enough for methods of inquiry that will serve education well. We have tried, at least since the turn of the century, to develop a science of education and to employ in practice a technological system that reflects the most efficient methods of industry. The procedures that have been developed have not been a rousing success. The directions our efforts have taken are understandable. One can obtain a real sense of intellectual security from doing work that appears to be scientifically grounded, that has all of the features of a replicable, quantitative, measurement oriented system. If only such a system could be developed we would have a reliable knowledge base that could be used to guide practice. We could say to the tax paying public with a certain degree of confidence and pride that we could achieve the aims they expect, and we could hold our heads high among our peers in academe because we, too, would have, at last, a solid rock on which to stand.

Frankly, the aim of developing a foolproof method of teaching, program planning, or evaluating thrills me not. I receive no pleasure from the prospect of a closed, yet effective system. I suspect the reason for my reaction is because I take great pleasure in the journey. I welcome ambiguity and uncertainty and because I believe that, the quality of inquiry is as least as important as arriving at the church on time.

But even if such preferences are dismissed as the perverse tastes of a middle aged academic, there are other reasons for rejecting a view that has as its aim the discovery of a more or less foolproof system for doing anything significant in education. That reason deals with the nature of the enterprise.

We who work in and study education are engaged in a field that has 'no nature'. By that I mean that the ways in which a child learns or a teacher teaches or an educator evaluates may be other than the way they are. There are an infinite number of ways to teach, to learn, and to evaluate. Furthermore, the ways that are effective in some contexts may be ineffective in others. Even 'the same' context is not the same over time. Generalizations in education are tentative in a way that H_2O is not. What one needs therefore to deal with educational questions are not certain or near certain answers or foolproof methods, but a sensitivity to context, an appreciation for nuance, a set of skills that one can use with both virtuosity and flexibility, and a variety of intellectual frameworks that allows one to see the situation from different perspectives. What truly is useful are conceptual frameworks that enable one to raise fresh questions and to interpret what one sees with the kind of qualification that the situation warrants.

Such a conception of the 'nature' of educational problems is antithetical to the aspirations and procedures that have pervaded educational thought in America since the turn of the century. Our most salient and most respected views have been technological and industrial in character. There was a time not so long ago when we were looking for 'the one best method'[1] for teaching reading, or mathematics, or writing. There was a time not so long ago when we hoped to create a teacher-proof curriculum.[2] There was a time when we patiently awaited an educational break-through of the kind that gave us radar, penicillin, and the laser beam. And there was a time – about eighty years ago, but which has returned in the guise of time on task – when the movements of teachers in their classrooms were measured with a stop-watch in order to make them more efficient.[3] While we no longer clock teachers, we do measure students' academic engaged time. As a 'can do' society we very much would like to maximize our efficiency and what better way than to create a technology that was capable of doing this.

One technology that was developed, and in some ways the most

2

successful, was the technology of testing. The first efforts to develop mental tests scientifically were found in the work of Galton in England[4] in the 1870s and later in Binet's work in France[5] in the 1900s. But the major advance in testing in America occurred when the Alpha and Beta Tests were developed at the beginning of the First World War.[6] Designed by American psychologists to enable the Army to select officer candidates from the large pool of enlisted men that had been recuited and to help identify those men who could not read, the Army Alpha and Beta became a kind of demonstration of the power of social science to solve practical problems.

The tack taken to devise these tests had a significant and enduring influence on educational evaluation in the schools. First, tests became *the* vehicle through which evaluation was to occur. In the minds of thousands of teachers and millions of students, to evaluate meant to test. Second, the major aim of the Alpha and Beta approach to test construction was to sort out people, to select the most able from the less able, to identify the extent to which men could read. The model that was used was a statistical one: the bell shaped curve became the expected distribution for human performance and the reliability of the tests themselves was predicated on a variance of scores that approximated the normal distribution. This meant that test items that almost all students answered correctly, as well as those that were missed by almost all were eliminated from the final version of the tests since those test items did not contribute to the test's statistical reliability. Third, those forms of human performance that were difficult to test were frequently omitted from the test battery that eventually was created. If a behaviour, skill or a form of knowledge could not be reliably tested according to statistical criteria, that behaviour, skill, and knowledge would be dropped from the test. The consequences of such an approach to educational evaluation were and are substantial. One of the most important of these consequences was that curriculum priorities were shaped by what those who made tests were able to measure rather than through educational deliberation, or by appealing to a philosophy of education. This is not, incidentally, to suggest that this way of formulating educational priorities was formalized and publicly articulated. No educator I ever encountered has said to me that tests define all that he or she believed important. Nevertheless, operationally, tests have driven the curriculum. The scores that they yield provide a comparatively unambiguous criterion that purportedly relates to what is educationally important. These scores are given public visibility in the United States by being published in the newspapers, often in rank order for grade and school within a local education authority. These published test scores seldom enjoy the benefits of interpretation. In addition, because the tests that are used to assess achievement in schools are produced by technically competent test developers and carry the aura of authority and because they are used nationally, the norms derived are national norms, encouraging comparisons not only within, but across districts and regions.

A further consequence of using tests to determine what has been learned in school has to do with the form of representation that tests employ. By 'form of representation' I mean the device or devices humans use to convey what they have come to know.[7] Tests tend to rely upon numbers to do this. Number is a conventional device that is employed to convey quantity and to describe relationships among empirical and non-empirical 'matters'. Numbers are extraordinarily useful. When we want to know how much carpeting we will need to cover a floor, I can think of no better device to use than number. Yet number is not equally useful for everything. If we want to convey something about the distinctive features of a student's work, descriptive prose is likely to be much more informative. If we want to relate the way in which a teacher manages his or her classroom, a literary narrative might be even better than descriptive prose. Not only do statistical criteria limit what test makers believe they can legitimately include, the manner through which information is provided also constrains – just as it makes possible – the kind of information that can be conveyed. We have not reflected much in education about the significance of the forms of representation we use on what we know and what we believe.

For all of the foregoing reasons the way in which we have conceptualized educational evaluation has impeded our understanding of both the consequences and the processes of schooling. Evaluation has, I reiterate, been regarded as analogous to testing. It has defined educational priorities in the curriculum by virtue of the public status test scores have received. It has limited our understanding of the processes of educational practice by its neglect of the conditions that account for the outcomes that have been measured. It has neglected large areas of important educational outcomes by employing forms of representation that cannot describe certain significant features of a student's work. And it has encouraged teachers to focus upon teaching bits and pieces of information because of the ways in which tests have been constructed.

It takes little reflection to recognize that evaluation is a term far broader than testing. Evaluation deals with appraising the value of some object, enterprise, or activity. Evaluation is ineluctably value-oriented. Without a conception of virtue, one cannot evaluate anything. One can measure, one can test, but one cannot evaluate. If I measure the length of the room in which I am now sitting, I describe it quantitatively. I am not evaluating it. If I give a student a test of handwriting, I prepare a device or situation that will elicit from that student a response in which I am interested. I may be interested in the way in which the student shapes his letters, but interest does not mean that I am obliged to make value judgments about what I discover. I might simply want to describe or classify what I see.

Just as clearly one can evaluate without measuring or testing. When we go to see a film, we typically evaluate its quality both during and after the time we are in the theatre. We do not measure the film and we certainly don't give it a test. The film is there to be seen and if we have the price of admission, we can see it and, more often than not, make some judgments about its quality.

Evaluation is ubiquitous in our lives and is a critical part of any responsible educational enterprise. The reason this is so is straightforward. Education is a normative enterprise: we seek virtue, not mere change. Educational evaluation is a process that, in part, helps us determine whether what we do in schools is contributing to the achievement of virtuous ends or whether it is antithetical to those ends. That there are many versions of virtue is undoubtedly true. It is one of the factors that makes education more complex than medicine. Except for a slight variability, 98.6 degrees is a normal temperature in Iceland as well as in Brazil. The educational situation is different. Even within a particular culture, community, or neighbourhood there is comparatively wide variability with respect to the educational values that are regarded as important. This makes educational evaluation a difficult and complex task, yet in the end some values must be advanced, some judgments must be made about the quality of what has or is taking place. Unless this is done we have no way of knowing whether we are educating or mis-educating.

I indicated, perhaps too briefly, that educational evaluation was only partly concerned with the outcomes of teaching. There can be no question that the outcomes of teaching – when they can be known – are of central importance. But what creates or contributes to such outcomes are just as important. If we are to be in a position more effectively to achieve the values we cherish, the factors that create or contribute to those outcomes need to be identified. If we want to understand why we get what we get from our schools, we need to pay attention not simply to the score, but to the ways in which the game is played. The process of educational practice is the *sine qua non* of education. How does teaching proceed? What kinds of relationships are established in class? What is the level of engagement of the students being taught? How about the curriculum? What is its quality? Are the ideas and skills being taught important ones? Are the students being helped to see the relationships between what they are studying in school and the problems they encounter outside of the school? What relationships are drawn across the subjects students study? Are the various content areas isolated entities or are students encouraged to learn how, for example, science and history relate to each other? What muted (or not so muted) messages do teachers give to students about the importance of learning what they are teaching? Are those messages ones that emphasize the consummatory or intrinsic aspects of inquiry or do they emphasize the getting of good grades and the passing of up-and-coming tests?

To neglect such aspects of school practice is to miss much of what is of central importance in schools. Educational evaluation *as an educational enterprise* has the processes of classroom life as a major focus. Such attention requires more than an anthropological intent. Anthropologists typically wish not only to appear invisible within the cultures they study, they have no professional mission to change what they find. Margaret Mead was not interested in improving Samoan life.[8] As distressful as the life of the Ik appeared to Colin Turnbull, he had no interest whatsoever in making things better.[9] Clifford Geertz studied cock fights in Balanese culture but was not at all moved to improve the way in which this ritual took place.[10] His interest, as is true of virtually all anthropologists, is not to improve but to understand. Such luxuries are not the lot of educational evaluators. Again, education is a normative enterprise. By normative I mean value-oriented. We study a situation, a student, a set of products not simply to understand them but to help improve them or to understand how they got the way they are so that we will be better able to work with others like them. Such commitments are a far cry from those of the so-called value-free social scientist who wishes to appear interested only in analysis and explication. The biochemist seeks to explain. The physician seeks to heal. It is in the latter sense that education is a calling. Teachers have a mission.

Embedded in the foregoing is the argument that the subject matters of educational evaluation are not simply those defined by what tests test. Nor are they simply the outcomes of our efforts as teachers.

To borrow an acronym from Dan Stufflebeam, our interest is the evaluation of what he called CIPP: Context, Input, Process, and Product.[11] Stufflebeam's terminology is not as felicitous as I would like, but his focus is on the mark. We are, or ought to be, concerned with the context in which teaching and learning take place, with the quality of the input or curriculum to which students have access, and in the pedagogical processes employed by the teacher as students and teacher interact. Finally, we are interested in the product, or more aptly the outcomes of the foregoing. A full blown effort to evaluate a school or classroom will in some way attend to all of these dimensions.

The manner in which such attention is provided is what this book focuses upon. The major philosophical orientation to evaluation in education has been rooted in the social sciences. The social sciences have important utilities, but deserve no monopoly on how evaluators work. My aim, not only in this book but in my work in general, is to help articulate the ways in which artistic and humanistic approaches to evaluation might be pursued. *Any* framework, *any* form of representation, and *any* methodology has limited parameters. Once it is granted that the modes of knowing and the forms through which what one knows is represented are multiple, it makes no sense to restrict inquiry to a single form. Bias in one's observations and conclusions is a function of not only what is inadvertently put in, but what is inadvertently left out. If we leave out of our considerations and reports what our vehicle cannot contain, we provide a limited, indeed a distorted perspective. To fish for trout in a stream using bait designed to catch salmon and to conclude from our failed efforts that no trout are there, is to draw what might very well be an erroneous conclusion. Our nets define what we shall catch.[12] If there is one message I would like to convey in this book it is the desirability of weaving many types of nets. We need not be fettered by tradition. And, as a matter of fact, tradition is changing. The range of professionally legitimate ways to conduct educational evaluation, and even to talk about teaching, has over the past decade expanded significantly. Simply reflect on the work of Phillip Jackson,[13] Sara Lightfoot,[14] Maxine Greene,[15] Elizabeth Vallance,[16] Gail McCutcheon,[17] Tom Barone,[18] George Willis,[19] Madeline Grumet,[20] Rob Walker,[21] Robert Stake[22] – the list could go on.

I said in the first sentence of this introduction that the articles that constitute this book are autobiographical in character. My earliest interests as a boy were in the visual arts. I later studied painting, was a painter, and later still a commercial artist. But more than my engagement in the art of making visual images was the kind of experience that such work provided. The experience that I had as a painter and, I must confess, as a lover of art made it possible for me to think about education, and teaching, and evaluation in terms that were not derived exclusively from the social sciences, the fields in which I was trained at the University of Chicago. There are two dimensions that are central for an artistic perspective on anything to be achieved. One dimension deals with the way in which things are attended to. In typical modes of seeing classification, recognition, the assignment of names to qualities is the standard task. We see a tree and call it an oak. We see a person and recognize her as our neighbour. We look at a classroom and conclude that the students are engaged in their work. We observe a teacher and determine that she is lecturing. The observation of particulars is used as an instrumentality for classification and labelling. When these tasks are completed, and they are often completed in micro-seconds, we move on to another event, person, or object.

Artistic perception is not focused primarily on recognition and labelling, it is concerned with exploring the characteristics that constitute the complex array of qualities that we encounter. How are those qualities patterned? What do they convey? Which are most dominant among them? When such questions are raised they are in the service of more experience. What artistic perception is after is more perception and the sense of life that it generates. Categories, labels, frameworks are sometimes used, but they are used as tools with which to deepen and broaden our experience. In the social sciences qualities are typically used to generate categories. In artistic perception we want to read the qualities that characterize a particular student's work. We want to experience the pervasive qualities of *this* classroom, *this* school, *this* teacher. The extent to which such experience will be secured is related to the categories we have in our heads, our interests at the time, and the extent to which those antennae called the senses have been refined. When they are and when we see what others miss, we are regarded as perceptive. When we can manipulate the images we have encountered in our mind's eye to explore and play with alternatives that cannot be encountered in the empirical world, we are called imaginative. The outer eye gives us the world, the inner eye gives us possibilities to pursue.

The metaphor of inner and outer eye should not be taken too literally. We 'see' with more than our eyes: our ears help us see, as do our nose, our sense of touch, and so forth. The smell of stale milk and chalk dust ineluctably informs us that we are in an elementary school classroom. The cadence and tone of a teacher's voice speaks reams about how that teacher feels about what is going on.

Perception of the qualitative events that surround us is but one part of the task of artistically oriented work in education. A second dimension and equally as important is the character of the form that is created by the percipient to disclose what he or she has experienced.

Artistic expression is defined by the way in which the forms used to carry a message are treated. In conventional modes of expression, elements within a system are used according to a set of codified rules. What the message conveys is both made possible and constrained by the rules to which the elements adhere. The stricter the discipline, the less scope there is for violating these rules or for misinterpreting the meaning of the elements. Simple arithmetic is a classic case in point. The meaning of an arithmetic statement is defined by the terms of the system. Neither the formulation of the statement nor its interpretation is subject to the tastes of individuals. In artistic forms meanings are shaped by the way in which the form is made. A literary description and a non-literary description of a situation differ because of the manner in which the language describing the situation has been crafted: form is part of the content. In the arts, form is intentionally crafted to constitute that content.

When science is an art, as it is in the context of discovery[23] and in those cases when theoretical formulations are themselves aesthetic, we undergo experience akin to art. A new theory has an elegance that thrills us, a fresh interpretation of an old, time-worn set of circumstances awakens our interest and sheds new light on an old problem. In such circumstances science has an artistic or aesthetic character. The scientist like the artist is a maker of forms, one of the important differences resides in the qualities with which each works. The work of the scientist is carried by symbols that typically are at one level removed from the phenomena of interest. We use the symbol to travel somewhere else. The artist works directly with qualities and conveys meaning by the way in which those qualities are themselves formed.[24]

For educational evaluation this means that the form of the qualities we use: the particular words we select, the sentences we construct, the cadence, tempo, tone, and tenor of our language is a primary means for conveying what our (hopefully) refined sensibilities have revealed to us. We have the task – ubiquitous in human experience – of creating an equivalent in the public world for the ideas and feelings we have construed in the private world.[25] And because each form that we are able to employ to accomplish this magical feat enables us to convey unique aspects of what we have experienced, each form of representation makes a unique contribution to our grasp of the world. The expansion of our expressive repertoire, when complemented by refined sensibilities, is an achievement of signal importance in our efforts to improve education.

The articles in this book represent not only an autobiographical statement with respect to my deep interest in the arts, they are autobiographical in another sense as well. They represent roads that I have travelled to date. Some of what I have had to say, brought together in one volume, will undoubtedly be redundant. New notions do not emerge with every writing. Common schematic notions are, I suppose, necessary if one has to have some degree of coherence and continuity in one's life. In any case, I regard these articles as markers along the way, signposts that remind me of where I have been. They are not surely, and have never been regarded by me as 'definitive statements'. I do not know what a definitive statement is.

I make this last statement to encourage readers to regard my work as 'work in progress'. I am not yet finished as a person and have no expectation that my work should be. What I produce is stuff for your consideration – let's call it a stimulus for thought. If it does provide such stimulation, I shall be content. If you find that you can use the ideas I have explored to improve the quality of education, I shall be delighted.

Elliot W. Eisner
Stanford University
May 1984

Notes

1. TYACK, D. (1974) *The One Best System*, Cambridge, Massachusetts: Harvard University Press.
2. The concept of 'teacher proof curriculum', was much discussed during the height of the curriculum reform movement in the United States during the 1960s. That aspiration, I am happy to say, is no longer salient in education circles.
3. For the discussion of the efficiency movement in education see CALLAHAN, R. (1964) *Education and the Cult of Efficiency*, Chicago: The University of Chicago Press.
4. CREMIN, L.A. (1961) *The Transformation of the School*, New York: Vintage Books, p. 186.

5. *Ibid.*
6. *Ibid.*, p. 187.
7. The Concept 'Form of Representation' is discussed in detail in EISNER, E.W. (1982) *Cognition and Curriculum: A Basis for Deciding What to Teach*, New York: Longman, Inc.
8. MEAD, M. (1928) *Coming of Age in Samoa*, New York: Blue Ribbon Books.
9. TURNBULL, C.M. (1972) *The Mountain People*, New York: Simon & Schuster.
10. GEERTZ, C. (1973) *The Interpretation of Culture: Selected Essays*, New York: Basic Books.
11. STUFFLEBEAM, D. *et al.* (1971), *Educational Practice and Decision Making*, Itasca, Ill.: Peacock Publishers.
12. I borrow this notion from Karl Popper who, in *The Logic of Scientific Discovery* writes 'Theories are nets, he who casts will catch'.
13. JACKSON, P. (1968) *Life in Classrooms*, New York: Holt, Rinehart and Winston.
14. LIGHTFOOT, S. (1983) *The Good High School*, New York: Basic Books.
15. GREENE, M. (1973) *Teacher as Stranger: Educational Philosophy for the Modern Age*, Belmont, Calif.: Wadsworth Publishing Company.
16. VALLANCE, E. (1980) 'The hidden curriculum and qualitative inquiry as states of mind', *Journal of Education*, vol. 162, No. 1, Winter.
17. MCCUTCHEON, G. (1981) 'On the interpretation of classroom observations', *Educational Researcher*, vol. 10, No. 5, May.
18. BARONE, T. (1983) 'Things of use and things of beauty: the swain County Michigan School Arts Program', *Daedalus*, vol. 112, No. 3, Summer.
19. WILLIS, G. (1978) *Qualitative Evaluation: Concepts and Cases in Curriculum Criticism*. Berkeley, Calif.: McCutchan Pub. Corp.
20. GRUMET, M. (1983) 'The line is drawn', *Educational Leadership*, vol. 40, No. 4, January.
21. WALKER, R. and ADELMAN, C. (1975) *A Guide to Classroom Observation*, London: Methuen and Co. Ltd.
22. STAKE, R. (Ed.), (1975) *Evaluating the Arts in Education: A Responsive Approach*, Columbus, Ohio: Merrill.
23. See KARL POPPER, *op. cit. The Logic of Scientific Discovery*.
24. The preceding views have been substantially informed by DEWEY, J. (1934) *Art As Experience*, New York: Minton, Balch & Company.
25. EISNER, E.W. *op. cit.*

1 Franklin Bobbitt and the 'Science' of Curriculum Making[1]

The 1920s were a fruitful decade in American education. The scientific study of education had survived its infancy; the survey movement was well into its adolescence. Thorndike and Judd had, through their work, established themselves as leaders in scientific education; the innovations and methods which were initiated twenty years earlier were beginning to bear fruit.

Yet despite the growing abundance of new tools and methods, few people were ready or willing to take on what is perhaps the most complex educational task of all, the systematic and scientific development of curriculum. Dewey's *The Child and the Curriculum*,[2] published in 1902, was a philosophical statement, persuasive and insightful to be sure, but was not easily translatable into practical terms. Kilpatrick's *The Project Method*[3] dealt with a piece of the curriculum problem but left out much that the practical schoolman wanted and needed to reconstruct curriculums. While a few men, such as Frederick Bonser,[4] W.W. Charters,[5] and David Snedden,[6] had made important beginnings in applying scientific principles to solve curriculum problems, for the most part the task of constructing curriculums was a mixture of practical know-how and tradition. The goal of developing a scientific *system* of curriculum construction was yet to come. Charles H. Judd describes the state of affairs in 1922 this way:

> Not only is the problem of curriculum-construction inherently baffling, but there are few individuals, and practically no recognized agency, in school systems that make this problem a special subject of attention. There is plenty of social machinery to check up a course after it is once launched. The principal of a school, the district superintendent, the college inspector, or the examining board, are all at hand to decide whether the class is

doing well in the course. Suppose, however, that by some exercise of wisdom we had reached the conclusion that the subject ought to be thoroughly overhauled. Whom would we expect to do the overhauling? Would the principal regard it as his task? Or the superintendent, or the inspector?

The question arises: Can a substitute for initiative be found in some kind of systematic procedure that will bring to the door of the school new ideas as fast as these ideas are produced? Can we find some way, other than the brilliant inspiration of the reformer, to break into the complaisant routine of the schools? In answer to such questions one can project a plan of organized revision which shall lead to an annual overhauling of the curriculum. The mere suggestion of such a plan serves perhaps better than any extended argument to show how far we are at the present moment from any study of the problem and certainly from any solution.

It is hoped that the net impression produced by the discussion will be one of conviction that there is here a broad field for the exercise of scientific ingenuity. While the testing movement and certain other lines of scientific work in education are becoming so highly routinized that they fail at times to stimulate workers to original and constructive efforts, the re-making of the curriculum with its manifold problems and possibilities seems to offer unbounded and inviting opportunities for the exercise of all the genius that educational workers can contribute.[7]

The ideas of social efficiency, scientific management, experimentalist theory, and psychological measurement were a part of the educational context of the day. The beginnings of scientific inquiry in education had already been made, and piecemeal investigations had done much to generate debate and controversy. But the systematic general formulation of methods of curriculum construction had hardly been approached.

Franklin Bobbitt was one of those dedicated to the construction of a science of education and, more than most, concerned himself with the application of scientific principles to the practical problems of schooling. *How To Make a Curriculum*,[8] published in 1924, is an effort to demonstrate how such principles could be used intelligently to go about the task of curriculum building; indeed much of the book's material was derived from the curriculum work that Bobbitt guided for the schools in Los Angeles, California. As a consultant to the Los Angeles school system, Bobbitt was asked to assume responsibility for developing and supervizing the construction of the curriculum of the junior high school, and although his employers recognized that 'Dr. Bobbitt does not figure as a specialist in the junior high school realm ... the underlying principles of curriculum making are universal and should apply fairly well to any consecutive group of grades.'[9]

Thus it was that Bobbitt set out to operationalize as best he could some of the principles he had laid down six years earlier in his book, *The Curriculum*.[10] What were those principles? How were they employed empirically? On what educational assumptions did they rest?

Bobbitt seemed quite aware of the fact that in order to speak intelligently about as complex a problem as the construction of the curriculum, useful distinctions would need to be framed – and this he did. Distinctions between the play and work aspects of education, between antecedent and objective performance, between the general and the vocational curriculum were only a few that he employed in *The Curriculum*. These distinctions he used and elaborated upon in *How To Make a Curriculum*.

How To Make a Curriculum contains nineteen chapters which can be divided into three general sections. The first section deals with the generic problems of curriculum construction, such as the rationale to be employed, the procedures to be used in formulating educational objectives, and the criteria and characteristics of pupil activities. The second section consists of exemplary educational objectives and curriculum experiences in a variety of subject areas of life domains. The third section of the book presents suggestions for administrators and others in supervisory positions.

For Bobbitt the solution to educational problems could most efficiently be obtained if the procedures of science could be employed, and this he believed was possible. Although he reiterated throughout his work that the educational sciences were still in a relatively undeveloped state, the tools that were available could be used with profit and, if so used, could eliminate waste. The tool that was perhaps most important was the survey or task analysis; and its importance rested upon the assumption that education, insofar as it is carried on in the school, was to prepare children to assume their roles as productive adult citizens. The school was, after all, a social institution. Its support came from the community, and its products ought to feed back into the community to replenish and maintain the society which made education possible in the first place. Bobbitt did not view this function as antithetical or incompatible with the personal or idiosyncratic development of the child. He saw the one as a precondition for the development of the other. Children were, to be sure, unequally endowed, but each ought to have an opportunity to develop his potentialities. And these could not really come to fruition unless they could be employed in some socially useful way. The common skills that man needed to live a socially useful life were what, in Bobbitt's view, constituted the general curriculum of the school. And it was this curriculum which was to be the primary and dominant program of the schools from kindergarten to the junior college.

'Education,' Bobbitt writes, 'is primarily for adult life, not for child life. Its fundamental responsibility is to prepare for the fifty years of adulthood, not for the twenty years of childhood and youth.'[11]

But granted the notion that education is to be useful and that it ought to serve the individual throughout life, how is such a functional education to be achieved? In 1893 the Committee of Ten, like subsequent national committees, thought they had the answer, but they had viewed education too narrowly, Bobbitt believed. Their focus was on the subject matters to be learned not on the tasks to be performed. Thus, the educational programs that the Committee of Ten advocated were inefficient and ineffective; they rested on an antiquated conception of mind as muscle. Had not Thorndike and Woodworth demonstrated the limited transfer value of subjects supposedly suited to mental disciplines.[12] Was not the social order changing rapidly, and did not the curriculum of the school need to keep pace with these changes? Bobbitt's answers were affirmative and his solution straightforward. For this solution we must go back six years to 1918. In *The Curriculum* he writes:

> The central theory [of curriculum] is simple. Human life, however varied, consists in the performance of specific activities. Education that prepares for life is one that prepares definitely and adequately for these specific activities. However numerous and diverse they may be for any social class they can be discovered. This requires only that one go out into the world of affairs and discover the particulars of which their affairs consist. These will show the abilities, attitudes, habits, appreciations and forms of knowledge that men need. These will be the objectives of the curriculum. They will be numerous, definite and particularized. The curriculum will then be that series of experiences which children and youth must have by way of attaining those objectives.[13]

Educational objectives and their formulation constituted the hub of curriculum planning. The first step for Bobbitt was to identify the domains of activity or responsibility in which all children should develop skills. To do this he 'surveyed' twenty-seven hundred 'cultivated and well trained adults.'[14] Fifteen hundred of this group had been students in his course, 'The Curriculum,' given in the Department of Education at the University of Chicago. The remainder of the group was composed of school personnel in Los Angeles, where he had served as a consultant. From the suggestions of this group he identified ten major fields of experience, the first nine of which the curriculum of the school should deal with. These were: (1) language activities, (2) health activities, (3) citizenship activities, (4) general social activities, (5) spare-time activities, (6) keeping oneself mentally fit, (7) religious activities, (8) parental activities, (9) unspecialized or non-vocational activities, and (10) the labor of one's calling.[15]

Once having identified the significant areas of human life for which schools have responsibility, it was a simple matter to follow this logic through in an attempt to identify the array of tasks that one needed to perform well within each of these domains. This Bobbitt did with meticulous care: The list he presents in *How To Make a Curriculum* contains 160 educational objectives which range from items such as 'ability to use language in all ways required for proper and effective participation in community life,'[16] to 'ability to make one's sleep contribute in maximum measure to the development and maintenance of a high level of physical vitality.'[17]

What we see in this approach is a serious effort to make curriculum planning rational and education meaningful, to build a curriculum for the schools that was not a product of armchair speculation but a product of the systematic study of society and the demands it makes on men. The survey movement, which began in 1892 with Rice's studies of the performance of students and teachers in the nation's schools, brought in its development a variety of tools that could be employed in order to identify areas of pupil strength and weakness.[18] Cubberley,[19] Sears,[20] Snedden,[21] and others had all conducted important investigations of educational progress. W.W. Charters, for example, had constructed elaborate studies of academic achievement in the language arts.[22] If the tools these men employed could be used to make the school more efficient in improving its means, perhaps they could be used to formulate educational ends as well. Bobbitt apparently believed this was possible, since he calls people using such tools 'curriculum discoverers.' In this view, the objectives of the curriculum are discovered by finding out what successful or skilled individuals do in life.

The difference between what these competent adults do and what children are able to do constitutes the gap to be reduced through curriculum experience. He outlines the steps to be followed succinctly:

Step 1: Divide life into major activities.
Step 2: Analyze each major activity into specific activities. This process is to continue until he, the curriculum discoverer, has found the quite specific activities that are to be performed.
Step 3: The activities once discovered, one can then see the objectives of education.[23]

In taking this approach to curriculum construction, a number of consequences followed. First, the array of objectives that were formulated reached the hundreds and once 'discovered' needed to be graded and placed in sequence. Second, since Bobbitt viewed with disdain what he believed were academic and unrealistic assumptions employed by previous curriculum committees, he laid emphasis on the formation of objectives that were related to life. Thus, the objectives were to be stated in activity or, as we say today, in behavioral terms. The student, for Bobbitt, was not a receptacle to be filled but an active organism that needed 'unfoldment,' a term he used throughout his writings. A third consequence of this approach to curriculum construction was a lack of sufficient attention to the is-ought problem in formulating educational ends. While Bobbitt was aware of the fact that people disagree about the ends of education, he did not adequately speak to this issue in his work. It appeared rational to him to employ scientific procedures to 'discover' what the ends of education shall be. And since the society which provided the subject matter for such study was changing, the continuous study of society was an important aspect of curriculum development.

It may be argued fairly that this view is socially adaptive rather than reconstructive in nature. It rests upon the assumption that the end of education is the production of citizens who will be able to perform well in the existing, albeit changing, social order.[24] Bobbitt writes: 'The School is not an agency of social reform. It is not directly concerned with improving society. Its responsibility is to help the growing individual continuously and consistently to hold to the type of human living which is the best practical one for him. This should automatically result in an enormous improvement in society in general. But this improvement is not a thing directly aimed at. It is only a by-product.'[25]

Bobbitt was no social reconstructionist. Although he apparently was sympathetic to some of the insights of experimentalism, the tenor of his educational philosophy was conservative in character.

A fourth consequence of the approach he took in constructing curriculum deals within the variety of personnel he believed was needed for making curriculum decisions. Since he believed that life required the use of a diversity of skills and since education was to prepare the young adequately to use those skills, it was not likely that any one individual – a superintendent, curriculum co-ordinator, or teacher – would have the competence necessary for their identification. Thus, it was important to draw upon the resources of skilled personnel in the community for aid in curriculum making. 'Specialized groups, within the community,' Bobbitt writes, 'should be held responsible for specially expert services in locating the abilities involved in those portions of the field with which they have to do. This principle is especially clear in locating the vocational abilities. Salesmen and supervisors of salesmen are especially competent in pointing out the abilities which are needed by salesmen. Printers are specially competent to point out the abilities needed by successful printers. . . . The principle applies also outside of the vocational field. Physicians and nurses possess specialized ability to assist in formulating the objectives of health education.'[26] Bobbitt goes on to identify the potential curriculum contributions of civic and social workers, of religious leaders, and of specialists in the field of recreation. While the educationist has the primary responsibility for providing leadership and cohesiveness to the larger educational map, he lacks the skills necessary for laying out the details. Thus, for Bobbitt, curriculum construction was in a significant sense a community enterprise in which the co-ordination of the judgment of specialists was crucial.

A fifth consequence of this view was the belief that, while a curriculum could be effectively planned within a school system or district, it was not likely to be planned effectively for a state or nation. The reason for this belief is not so much due to a commitment to the local control of the schools but more a realization of the difficulties inherent in the latter approach.

The curriculum, which he viewed as a general map of the educational terrain to be covered with general means identified to carry the student successfully on this journey, needed to take into account the pupils, their backgrounds and capabilities.[27] The larger the domain to be covered by any single curriculum 'map,' the less it was likely to be useful in the particular school or classroom. This belief became so significant that two years *after* the publication of *How To Make a Curriculum* he differentiated between the general and the individual curriculum, saying that the general curriculum, while important as an overall map, was not the most important curriculum at all.[28] What was most important was the particular or individual curriculum that the classroom teacher built for her pupils. The experimentalist's concern for individual differences appeared to have an impact on Bobbitt's thinking.

Bobbitt emphasized, however, that although the teacher needed to play a significant role in the planning of the individual curriculum and although scientific survey and measurement tools could be used to locate particular deficiencies having educational import, 'The major task of curriculum-making at present is the discovery of the goals in a general way and this general planning of the general outlines of the routes.'[29] This was the first and the basic step in curriculum work. And this step called for a conception of education itself; it required a point of view regarding the unique functions of the school. And this Bobbitt attempted to formulate.

Bobbitt held that education existed on two levels: the foundational and the functional. The foundational level developed the child's powers as a by-product of normal play activity. Such development, he believed, was not formed in relation to specific tasks to be performed. It was a natural process of 'unfoldment.'

Functional education, however, is related directly and consciously to the tasks that are to be done; it is the systematic attempt to prepare the child to exercise power in the performance of life's duties. And it is this latter type of education – the functional type – for which schools have a unique responsibility.

But Bobbitt went on to say that, although a part of functional education deals with vocational preparation, he was concerned in *How To Make a Curriculum* only with those human tasks that were common to all men; thus his concern was with the general rather than the special or vocational aspects of education. These latter aspects should, he believed, be reserved for the collegiate years and beyond. He abhorred inflicting courses that had only vocational utility upon the general school population – trigonometry, and in many cases algebra, physics, drawing, practical arts, Spanish, and economic geography frequently were employed this way.[30] 'Never,' he italicized in his book, 'will a subject be placed in the general training for all persons simply because it's of specialized value for certain occupations.'[31]

Thus far I have attempted to identify the principles and premises upon which Bobbitt's work rested. It is clear that he was concerned with relating education to life, that he focused upon the social demands of the society for the formulation of educational objectives, that he emphasized the active role of the student in learning. In many ways he shared with the experimentalists a concern for the education of the whole child. And like the experimentalists, he was concerned with the use of science in educational planning while recognizing the limitations of the young, if lusty, child. His work lacked the jargon or, in a more positive sense, the technical precision and language of a Dewey. But Bobbitt believed that clarity was a virtue and that ordinary discourse would go a long way as long as thought was not muddled. His book is a monument to this belief. In spite of the variety of concepts that he framed for thinking about curriculum, it is a book that is comprehensible – one that applies the common sense and straightforward logic of a practical educator.

Given these qualities, how was the book received? The *Peabody Journal of Education* called it 'A very important book: the school library ought not to be without it.'[32] The *Educational Review* saw it as 'a marvelous piece of work . . . remarkably readable and as definite as a manual. It will be studied by superintendents for many a day.'[33] David Snedden of Teacher's College, writing in the *School Review*, was enthusiastic enough to say: 'Professor Bobbitt's latest book represents thinking and work in education so advanced and sound that, if the phrase were not hackneyed, it would deserve to be called "epoch-making."'[34]

Henry Harap, however, who himself had some things to say about curriculum theory was somewhat less enthusiastic.[35] Writing in *School and Society*, Harap found the book useful but incomplete – an admirable first step, but in Harap's view, 'The author's work is not done.'[36] Although Harap's review of the work was generally favorable, it lacked the accolades that the previous reviewers accorded.

Boyd Bode was even less enthusiastic than Harap. And as one might expect, the rub in Bobbitt's *How To Make a Curriculum* for philosopher Bode was the blunder of believing, as he thought Bobbitt did, that scientific methods could yield educational ends. Bode's comments are pungent when he writes, 'Bobbitt's *How To Make a Curriculum* conveys the idea that the question of ideals is at bottom just a question of 'scientific analysis. . . .' The author seems to be unaware that in the scheme the cart is placed before the horse. How such analyses are to be made unless we know in advance which persons are good citizens, good parents, and true believers is not clear. It is assumed that if we dug up the facts by means of scientific analysis, the appropriate ideals will come to the surface too. But this simply means that science, like patriotism, may be used as a cover for prejudice and as an obstacle to progress.' Bode concludes his review by saying, 'In other words there is no social vision or program to guide the process of curriculum construction.'[37] A more devastating comment could hardly have been made.

Bode put his finger on a significant weakness in the book, one which Bobbitt probably recognized. Bobbitt was aware of the fact that men disagree to *some extent* as to what constitutes the good life. But the social order was not without its share of reasonable men, and some consensus existed. Furthermore, his practical bent left him ill-equipped to wait to construct curriculums until the philosopher's stone had been found. Bobbitt stuck out his practical neck, and it was roundly severed by one of the leading educational philosophers of the day.

Although Bode's criticism was telling, it was not the foible that he identified which weakened the impact of Bobbitt's work in the late twenties and thirties. The approach Bobbitt took, as indicated earlier, was rational, systematic, and meticulous. Education was for him a no-nonsense affair. And even though he shared some of the concerns of the experimentalists, the pervasive quality of his writing and his educational position lacked the romance that characterized theirs. While no one, least of all those experimentalists who called themselves 'Progressives,' could deny that education should prepare for life, the system and procedures that Bobbitt prescribed had a wooden quality to those who viewed the child as a budding organism who develops primarily from the inside out. Their conception of the child and of meaningful education was far more intimate in character. Yes, society should be studied by those who build curriculums, but the teacher should, at the same time, take her lead from the child. The Progressive spirit was not to be bridled by the formulation of hundreds of specific educational objectives because education as process and flux was a dynamic affair in which the teacher was to make educational capital out of the spontaneous developments emerging in the classroom. Furthermore, children did not progress in the neat systematic steps implied by Bobbitt's educational objectives. Listen as Ernest O. Melby's writing in 1935 says of the Progressive philosophy,

> This philosophy assumes that education is growth. It assumes that we shall choose such bodies of experience as will contribute to the growth of an individual child. It proceeds on the

assumption that the child is more important than the subject. *than outcomes*
The conflict between the traditional course-of-study notion of
education and that of a really dynamic and creative educational
concept is so direct and so vital that the prescribed course of
study in the traditional sense becomes one of the major
obstacles to a really creative and dynamic educational
program.... Were we to organize the school with primary
regard for the welfare of children we would probably make sure
that nowhere in that school do we have a book or pamphlet or
set of instructions which prescribes the subject-matter to be
taught to any group of children without regard to their needs,
interests, or abilities.[38]

In this sally by Melby, one can sense what the Progressives of the
thirties emphasized. It is not difficult to understand why Bobbitt's cool
approach did not capture their imagination. Bobbitt looked to the
society primarily for curriculum cues; the Progressives placed more
emphasis on the child. Bobbitt placed much more reliance on the use of
principle, science, and specificity; the Progressives more emphasis on
art and the idiosyncratic aspects of instruction. In short, the hundreds
of objectives that needed to be formulated in Bobbitt's approach caused
it to collapse under its own weight; as practical and rational as it
appeared, it did not mesh well with the vision of education advanced by
Rugg, Mearns, Shumaker, Melby, Zirbes, and Brim. And as might be
expected, their work neglected or omitted reference to Bobbitt. *The
Child-centered School*,[39] for example, makes no mention of his work; the
same is true for *The Activity Movement*[40] and other works hoisting the
Progressive banner.

If Bobbitt's work had little impact on the Progressive movement
of the thirties because it laid too little emphasis on the role of the child
in curriculum construction, it was neglected by the essentialists and
rational humanists for other reasons. Robert Maynard Hutchins, for
example, while not attending to the problems of elementary education,
nevertheless represents a position to which the essentialists subscribed.
For Hutchins the assumption that social analysis could be used to
formulate educational objectives was indefensible. If we know anything about American society, he said, it is that it is changing – and
rapidly. What we need in education, Hutchins held, is not a philosophy
of adjustment or adaptation which 'was carried to its logical extreme in
a women's college in America, which based its curriculum on a job
analysis of the diaries of 323 mature women,'[41] but a return to the

dialectic examination of the greatest ideas formulated by the greatest writers who ever lived. And where are these to be found – in the great books. Thus Hutchins and others of his persuasion rejected Bobbitt's approach, not because it neglected the child, but because it neglected the very subject matter which they believed made human intelligence possible.

But if Bobbitt was neglected by the Progressives and essentialists, the ideas that he presented were of use to others. It is an old and familiar story now that the Progressive movement lost its strength in the late forties.[42] It's also familiar that the essentialists led by organizations and men such as The Council for Basic Education, Arthur Bestor, Admiral Rickover, and Albert Lynd gained in influence during this period. Their views of appropriate curriculum for American youth departed drastically from that advocated by the Progressives. But at the same time curriculum specialists who had a more theoretical bent were employing ideas similar to those advanced by Bobbitt twenty years earlier.

Among the most influential of these specialists were Ralph W. Tyler and Virgil Herrick. Tyler and Herrick had worked together in the Department of Education at the University of Chicago and, consonant with the spirit of that institution, were concerned with the development and application of theory and research to educational problems, the curriculum being of special interest to both. Tyler's approach to curriculum especially shows a quality similar to that of Bobbitt's, not in its conservative outlook or in its simplicity, but in its rationality. Tyler's curriculum rationale,[43] which was presented in part in *Toward Improved Curriculum Theory*,[44] was later published in monograph form as a syllabus for a course on curriculum that he taught, and, since its publication, has had wide dissemination at the University of Chicago and elsewhere. Tyler raises four questions that he believes a curriculum specialist ought to deal with in constructing curriculum for any educational level. These are, 'What educational purposes should the school seek to attain? What educational experiences can be provided that are likely to attain these purposes? How can these educational experiences be organized? How can we determine whether these purposes are being attained?[45] Tyler, like Bobbitt, attempts to provide a system for coping with the complex problem of curriculum construction, and like Bobbitt he emphasizes the importance of educational objectives stated in behavioral and content terms. But unlike Bobbitt, Tyler does not limit himself to the study of society for the selection of objectives or for the formulation of learning experiences. For Tyler, the psychologist and philosopher must also be consulted. But Tyler includes reference to philosophy only incidentally in his rationale, devoting only a few sentences to its role in curriculum construction, and when it is included, the philosopher's contribution is conceived of on the same level as the other specialists, who are to provide data for the formulation of objectives. Tyler, it seems, like Bobbitt, understates the importance of values as a guide to the selection of data sources he would use in making curriculum decisions.

Tyler and Herrick share another characteristic found in Bobbitt's work. This deals with the personnel needed for curriculum construction. Tyler and Herrick write in their concluding statement to the 1947 conference on curriculum theory, 'Curriculum development by its very nature is a co-operative problem. No one person is going to be able to encompass all the knowledge or perceive all the problems that would be essential in the formulation of an adequate conception of curriculum.'[46]

A major difference exists, however, in the ways in which they would go about using specialists. Tyler and Herrick would have specialists not only provide data relevant for curriculum decision making but would use specialists to screen each other's recommendations. Thus, the psychologist would presumably be in a position to say whether a particular activity to be performed or a generalization to be learned was appropriate for the cognitive abilities of a child of a particular age. Their use of specialists goes well beyond the recommendations advanced by Bobbitt.

But the ideas that Bobbitt formulated are related not only in the work of Herrick and Tyler but in the work of Benjamin Bloom and John I. Goodlad, two men who studied under Tyler and Herrick. The benchmark that these men share with Bobbitt is the rational, systematic, and social orientation they bring to curriculum theory. Bloom employs recommendations regarding the formulation and use of educational objectives that Bobbitt, I believe, would have applauded.[47] And Goodlad, in attempting to extend the work of Tyler, would receive similar bows.[48] Bloom's recommendations for the construction of curriculum centers, which would apply some of the recommendations made in Tyler's work, carry the spirit of Bobbitt's approach even further.[49]

It should be mentioned that I am not here attempting to deal with historical causality. I am certain that most of us do not know where we have gotten most of our ideas. What I do see in the work of Virgil Herrick, Ralph Tyler, Benjamin Bloom, and John Goodlad are family resemblances to many of the ideas formulated in *How To Make a Curriculum*. But most of all I see some of the same rational spirit, even if less conservative and considerably more complex.

When one looks back at Franklin Bobbitt's contributions to the curriculum field, an interesting picture emerges. If Bobbitt attended to the analysis of life's duties, he neglected the logical difficulties of moving from 'is' to 'ought.' As much as he wanted to use scientific procedures to formulate curriculums, he paid little attention to the assessment of educational outcomes. In spite of the fact that he considered the curriculum-building process complex, he underestimated the dynamic character of the teacher's tasks. Even though he attempted to build a conception of education that would provide the foundation for his curriculum recommendations, he neglected previous scholarship in his own field upon which he might have built. Although he valued clarity and specificity in formulating educational ends, this very specificity became a quagmire from which teachers wanted to escape.

But these observations are easy in retrospect. It is always easier to look back and to say what should have been. Franklin Bobbitt, the cool pragmatic conservative, should be viewed in the context of his day. And for his day, I think he moved his team forward.

Notes

1. I wish to express my gratitude to Professor EMERITUS JESSE B. SEARS and to Professor LAWRENCE THOMAS of Stanford University for very helpful critical comments in the preparation of this manuscript.
2. DEWEY, J. (1902) *The Child and the Curriculum* Chicago, University of Chicago Press.
3. KILPATRICK, W.H. (1918) 'The Project Method, the Use of the Purposeful Act in the Educative Process,' in *Teachers College Bulletin* New York, 12 October.
4. BONSER, F.G. (1921) *The Elementary School Curriculum* New York, Macmillan Co.
5. CHARTERS, W.W. (1923) *Curriculum Construction* New York, Macmillan Co.
6. SNEDDEN, D. (1921) *Sociological Determination of Objectives in Education* Philadelphia and London, J.B. Lippincott Co.
7. JUDD, C.H. (1922) 'The Scientific Technique of Curriculum-Making,' in *School and Society*, XV, No. 367, January, pp. 1–11. It might also be mentioned that the *Encyclopedia of Education*, edited by Paul Monroe and published in 1911, does not include a section on 'Curriculum' but instead

refers the reader to the section on 'Theory of Course of Study.' None of the references cited by the author of this section, John Dewey, even mentions the word 'curriculum' in its title.

8. BOBBITT, F. (1924) *How To Make a Curriculum* Boston, Houghton Mifflin Co.

9. DORSEY, S.M. (1924) 'Reconstruction of the Junior High School Curriculum in Los Angeles,' in *Chicago Schools Journal*, VII, September, pp. 1–6.

10. BOBBITT, F. (1918) *The Curriculum* Boston, Houghton Mifflin Co.

11. BOBBITT, F. (1924) *op. cit.*, p. 8.

12. THORNDIKE, E.L. and WOODWORTH, R.S. (1901) 'The influence of Improvement on One Mental Function upon the Efficiency of Other Functions,' in *Psychological Review*, May.

13. BOBBITT, F. (1918) *op. cit.*, p. 42.

14. BOBBITT, F. (1924) *op. cit.*, p. 10.

15. *Ibid.*, pp. 8–9.

16. *Ibid.*, p. 11.

17. *Ibid.*, p. 13.

18. For a discussion of Rice's work, see CREMIN, L. (1961) *The Transformation of the School* New York, Alfred A. Knopf, Inc., pp. 3–8.

19. CUBBERLEY, E.P. (1915) *Report of the Survey of the Public School System of Salt Lake City, Utah* Salt Lake City, Utah, Grocer Printing Co.

20. SEARS, J. (1915) *Spelling Efficiency in Oakland's Schools* Oakland; and (1922) *The Technique of the Public School Survey* Bloomington, Ill., Public School Publishing Co.

21. SNEDDEN, *op. cit.*

22. For a view of the use of survey methods in curriculum construction, see Charters, *op. cit.*

23. BOBBITT, F. (1926) 'The Orientation of the Curriculum Makers,' in RUGG, H. (Ed.), *The Foundations and Technique of Curriculum Construction* (26th Yearbook of the National Society for the Study of Education, Part II) Bloomington, Ill., Public School Publishing Co., p. 9.

24. For an interesting and critical appraisal of Bobbitt's work and its relation to scientific management in education, see CALLAHAN, R.E. (1962) *Education and the Cult of Efficiency* Chicago, University of Chicago Press.

25. BOBBITT, 'The Orientation of the Curriculum Maker,' p. 54.

26. *Ibid.*, pp. 38–39.

27. BOBBITT, F. (1924) *op. cit.*, p. 1 and *passim*.

28. BOBBITT, 'The Orientation of the Curriculum Maker,' p. 47.

29. BOBBITT, F. (1924) *op. cit.*, p. 5.

30. *Ibid.*, p. 67.

31. *Ibid.*

32. 'New Books on Our Shelf,' in *Peabody Journal of Education*, II, July, 1924–May, 1925, p. 226.

33. 'Educational Review of Books,' in *Educational Review*, LXVIII, June–December, 1924, pp. 111–12.

34. DAVID SNEDDEN, review of *How To Make a Curriculum*, in *School Review*, XXXII, January–December, 1924, pp. 468–69.

35. HENRY HARAP was very active in curriculum work, writing and editing a

variety of widely used materials in this field. He is the author of *The Technique of Curriculum Making* New York, Macmillan Co., 1928.

36. HENRY HARAP, review of *How To Make a Curriculum*, in *School and Society*, XIX, January–June, 1924, pp. 771–72.

37. BOYD BODE, review of *How To Make a Curriculum*, in *Educational Administration and Supervision*, X, No. 7, October, 1924, pp. 471–74.

38. MELBY, E.O. 'Organizing Educational Forces for Curriculum Development,' in HARAP, H. (Ed.), (1937) *The Changing Curriculum* (10th Yearbook, Department of Supervisors and Directors of Instruction) New York, D. Appleton-Century Co. p. 128.

39. RUGG, H. and SHUMAKER, A. (1928) *The Child-centred School* New York, World Book Co.

40. HISSONG, C. (1932) *The Activity Movement* Baltimore, Warwick and York.

41. HUTCHINS, R.M. (1953) *The Conflict in Education in a Democratic Society* New York, Harper and Co.

42. For an important statement on the development, decline, and fall of the Progressive movement in American education, see CREMIN, L. (1961) *op. cit.*

43. TYLER, R.W. (1950) *Basic Principles of Curriculum and Instruction Syllabus for Education 360* Chicago, University of Chicago Press.

44. HERRICK, V.E. and TYLER, R.W. (Eds.) (1950) *Toward Improved Curriculum Theory* ('Supplementary Educational Monographs,' No. 71) Chicago, University of Chicago Press.

45. TYLER, *op. cit.*

46. HERRICK and TYLER, 'Next Steps in the Development of a More Adequate Curriculum Theory,' *Toward Improved Curriculum Theory*, p. 120.

47. The classic effort to give operational meaning to educational objectives is, in my estimation, to be found in BLOOM, B. (Ed.), *The Taxonomy of Educational Objectives. Handbook I: The Cognitive Domain* New York, Longmans, Green and Co.

48. JOHN I. GOODLAD's work on curriculum is found in a variety of sources; among them are, 'Illustrated Programs and Procedures in Elementary Schools,' in HENRY, N.B. (Ed.) (1958) *The Integration of Educational Experiences* (57th Yearbook of the National Society for the Study of Education) Chicago, University of Chicago Press; (1959) *The Nongraded Elementary School* New York, Harcourt, Brace and Co. This latter book was written with ROBERT H. ANDERSON of Harvard University. Also see (1964) *School Curriculum Reform* New York, Fund for the Advancement of Education; 'The Curriculum,' in GOODLAD, J.I. (Ed.), (1966) *The Changing American School* (65th Yearbook of the National Society for the Study of Education, Part II) Chicago, University of Chicago Press.

49. To understand how various personnel are to be used in curriculum development, see BLOOM, B. (1965) 'The Role of the Educational Sciences in Curriculum Development,' in *International Journal of Educational Sciences*, Spring.

2   Educational Objectives: Help or Hindrance?[1]

If one were to rank the various beliefs or assumptions in the field of curriculum that are thought most secure, the belief in the need for clarity and specificity in stating educational objectives would surely rank among the highest. Educational objectives, it is argued, need to be clearly specified for at least three reasons: first, because they provide the goals toward which the curriculum is aimed; second, because once clearly stated they facilitate the selection and organization of content; third, because when specified in both behavioral and content terms they make it possible to evaluate the outcomes of the curriculum.

It is difficult to argue with a rational approach to curriculum development – who would choose irrationality? And, if one is to build curriculum in a rational way, the clarity of premise, end or starting point, would appear paramount. But I want to argue in this paper that educational objectives clearly and specifically stated can hamper as well as help the ends of instruction and that an unexamined belief in curriculum as in other domains of human activity can easily become dogma which in fact may hinder the very functions the concept was originally designed to serve.

When and where did beliefs concerning the importance of educational objectives in curriculum development emerge? Who has formulated and argued their importance? What effect has this belief had upon curriculum construction? If we examine the past briefly for data necessary for answering these questions, it appears that the belief in the usefulness of clear and specific educational objectives emerged around the turn of the century with the birth of the scientific movement in education.

Before this movement gained strength, faculty psychologists viewed the brain as consisting of a variety of intellectual faculties. These faculties, they held, could be strengthened if exercised in appropriate ways with particular subject matters. Once strengthened, the faculties could be used in any area of human activity to which they were applicable. Thus, if the important faculties could be identified and if methods of strengthening them developed, the school could concentrate on this task and expect general intellectual excellence as a result.

This general theoretical view of mind had been accepted for several decades by the time Thorndike, Judd, and later Watson began, through their work, to chip away the foundations upon which it rested. Thorndike's work especially demonstrated the specificity of transfer. He argued theoretically that transfer of learning occurred if and only if elements in one situation were identical with elements in the other. His empirical work supported his theoretical views, and the enormous stature he enjoyed in education as well as in psychology influenced educators to approach curriculum development in ways consonant with his views. One of those who was caught up in the scientific movement in education was Franklin Bobbitt, often thought of as the father of curriculum theory. In 1918 Bobbitt published a signal work titled simply *The Curriculum*.[2] In it he argued that educational theory is not so difficult to construct as is commonly held and that curriculum theory is logically derivable from educational theory. Bobbitt wrote in 1918:

> The central theory is simple. Human life, however varied, consists in its performance of specific activities. Education that prepares for life is one that prepares definitely and adequately for these specific activities. However numerous and diverse they may be for any social class, they can be discovered. This requires that one go out into the world of affairs and discover the particulars of which these affairs consist. These will show the abilities, habits, appreciations, and forms of knowledge that men need. These will be the objectives of the curriculum. They will be numerous, definite, and particularized. The curriculum will then be that series of experiences which childhood and youth must have by way of attaining those objectives.[3]

In The Curriculum, Bobbitt approached curriculum development scientifically and theoretically: study life carefully to identify needed skills, divide these skills into specific units, organize these units into experiences, and provide these experiences to children. Six years later, in his second book, *How To Make a Curriculum*,[4] Bobbitt operationalized his theoretical assertions and demonstrated how curriculum components – especially educational objectives – were to be formulated. In this book Bobbitt listed nine areas in which educational objectives are to be specified. In these nine areas he listed 160 major educational objectives which run the gamut from 'Ability to use language in all ways required for proper and effective participation in community life' to 'Ability to entertain one's friends, and to respond to entertainment by one's friends.'[5]

Bobbitt was not alone in his belief in the importance of formulating objectives clearly and specifically. Pendleton, for example, listed, 1,581 social objectives for English, Guiler listed more than 300 for arithmetic in grades 1–6, and Billings prescribed 888 generalizations which were important for the social studies.

If Thorndike was right, if transfer was limited, it seemed reasonable to encourage the teacher to teach for particular outcomes and to construct curriculums only after specific objectives had been identified.

In retrospect it is not difficult to understand why this movement in curriculum collapsed under its own weight by the early 1930's. Teachers could not manage fifty highly specified objects, let alone hundreds. And, in addition, the new view of the child, not as a complex machine but as a growing organism who ought to participate in planning his own educational program, did not mesh well with the theoretical views held earlier.[6]

But, as we all know, the Progressive movement too began its decline in the forties, and by the middle fifties, as a formal organization at least, it was dead.

By the late forties and during the fifties, curriculum specialists again began to remind us of the importance of specific educational objectives and began to lay down guidelines for their formulation. Rationales for constructing curriculums developed by Ralph Tyler[7] and Virgil Herrick[8] again placed great importance on the specificity of objectives. George Barton[9] identified philosophic domains which could be used to select objectives. Benjamin Bloom and his colleagues[10] operationalized theoretical assertions by building a taxonomy of educational objectives in the cognitive domain; and in 1964, Krathwohl, Bloom, and Masia[11] did the same for the affective domain. Many able people for many years have spent a great deal of time and effort in identifying methods and providing prescriptions for the formulation of educational objectives, so much so that the statement 'Educational objectives should be stated in behavioral terms' has been elevated – or lowered – to almost slogan status in curriculum circles. Yet, despite these efforts, teachers seem not to take educational objectives seriously – at least as they are prescribed from above. And when teachers plan curriculum guides, their efforts first to identify over-all educational aims, then specify school objectives, then identify educational objectives for specific subject matters, appear to be more like exercises to be gone through than serious efforts to build tools for curriculum planning. If educational objectives were really useful tools, teachers, I submit, would use them. If they do not, perhaps it is not because there is something wrong with the teachers but because there might be something wrong with the theory.

As I view the situation, there are several limitations to theory in curriculum regarding the functions educational objectives are to perform. These limitations I would like to identify.

Educational objectives are typically derived from curriculum theory, which assumes that it is possible to predict with a fair degree of accuracy what the outcomes of instruction will be. In a general way this is possible. If you set about to teach a student algebra, there is no reason to assume he will learn to construct sonnets instead. Yet, the outcomes of instruction are far too numerous and complex for educational objectives to encompass. The amount, type, and quality of learning that occur in a classroom, especially when there is interaction among students, are only in small part predictable. The changes in pace, tempo, and goals that experienced teachers employ when necessary and appropriate for maintaining classroom organization are dynamic rather than mechanistic in character. Elementary school teachers, for example, are often sensitive to the changing interests of the children they teach, and they frequently attempt to capitalize on these interests, 'milking them' as it were for what is educationally valuable.[12] The teacher uses the moment in a situation that is better described as kaleidoscopic than stable. In the very process of teaching and discussing, unexpected opportunities emerge for making a valuable point, for demonstrating an interesting idea, and for teaching a significant concept. The first point I wish to make, therefore, is that the dynamic and complex process of instruction yields outcomes far too numerous to be specified in behavioral and content terms in advance.

A second limitation of theory concerning educational objectives is its failure to recognize the constraints various subject matters place upon objectives. The point here is brief. In some subject areas, such as mathematics, languages, and the sciences, it is possible to specify with great precision the particular operation or behavior the student is to perform after instruction. In other subject areas, especially the arts, such specification is frequently not possible, and when possible may not be desirable. In a class in mathematics or spelling, uniformity in response is desirable, at least insofar as it indicates that students are able to perform a particular operation adequately, that is, in accordance with accepted procedures. Effective instruction in such areas enables students to function with minimum error in these fields. In the arts and in subject matters where, for example, novel or creative responses are desired, the particular behaviors to be developed cannot easily be identified. Here curriculum and instruction should yield behaviors and products which are unpredictable. The end achieved ought to be something of a surprise to both teacher and pupil. While it could be argued that one might formulate an educational objective which specified novelty, originality, or creativeness as the desired outcome, the particular referents for these terms cannot be specified in advance. One must judge after the fact whether the product produced or the behavior displayed belongs in the 'novel' class. This is a much different procedure than is determining whether or not a particular word has been spelled correctly or a specific performance, that is, jumping a 3-foot hurdle, has been attained. Thus, the second point is that theory concerning educational objectives has not taken into account the particular relationship that holds between the subject matter being taught and the degree to which educational objectives can be predicted and specified. This, I suppose, is in part due to the fact that few curriculum specialists have high degrees of intimacy with a wide variety of subject matters and thus are unable to alter their general theoretical views to suit the demands that particular subject matters make.

The third point I wish to make deals with the belief that objectives stated in behavioral and content terms can be used as criteria by which to measure the outcomes of curriculum and instruction. Educational objectives provide, it is argued, the standard against which achievement is to be measured. Both taxonomies are built upon this assumption since their primary function is to demonstrate how objectives can be used to frame test items appropriate for evaluation. The assumption that objects can be used as standards by which to measure achievement fails, I think, to distinguish adequately between the application of a standard and the making of a judgment. Not all – perhaps not even most – outcomes of curriculum and instruction are amenable to measurement. The application of a standard requires that some arbitrary and socially defined quantity be designated by which other qualities can be compared. By virtue of socially defined rules of grammar, syntax, and logic, for example, it is possible to quantitatively compare and measure error in discursive or mathematical statement.

Some fields of activity, especially those which are qualitative in character, have no comparable rules and hence are less amenable to quantitative assessment. It is here that evaluation must be made, not primarily by applying a socially defined standard, but by making a human qualitative judgment. One can specify, for example, that a student shall be expected to know how to extract a square root correctly and in an unambiguous way, through the application of a standard, determine whether this end has been achieved. But it is only in a metaphoric sense that one can measure the extent to which a student has been able to produce an aesthetic object or an expressive narrative. Here standards are unapplicable; here judgment is required. The making of a judgment in distinction to the application of a standard implies that valued qualities are not merely socially defined and arbitrary in character. The judgment by which a critic determines the value of a poem, novel, or play is not achieved merely by applying standards already known to the particular product being judged; it requires that the critic – or teacher – view the product with respect to the unique properties it displays and then, in relation to his experience and sensibilities, judge its value in terms which are incapable of being reduced to quantity or rule.

This point was aptly discussed by John Dewey in his chapter on 'Perception and Criticism' in *Art as Experience*.[13] Dewey was concerned with the problem of identifying the means and ends of criticism and has this to say about its proper function:

> The function of criticism is the reeducation of perception of works of art; it is an auxiliary process, a difficult process, of learning to see and hear. The conception that its business is to appraise, to judge in the legal and moral sense, arrests the perception of those who are influenced by the criticism that assumes this task.[14]

Of the distinction that Dewey makes between the application of a standard and the making of a critical judgment, he writes:

> There are three characteristics of a standard. It is a particular physical thing existing under specifiable conditions; it is *not* a value. The yard is a yard-stick, and the meter is a bar deposited in Paris. In the second place, standards are measures of things of lengths, weights, capacities. The things measured are not values, although it is of great social value to be able to measure them, since the properties of things in the way of size, volume,

weight, are important for commercial exchange. Finally, as standards of measure, standards define things with respect to *quantity*. To be able to measure quantities is a great aid to further judgments, but it is not a mode of judgment. The standard, being an external and public thing, is applied *physically*. The yard-stick is physically laid down upon things to determine their length.[15]

And I would add that what is most educationally valuable is the development of that mode of curiosity, inventiveness, and insight that is capable of being described only in metaphoric or poetic terms. Indeed, the image of the educated man that has been held in highest esteem for the longest period of time in Western civilization is one which is not amenable to standard measurement. Thus, the third point I wish to make is that curriculum theory which views educational objectives as standards by which to measure educational achievement overlooks those modes of achievement incapable of measurement.

The final point I wish to make deals with the function of educational objectives in curriculum construction.

The rational approach to curriculum development not only emphasizes the importance of specificity in the formulation of educational objectives but also implies when not stated explicitly that educational objectives be stated prior to the formulation of curriculum activities. At first view, this seems to be a reasonable way to proceed with curriculum construction: one should know where he is headed before embarking on a trip. Yet, while the procedure of first identifying objectives before proceeding to identify activities is logically defensible, it is not necessarily the most psychologically efficient way to proceed. One can, and teachers often do, identify activities that seem useful, appropriate, or rich in educational opportunities, and from a consideration of what can be done in class, identify the objectives or possible consequences of using these activities. MacDonald argues this point cogently when he writes:

> Let us look, for example, at the problem of objectives. Objectives are viewed as directives in the rational approach. They are identified prior to the instruction or action and used to provide a basis for a screen for appropriate activities.
>
> There is another view, however, which has both scholarly and experiential referents. This view would state that our objectives are only known to us in any complete sense after the completion of our act of instruction. No matter what we

thought we were attempting to do, we can only know what we wanted to accomplish after the fact. Objectives by this rationale are heuristic devices which provide initiating consequences which become altered in the flow of instruction.

In the final analysis, it could be argued, the teacher in actuality asks a fundamentally different question from 'What am I trying to accomplish?' The teacher asks 'What am I going to do?' and out of the doing comes accomplishment.[16]

Theory in curriculum has not adequately distinguished between logical adequacy in determining the relationship of means to ends when examining the curriculum as a *product* and the psychological processes that may usefully be employed in building curriculums. The method of forming creative insights in curriculum development, as in the sciences and arts, is as yet not logically prescribable. The ways in which curriculums can be usefully and efficiently developed constitute an empirical problem; imposing logical requirements upon the process because they are desirable for assessing the product is, to my mind, an error. Thus, the final point I wish to make is that educational objectives need not precede the selection and organization of content. The means through which imaginative curriculums can be built is as open-ended as the means through which scientific and artistic inventions occur. Curriculum theory needs to allow for a variety of processes to be employed in the construction of curriculums.

I have argued in this paper that curriculum theory as it pertains to educational objectives has had four significant limitations. First, it has not sufficiently emphasized the extent to which the prediction of educational outcomes cannot be made with accuracy. Second, it has not discussed the ways in which the subject matter affects precision in stating educational objectives. Third, it has confused the use of educational objectives as a standard for measurement when in some areas it can be used only as a criterion for judgment. Fourth, it has not distinguished between the logical requirement of relating means to ends in the curriculum as a product and the psychological conditions useful for constructing curriculums.

If the arguments I have formulated about the limitations of curriculum theory concerning educational objectives have merit, one might ask: What are their educational consequences? First, it seems to me that they suggest that in large measure the construction of curriculums and the judgment of its consequences are artful tasks. The methods of curriculum development are, in principle if not in practice, no different from the making of art – be it the art of painting or the art of science. The identification of the factors in the potentially useful educational activity and the organization or construction of sequence in curriculum are in principle amenable to an infinite number of combinations. The variable teacher, student or class group requires artful blending for the educationally valuable to result.

Second, I am impressed with Dewey's view of the functions of criticism – to heighten one's perception of the art object – and believe it has implications for curriculum theory. If the child is viewed as an art product and the teacher as a critic, one task of the teacher would be to reveal the qualities to the child to himself and to others. In addition, the teacher as critic would appraise the changes occurring in the child. But because the teacher's task includes more than criticism, he would also be responsible, in part, for the improvement of the work of art. In short, in both the construction of educational means (the curriculum) and the appraisal of its consequences, the teacher would become an artist, for criticism itself when carried to its height is an art. This, it seems to me, is a dimension to which curriculum theory will someday have to speak.

Notes

1. This is a slightly expanded version of a paper presented at the fiftieth annual meeting of the American Educational Research Association, Chicago, February, 1966.
2. BOBBITT, F. (1918) *The Curriculum* Boston, Houghton Mifflin Co.
3. *Ibid.*, p. 42.
4. BOBBITT, F. (1924) *How to Make a Curriculum* Boston, Houghton Mifflin Co.
5. *Ibid.*, pp. 11–29.
6. For a good example of this view of the child and curriculum development, see Department of Supervisors and Directors of Instruction, National Education Association and Society for Curriculum Study (1937) *The Changing Curriculum, Tenth Yearbook*, New York, Appleton-Century Crofts Co.
7. TYLER, R.W. (1951) *Basic Principles of Curriculum and Instruction* Chicago, University of Chicago Press.
8. HERRICK, V.E. The Concept of Curriculum Design, in HERRICK, V.E. and TYLER, R.W. (Eds) (1950) *Toward Improved Curriculum Theory,* (Supplementary Educational Monographs, No. 71) Chicago, University of Chicago Press, pp. 37–50.
9. BARTON, G.E. JR., 'Educational Objectives: Improvement of Curriculum Theory about Their Determination,' *ibid.*, pp. 26–35.

10. Bloom, B. *et al.* (Ed.), (1956) *Taxonomy of Educational Objectives, Handbook 1: The Cognitive Domain* New York, Longmans, Green and Co.
11. Krathwohl, D. Bloom, B. and Masia, B. (1964) *Taxonomy of Educational Objectives*, Handbook II: *The Affective Domain* New York, David McKay, Inc.
12. For an excellent paper describing educational objectives as they are viewed and used by elementary school teachers, see Jackson, P.W. and Belford, E. (1965) 'Educational Objectives and the Joys of Teaching,' in *School Review*, LXXIII pp. 267–91.
13. Dewey, J. (1934) *Art as Experience* New York, Minton, Balch and Co.
14. *Ibid.*, p. 324.
15. *Ibid.*, p. 307.
16. MacDonald, J.B. (1965) 'Myths about Instruction,' in *Educational Leadership*, XXII, No. 7, May, pp. 613–14.

3 Instructional and Expressive Educational Objectives: Their Formulation and Use in Curriculum

The concept of educational objectives holds a central position in the literature of curriculum; yet the way in which educational objectives should be formulated – if at all – continues to be the subject of professional debate. This chapter will examine the concept 'educational objectives,' its evolution in educational literature and the research which has been undertaken to appraise its usefulness. A primary function of the chapter is to distinguish between two types of objectives – instructional and expressive. This distinction might prove useful for ameliorating the arguments of those holding contrasting views on their usefulness in curriculum theory and instruction.

There is little need to document the fact that educational literature has devoted much attention to the character and the methods through which educational objectives are to be formulated. Bloom et al. (1956), Gagné (1967), Krathwohl, Bloom and Masia (1964), Mager (1962), Tyler (1950), and others have worked diligently at the task of clarifying, classifying, and specifying the manner in which objectives are to be formulated and the characteristics they are to have once developed. Through the efforts of these writers a number of characteristics necessary for having a useful statement of objectives have been identified. For one, it is argued that educational objectives should describe pupil behavior, not teacher behavior; that is, they should describe how pupils are to perform after having had educational experiences. Second, objectives should describe both the behavior to be displayed and the content in which the behavior is to occur. Thus, not just critical thinking is to be identified but critical thinking in history or mathematics or biology. Third, objectives should be stated at a level of specificity that makes it possible to recognize the behavior should it be displayed, thus avoiding the pitfalls of making inferences to non-empirical phenomena such as mental events. (The reader should note that the example of critical thinking just offered would not pass muster.)

These and other rules or principles have been offered to the would-be curriculum maker to facilitate his labors in the field of education. For once having formulated objectives that meet such criteria, a number of subsequent functions are facilitated. First, a clear statement of educational objectives gives direction to curriculum planning. Second, they provide criteria for selecting content and organizing curriculum activities. Third, they provide cues for formulating evaluation procedures inasmuch as evaluation should proceed from specifications set forth by objectives.

Tyler (1950), in describing the importance of educational objectives in his rationale for curriculum development, states,

> By defining these desired educational results [educational objectives] as clearly as possible the curriculum-maker has the most useful set of criteria for selecting content, for suggesting learning activities, for deciding on the kind of teaching procedures to follow, in fact to carry on all the further steps in curriculum planning. We are devoting much time to the setting up and formulations of objectives because they are the most critical criteria for guiding all the other activities of the curriculum-maker.[1]

And Gagné (1967) writing in the first AERA monograph of the Curriculum Evaluation Series goes beyond Tyler in emphasizing the importance of educational objectives by reducing content to objectives. He writes:

> Possibly the most fundamental reason of all for the central importance of defining educational objectives is that such definition makes possible the basic distinction between content and method. It is the defining of objectives that brings an essential clarity into the area of curriculum design and enables both educational planners and researchers to bring their practical knowledge to bear on the matter. As an example of the kind of clarification which results by defining content as 'descriptions of the expected capabilities of students,' the following may be noted. Once objectives have been defined, there is no step in curriculum design that can legitimately be entitled 'selecting content.'[2]

Here we have two distinguished students of education emphasizing the importance of educational objectives. Each of these statements, as well as the statements of other thoughtful citizens of the educational community, affirms belief in the importance of educational objectives as a boon to teaching, curriculum making, and educational planning.

And yet, and yet ... if we reflect on our own teaching or observe the teaching behavior of others, if we compare the courses of the 'haves' and 'have nots' of educational objectives, we are, I believe, hard pressed to identify the power they are believed to have by their advocates. Why is it that teachers do not eagerly use tools that would make their lives easier? Perhaps because they are ignorant of how objectives should be specified ... perhaps. But why should those who know how objectives are to be specified disregard them in their own course work? Perhaps because they have acquired 'bad' professional habits ... perhaps. Is it possible that the power and utility assigned to objectives in theoretical treatises are somewhat exaggerated when tested in the context of the classroom? Is it possible that the assumptions on which prescriptions about objectives are based are somewhat oversimplified? Is it also possible that the prescription of a set of procedures for the formulation of objectives and the identification of appropriate criteria for their adequacy implicitly contain an educational *Weltanschauung* that is not shared by a substantial proportion of those who are responsible for curriculum planning and teaching in America's schools?

The formulation of educational means is never a neutral act. The tools employed and the metaphors used to describe education lead to actions which are not without consequences with respect to value. Many of the metaphors used to describe the importance and function of educational objectives have been associated with conceptions of education which I believe are alien to the educational values held by many of those who teach. These metaphors are not new; they have been with educators for some time, and it will be fruitful, I believe, to compare some of the arguments and metaphors used today with conceptions of education developed within the past fifty years.

It seems to me that three metaphors can be used to characterize dominant views about the nature of education – at least as it has been conceived and carried on in American schools. These metaphors are *industrial, behavioristic,* and *biological.*

The industrial metaphor was perhaps most influential in education during the first and second decades of this century, a period in which the efficiency movement emerged. This movement, described brilliantly by Callahan (1962), adopted and adapted industrial methods – especially time and motion study – to improve the educational process and make it more efficient. Under pressure from local boards of education and the muckraking magazines of the early twentieth century, school administrators tried to protect their positions and to reduce their vulnerability to public criticism by employing methods developed by Francis Taylor in industry in order to improve the efficiency of the school. If the school could be managed scientifically, if the procedures which had been employed so successfully in the production of steel could be used in schooling, education might become more efficient and school administrators would have a mantle to protect themselves from the barrage of criticism that befell them during these times. With the adoption of scientific methods they would have evidence that they were not running a 'loose shop.'

To bring about this metamorphosis in the schools certain tasks had to be accomplished. First and foremost, quantitative and qualitative standards had to be formulated for judging the educational product. Second, time and motion studies had to be made to identify the most efficient means. Third, nothing that could be routinized and prescribed was to be left to the judgment of the worker since his decisions might lead to inefficiency and error. Fourth, the quality of the product was to be judged not by the workers in the school but by the consumers of the product – in this case, society. Fifth, the tasks were to be divided into manageable units so that they could be taught and evaluated at every step along the production line. From these prescriptions for practice, prescriptions taken from industrial management, emerged metaphors through which education was viewed. These metaphors, like the means, were industrial in character. The school was seen as a *plant*. The *superintendent* directed the operation of the plant. The teachers were engaged in a job of *engineering*, and the pupils were the *raw material* to be processed in the plant according to the demands of the *consumers*. Furthermore, the product was to be judged at regular intervals along the production line using *quality control standards* which were to be quantified to reduce the likelihood of error. *Product specifications* were to be prescribed before the raw material was processed. In this way efficiency, measured with respect to cost primarily, could be determined.

The industrial metaphor, once having been imposed on schools, had several tragic consequences. Callahan (1962) identified these:

> The tragedy itself was fourfold: that educational questions were subordinated to business considerations; that administrators

were produced who were not, in any true sense, educators; that a scientific label was put on some very unscientific and dubious methods and practices; and that an anti–intellectual climate, already prevalent, was strengthened. As the business–industrial values and procedures spread into the thinking and acting of educators, countless educational decisions were made on economic or on non–educational grounds.[3]

Before comparing the educational assumptions embedded in the industrial metaphor with some of the assumptions and positions regarding educational objectives argued in the literature today, I should like to pass on to the second metaphor through which education has been viewed.

The behavioristic metaphor had its birth with efforts to construct a science of education and psychology. At the same time that school administrators were embracing the principles of scientific management in an effort to make schools more efficient, Thorndike, Watson, Judd and Bobbitt were trying to construct and employ scientific methods useful for the study and conduct of education. One part of the task, if it was to be accomplished at all, was to relinquish the heritage of a psychology that did not lend itself to scientific verification. Intra-psychic events, thoughts, and mental states couched in romantic language saturated with surplus meaning had to give way to careful, quantifiable descriptions of human behavior. The poetic and insightful language of a William James had to give way to the objective precision of a John Watson, if psychology was to become a science. By defining psychology as 'That division of natural science which takes human activity and conduct as its subject matter' Watson (1919), was able to attend to the observable event in order to accomplish two scientific goals: 'To predict human activity with reasonable certainty' and to formulate 'laws and principles whereby men's actions can be controlled by organized society'. Thorndike, although more broad ranging in his interest in and his concept of psychology, shared Watson's quest for precision in science and wrote of three stages in the description of human nature.

The first and most primitive stage is the postulation of mythical potencies. Conceptualizations of human nature through reified concepts could lead to little. Thorndike wrote: 'Science of this sort could prophesy very little of the behavior of any given man in any given situation.'[4]

A second and somewhat more advanced stage of description according to Thorndike (1921) consists:

... of more or less clearly described states of affairs to which man responds by more or less clearly described thoughts, movements, emotions or other responses ... We thus seek in this second stage of thought [about human nature] not a potency that vaguely produces large groups of consequences but bonds that unite particular responses or relations to particular situations or stimuli. Science of this sort leads to many successful prophesies of what a man will think or do in a given case, but these prophesies are crude and subject to variability and qualification.

What Thorndike sought was a precise, exact, objective science of human behavior, one without spiritual or metaphysical bogeymen.

In the third stage, behavior will be defined in terms of events in the world which any impartial observer can identify and, with the proper facilities, verify ... Science of this sort, by giving perfect identifiability and fuller knowledge, leads to completer and finer prophecy and control of human nature.

The significance of these views about the nature of science of psychology and education cannot in my opinion be overemphasized. If what education is after is a change in behavior – something that you can bring about and then observe – there is little use talking about the development of fugitive forms of non–empirical thought. If educational objectives are to be meaningful, they must be anchored in sense data and the type of data with which education is concerned is that of human behavior.

When one combines these assumptions with the research of Thorndike and Woodworth (1901) on the transfer of training research which wrecked the understructure of faculty psychology and which clearly demarcated the limits of transfer, it is easy to understand how curriculum writers could heed Thorndike's admonitions and prepare hundreds of specific, behaviorally defined objectives for the curriculum.[5] If transfer is indeed limited, as Thornike was thought to have demonstrated, it made little sense to prepare general statements of objectives referring to phenomena beyond the realm of observation. The formulation of educational objectives was to be stated in specific behavioral terms.

A third metaphor that can be used to characterize educational thought and practice during the twentieth century is biological in character. The birth of the child study movement in the 1880s, the development of egalitarian liberalism, but especially the ideas of Darwin, all had implications for conceiving the means and ends of education. With the advent of John Dewey, educationists had a powerful spokesman whose conception of man was biological. According to Dewey, man is an organism who lives not only in, but through, an environment. For Dewey, and for those who followed his lead, the child was not simply a matter to be molded but an individual who brings with him needs, potentialities, and experiences with which to transact with the environment. What was important educationally for Dewey was for the child to obtain increasing, intelligent control in planning his own education. To do this, to become a master of his own educational journey, required a teacher sympathetic to the child's background and talents. Educational experience was to be differentiated to suit the characteristics of a changing child; the cultivation of idiosyncracy was a dominant concern of those who held a biological view. Dewey (1915) writes:

> A truly scientific education can never develop so long as children are treated in the lump, merely as a class. Each child has a strong individuality, and any science must take stock of all the facts in its material. Every pupil must have a chance to show what he truly is, so that the teacher can find out what he needs to make him a complete human being. Only as a teacher becomes acquainted with each one of her pupils can she hope to understand childhood, and it is only as she understands it that she can hope to evolve any scheme of education which will approach either the scientific or the artistic standard. As long as educators do not know their individual facts they can never know whether their hypotheses are of value. But how are they to know their material if they impose themselves upon it to such an extent that each portion is made to act just like every other portion? If the pupils are marched into line, information presented to them which they are then expected to give back in uniform fashion, nothing will ever be found out about any of them. But if every pupil has an opportunity to express himself, to show what are his particular qualities, the teacher will have material on which to base her plans of instruction.[6]

The concept of education implied by the biological metaphor is one concerned neither with molding behavior through extrinsic rewards, nor with formulating uniform, quantifiable and objective standards through which to appraise achievement. Those who viewed (and view) education through the biological metaphor were (and are) much more concerned with the attainment of lofty goals, with helping children realize their unique potential, with the development of a sense of self-respect and intellectual and emotional autonomy which can be used throughout their lives. Educational practice in this view is an artful, emerging affair, one that requires teachers who are sensitive students of children and who follow as well as lead the children in the development of intelligence.[7]

The reason for identifying these strains in past educational thought is because I believe they are still with us. Indeed, I believe it is the differences in the metaphoric conception of education that, in part, account for the debates and differences regarding the use and the import of educational objectives. If education is conceived of as shaping behavior, then it is possible, indeed appropriate, to think of teachers as behavioral engineers. If the process of education is designed exclusively to enable children to acquire behaviors whose forms are known in advance, then it is possible to develop product specifications, to use quality control standards, and to identify terminal behaviors which students are to possess after having been processed properly. In this view the task of the teacher is to use scientifically developed materials which reduce error and thus make his task as a behavioral engineer more efficient. If the child is not interested in doing the task we set for him, the teacher's problem is not to find out what he is interested in but to motivate him. By establishing the appropriate reinforcement schedule we can mold the child in the image identified previously. In this view, it is not crucial to distinguish between the process of education and the process of training. The process of education enables individuals to behave intelligently through the exercise of judgment in situations that demand reflection, appraisal, and choice among alternative courses of action. The process of training develops specific types of behavioral responses to specific stimuli or situations.

If, however, education is viewed as a form of experience that has something to do with the quality of an individual's life, if it involves helping him learn to make authentic choices, choices that are a result of his own reflection and which depend upon the exercise of free will, then the problem of educational objectives takes a different turn.

What I am arguing is that the problem of determining how educational objectives should be stated or used is not simply a question of technique but a question of value. The differences between individuals regarding the nature and the use of educational objectives

46

spring from differences in their conceptions of education; under the rug of technique lies an image of man.

Compare for example the following two statements related to educational objectives:

> The behavioral technologist equates 'knowledge' and 'understanding' with behavior. He argues that there need not be any concern as to whether knowledge is basically behavior or not. The significant consideration is that the only tangible evidence of 'knowledge' is behavioral evidence.
>
> To sum up, then, the behavioral technologist approaches a problem by going through the following basic steps:
>
> 1 He specifies the behavior which the student is to acquire. (Behavior may be considered as evidence of knowledge.)
> 2 He specifies the relevant characteristics of the student, including the student's present level of knowledge.
> 3 He performs a behavioral analysis of the material to be taught. This involves 'atomizing' the knowledge to be imparted according to learning theory principles. The knowledge is broken down into concepts, discriminations, generalizations, and chains.
> 4 He constructs a teaching system or program by which the behavior may be built into the student's repertoire.
> 5 He tests the teaching system on sample students and revises it according to the results, until the desired result is obtained reliably in student after student.[8]

Now consider the following:

> The artist in the classroom in neither prevalent, nor, in fact particularly valued. He balks at established curricula, which makes administrators nervous and parents fearful, and oftentimes confuses children. He is constantly told that the school is for the students, and not a place for the teacher to push his pet fancies. When small avid groups of students congregate around him, he is reminded that school is for *all* the students, not just the few who see some perverse value in his unique conversations.
>
> So we begin with the fact that most teachers see themselves as professionals. In their training, they want to be shown how to become professional; they want to learn how to purvey the

wisdom of the culture in a reasonably standard and explicit way. In short, they want to know how to do their job ...

In these terms, the problem of teaching is construed less as the need for more creative artists to teach, but rather as the need for general scientific solutions to meet educational problems. We look not for unique personalities to provide a leavening for the flat culture; we create teams of increasingly specialized professionals to administer full-tested teaching 'systems.' The ultimate educational context then is not the free-flowing human dialogue; it is the student in the booth strapped up with a variety of teaching-learning devices monitored by a professional teacher. The implicit image is the operating room or the blood-cleansing kidney machine.[9]

What we have here are not merely two views related to the problem of stating educational objectives, but two radically different conceptions of the nature of education. The former conceives of education as the shaping of behavior; the latter as an emergent process guided through art.

Thus far I have indicated that the task of defining educational objectives rests upon a conception of value in education. In addition, I have indicated that the prescriptions offered for formulating educational objectives are related to the three metaphors through which education has been and is conceived: the industrial, the behavioristic, and the biological. These competing orientations, I am arguing, are implicit in the recommendations made by students of education as they go about the task of illuminating and improving the process of education by clarifying and prescribing the manner in which educational objectives are to be formulated and used.

As long as individuals in the educational field aspire toward different educational goals there can be no single set of research findings that will satisfy an individual who holds educational values different from those toward which the research was directed. While we can properly ask, for example, whether a clear statement of objectives on the part of the teacher facilitates curriculum planning, teaching, or student learning, and while, in principle, we can secure data to answer such questions, the significance of the answer depends not merely on the adequacy and precision of the research undertaken but on the goals toward which the educational program was directed. If education is seen as the practice of an art in which children have an opportunity to work as young apprentices with someone who himself is inquiring into a problem for which he has no answer, the relevance of concepts like terminal behavior, educational product, and deployment to learning stations, as well as research bearing upon them is likely to be considered beside the point educationally.

What of the research on educational objectives? What in fact has been found concerning the utility of educational objectives when specified according to criteria identified in the opening pages of this chapter?

A number of questions can be asked about educational objectives that are in principle amenable to empirical study. We can attempt to determine how in fact they are formulated by various groups such as curriculum developers, administrators and teachers, and it is possible to compare the methods used in their formulation to the recommendations of experts. We can determine the extent to which teachers have educational objectives and whether they meet the criteria for adequacy described by Tyler, Bloom, Gagné, and others. We can compare the curriculum planning behavior of those who have precise educational objectives with the planning of those who do not have precise educational objectives. We can determine the effect of clearly stated objectives on the process of instruction, and, perhaps most important, we can determine the relationship between clearly formulated educational objectives and student learning. Do teachers who know what they want students to be able to do as measured by the teachers' ability to state their objectives precisely (using criteria set forth by Mager, for example) have a greater effect on particular types of learning than teachers who do not? In short, we can ask questions about (1) the relationship between the way educational objectives are formulated and their quality; (2) the extent to which teachers have educational objectives; (3) the effect of educational objectives on curriculum planning; (4) the effect of educational objectives on instruction; and (5) the usefulness of educational objectives in facilitating learning.

Although such questions are complex they are important objects for empirical attention. When one looks for research on these questions, one soon finds that for the most part they have been neglected. There are some exceptions however. Margaret Ammons' study (1964) of the process and the product in curriculum development is one. In that study, Ammons set about to achieve three goals: to discover whether school systems used any systematic way of formulating educational objectives; to determine the relationship between the process used in formulating objectives and their quality; and to identify the extent to which factors thought to influence teacher appraisal of educational objectives do in fact influence such appraisal. Using a questionnaire on objectives Ammons selected a sample of school systems from a pool of 359 systems where it was possible to study the responses of board members, administrators, and teachers. At the end of her study Ammons states:

> The writer believes that this study has made the following contributions:
>
> 1 the discovery that some systems do not have objectives, as this term is defined here, to guide their educational programs;
> 2 the discovery that the school systems which participated in this study do not follow a process recommended by authorities to develop their educational objectives;
> 3 the discovery that teachers in this study appear to base their instructional programs on what they customarily have done rather than on the system's educational objectives;
> 4 the discovery that while no significant relation exists between process and product using the data collected for this study, there is enough relation to suggest further research before the process is discarded;
> 5 the possibility of using empirical tests to evaluate curriculum theories;
> 6 areas for further research have been identified.[10]

Gagné (1965) discusses the importance of educational objectives in the development of instructional systems. He refers to French's work in training apprentice Air Force mechanics and to Briggs and Bernards' work also in Air Force maintenance training as providing evidence on the effectiveness of instructional objectives. Evidence on the effectiveness of high level specification of objectives in educational settings is considerably more tenuous.

Although Nerbovig (1956) found that intermediate grade teachers who had participated in the formulation of objectives and who had longer experience as teachers used objectives more frequently in planning their curriculums, Ammons' findings contradict Nerbovig's.

In an interesting effort to create an instructional objectives preference list, Popham and Baker (1965) asked students to rate on a five-point scale instructional objectives arranged according to usefulness. One class of statements was both behaviorally stated and important, a second class behaviorally stated and unimportant, a third non-behaviorally stated and important, and a fourth non-behaviorally stated and not important. When the subjects' (in this case student teachers) lesson plans were surreptitiously observed with respect to the use of behaviorally defined objectives and correlated with the subjects' preferences as revealed in their ranking of objectives, $r = .25$ ($p < .05$). Although reported only as a note in the *Journal of Educational Measurement* the research by Popham and Baker appears promising; it suggests the type of enquiry needed to clarify the function of educational objectives in educational settings.

In view of the admonitions in curriculum literature to state objectives in behavioral terms, it is surprising to find such a paucity of empirical studies available. Most of the studies that have been undertaken were done in training systems in industry or in the military services. One would think – and hope – that there would be some differences between industrial and military training and education. In the *Review of Educational Research* John Goodlad (1960) wrote, 'There appear to be no studies establishing an actual relationship between increased clarification of educational objectives and improved discrimination in the selection of classroom learning opportunities for students.' With respect to quantitative empirical research in school settings the situation appears not to have changed much in the past eight years.

From the published studies of educational objectives one can conclude that:

1   a very limited amount of empirical data is available on the subject,
2   a narrow range of questions have been asked; and
3   most of the discussion on the usefulness of educational objectives has been based primarily upon rational analysis.

Now I have no bone to pick with the rational analysis of educational issues if empirical data are unavailable or unobtainable. Indeed, in a previous paper (1967a) I explicated some of the problems concerning high-level specification of educational objectives and such explication was a result of analysis rather than a result of conclusions based upon quantitative data. In that paper I identified a number of limitations in theory about high-level specification of objectives. Without elaborating on them here, they were as follows:

1   they tend to overestimate the degree to which it is possible to predict educational outcomes,
2   they tend to treat all subject matters alike regarding the degree of specificity possible in stating educational objectives,
3   they tend to confuse the application of a standard and the making of a judgment regarding the appraisal of educational outcomes,
4   they have tended to imply that the formulation of objectives should be a first step in curriculum development and hence have confused the logical with the psychological in educational planning.

In a subsequent paper (1967b), I argued further that those who have advocated high-level specification of objectives have not differentiated between establishing a direction and formulating an objective. I argued that much in school practice which is educational is a consequence of establishing directions rather than formulating objectives.

I see even more problems now. For one, if we follow Gagné's suggestions (1967) regarding the identity of content and objective, we would select or use no content which had no objective and therefore have objectives for each unit of content we selected. What would this mean in the classroom? If the suggestion were followed strictly, the teacher would have to formulate behaviorally defined objectives for each unit of content for each educational program for which she was responsible and in the elementary school she may teach in as many as fourteen subject areas.

Let's assume that a teacher has one unit of content to be learned by a group of thirty children for each of seven subject areas a day. Let's assume further that she has her class divided in thirds in order to differentiate content for students with differing abilities. This would mean that the teacher would have to formulate objectives for seven units of content, times five days a week, times three groups of students, times four weeks a month, times ten months a school year. She would therefore have to have 4,200 behaviorally defined objectives for a school year. A six-year school employing such a curriculum rationale would have to have 25,200 behaviorally defined educational objectives.

Aside from the question of the sheer feasibility of such a scheme, what those who object to such an approach are concerned with, I think, is that even if the scheme could be implemented, it would alter the type of relationship between the teacher and the student that they value. If a teacher focuses primarily on the attainment of clearly specified objectives, she is not likely to focus on other aspects of the educational encounter, for although clearly specified objectives provide windows, they also create walls. Those who are not enthusiastic about high-level specification of objectives are not eager, I believe, to look through the windows of those who conceive of education as behavioral engineering.

Can such differences in orientation to education be resolved when it comes to the issue of how, if at all, educational objectives should be formulated? The remainder of this chapter will elucidate a conception of educational objectives which might make this resolution possible.

As an institution responsible for the transmission of culture, the school is concerned with enabling students to acquire those intellectual codes and skills which will make it possible for them to profit from the contributions of those who have gone before. To accomplish this task an array of socially defined skills must be learned – reading, writing, and arithmetic are some examples of coding systems that are basic to further enquiry into human culture.

While school programs attempt to enable children to acquire these skills, to learn to employ the tools necessary for using cultural products, schools are also concerned with enabling children to make a contribution to that culture by providing opportunities for the individual to construe his own interpretation to the material he encounters or constructs. A simple repetition of the past is the surest path to cultural rigor mortis.

Given these dual concerns – helping children to become skilled in the use of cultural tools already available and helping them to modify and expand these tools so that the culture remains viable – it seems to me appropriate to differentiate between two types of educational objectives which can be formulated in curriculum planning. The first type is familiar to most readers and is called an *instructional objective*; the second I have called an *expressive objective*.

Instructional objectives are objectives which specify unambiguously the particular behavior (skill, item of knowledge, and so forth) the student is to acquire after having completed one or more learning activities. These objectives fit the scheme or criteria identified earlier. They are usually drawn from cultural products such as the disciplines and are laid out in intervals of time appropriate for the children who are to acquire them.

Instructional objectives are used in a predictive model of curriculum development. A predictive model is one in which objectives are formulated and activities selected which are predicted to be useful in enabling children to attain the specific behavior embodied in the objective. In this model, evaluation is aimed at determining the extent to which the objective has been achieved. If the objective has not been achieved, various courses of action may follow. The objective may be changed. The instructional method may be altered. The content of the curriculum may be revised.

With an instructional objective the teacher as well as the children (if they are told what the objective is) are likely to focus upon the attainment of a specific array of behaviors. The teacher in the instructional context knows what to look for as an indicator of achievement since the objective unambiguously defines the behavior. Insofar as the children are at similar stages of development and insofar as the curriculum and the instruction are effective, the outcomes of the learning activity will be homogeneous in character. The effective curriculum, when it is aimed at instructional objectives, will develop forms of behavior whose characteristics are known beforehand and, as likely as not, will be common across students – if not at the identical point in time, at some point during the school program.

The use of instructional objectives has a variety of educational ramifications. In preparing reading material in the social studies, for example, study questions at the beginning of a chapter can be used as cues to guide the student's attention to certain concepts or generalizations which the teacher intends to help the student learn. In the development of certain motor skills the teacher may provide examples of such skills and thus show the student what he is supposed to be able to do upon terminating the program. With the use of instructional objectives clarity of terminal behavior is crucial since it serves as a standard against which to appraise the effectiveness of the curriculum. *In an effective curriculum using instructional objectives the terminal behavior of the student and the objectives are isomorphic.*

Expressive objectives differ considerably from instructional objectives. An expressive objective does not specify the behavior the student is to acquire after having engaged in one or more learning activities. An expressive objective describes an educational encounter: It identifies a situation in which children are to work, a problem with which they are to cope, a task in which they are to engage; but it does not specify what from that encounter, situation, problem, or task they are to learn. An expressive objective provides both the teacher and the student with an invitation to explore, defer, or focus on issues that are of peculiar interest or import to the enquirer. An expressive objective is evocative rather than prescriptive.

The expressive objective is intended to serve as a theme around which skills and understandings learned earlier can be brought to bear, but through which those skills and understandings can be expanded, elaborated, and made idiosyncratic. With an expressive objective what is desired is not homogeneity of response among students but diversity. In the expressive context the teacher hopes to provide a situation in which meanings become personalized and in which children produce products, both theoretical and qualitative, that are as diverse as themselves. Consequently the evaluative task in this situation is not one of applying a common standard to the products produced but one of reflecting upon what has been produced in order to reveal its uniqueness and significance. In the expressive context, the product is likely to be as much of a surprise to the maker as it is for the teacher who encounters it.

Statements of expressive objectives might read:

1   To interpret the meaning of *Paradise Lost*,
2   To examine and appraise the significance of *The Old Man and the Sea*,
3   To develop a three-dimensional form through the use of wire and wood,
4   To visit the zoo and discuss what was of interest there.

What should be noted about such objectives is that they do not specify what the student is to be able to do after he engages in an educational activity; rather they identify the type of encounter he is to have. From this encounter both teacher and student acquire data useful for evaluation. In this context the mode of evaluation is similar to aesthetic criticism; that is, the critic appraises a product, examines its qualities and import, but does not direct the artist toward the painting of a specific type of picture. The critic's subject matter is the work done – he does not prescribe a blueprint of its construction.

Now I happen to believe that expressive objectives are the type that teachers most frequently use. Given the range and the diversity of children it is more useful to identify potentially fruitful encounters than to specify instructional objectives.

Although I believe that the use of expressive objectives is generally more common than the use of instructional objectives, in certain subject areas curriculum specialists have tended to emphasize one rather than the other. In mathematics, for example, much greater attention historically has been given to the instructional objective than in the visual arts where the dominant emphasis has been on the expressive.[11]

I believe that the most sophisticated modes of intellectual work – those, for example, undertaken in the studio, the research laboratory, and the graduate seminar – most frequently employ expressive rather than instructional objectives. In the doctoral seminar, for example, a theme will be identified around which both teacher and students can interact in an effort to cope more adequately with the problems related to the theme. In such situations educational outcomes are appraised after they emerge; specific learnings are seldom formulated in terms of instructional objectives. The dialogue unfolds and is followed as well as led. In such situations the skills and understandings developed are used as instruments for enquiring more deeply into the significant or puzzling. Occasionally such problems require the invention of new intellectual tools, thus inducing the creative act and the creative contribution. Once devised or fashioned these new tools become candidates for instructional attention.

Since these two types of objectives – instructional and expressive – require different kinds of curriculum activities and evaluation procedures, they each must occupy a distinctive place in curriculum theory and development. Instructional objectives embody the codes and the skills that culture has to provide and that make enquiry possible. Expressive objectives designate those circumstances in which the codes and the skills acquired in instructional contexts can be used and elaborated; through their expansion and reconstruction culture remains vital. Both types of objectives and the learning activities they imply constitute, to modify Whitehead's phrase, 'the rhythm of curriculum.' That is, instructional objectives emphasize the acquisition of the known while expressive objectives, emphasize its elaboration, modification, and, at times, the production of the utterly new.

Curriculum can be developed with an eye toward the alternating of such objectives. We can, I believe, study curriculum to determine the extent to which instructional and expressive educational objectives are employed, and we can raise questions about the types of relationships between them which are most productive for various types of students, for various types of learning, and for various subject matters.

In this chapter I have argued that the problem of formulating educational objectives is not simply a question of technique but is related directly to one's conception of education. The manner in which educational objectives are couched is, at base, a value decision. Second, I have tried to provide evidence of the differences among these values by examining the metaphors used by those who have contributed to the literature of the field. Third, I have cited empirical research aimed at examining the usefulness of educational objectives. Fourth, I have distinguished between two types of educational objectives – instructional and expressive – and indicated how they function in curriculum planning. The formulation and use of these objectives have implications for the selection of learning activities and for evaluation. The consequences of their use seem to me to be appropriate subject matter for research.

Discussion

POPHAM: This will be a discussion of Elliot Eisner's chapter. Who would like to start off?

SULLIVAN: I would be pleased to start. Elliot, I was wondering if you have changed your views recently. I know that your 1966 paper received fairly wide publicity and is still receiving it. I'm just curious as to how accurately it reflects your present views and how accurately the recent *School Review* issue reflects them.

EISNER: The recent *School Review* issue is a publication of the 1966 paper with relatively few modifications. There was a minor expansion, but it's essentially the same paper. I think that the major change is the one which appears in the present chapter; the conceptualization of what I think of as an expressive objective. At the time that I wrote the earlier paper, I didn't have that idea in mind. The major purpose of the paper at that time was simply to say that the process of education, or the conception of education, is not totally circumscribed by high level behavioral specifications of objectives and that there was another dimension to look at. In the current paper, an additional concept is introduced so that my position is not a matter of 'all or nothing' with respect to educational objectives. It is a position in which different kinds of objectives can be thought about which I think have implications for curriculum and evaluation.

POPHAM: I don't think the 1966 paper raises quite as nicely the metaphor concepts that you make very explicit in your current chapter. I'd like to examine these three metaphors more particularly because I think they are very accurate representations of differing value positions. You point out quite clearly that, as statements of value positions, they influence the way one thinks about objectives. So far I'm in complete agreement. What concerns me a little is that they seem to be statements

57

of value positions regarding means, not necessarily ends. That is, I think their focus is upon the procedures used by the teacher and by the schools in order to achieve some kind of desirable change in the learner, and I know that's very important. Let's assume for the moment that I could describe the 'good human being.' Wouldn't it be possible, perhaps, to use any of these three instructional approaches and produce one?

EISNER: I think in principle it would be possible. I don't see any a priori basis for saying that if you have a given end stated there might not be a variety of means for arriving at that end. Now whether, in fact, the conceptualization of education that people with different orientations hold are identical, whether the real difference is essentially in the means rather than the ends, is certainly something which can be argued about. If you read, for example, Callahan's work with respect to the efficiency movement in education and compare it with the goals that were formulated by experimentalists such as Dewey and the progressives who followed him, there would be, I think, no doubt in anyone's mind that the issue is not simply one of means, it is one of ends as well. I think different instructional approaches can relate to both ends as well as means.

POPHAM: I'm sure this is so. I think it's very easy to get the two muddled. I find people very frequently thinking about the ends question merged in some way with the means question. They can't seem to separate them. As far as your three metaphors are concerned, it would help if we made it very clear that at least to some extent they are pretty heavily involved with means rather than exclusively ends.

TYLER: I am confused about your differentiation between expressive objectives and instructional objectives. You indicate that expressive objectives describe an educational encounter. It identifies the situation in which children are to work or the task they are to engage in. But it does not specify what they are to learn from that encounter situation, problem, or task. And then you give some examples of expressive objectives. 'To interpret the meaning of *Paradise Lost*.' What's that? A task they are engaged in?

EISNER: Yes.

TYLER: 'To examine and appraise the significance of *The Old Man and the Sea*.' What's that?

EISNER: A task.

TYLER: How about 'To develop a three-dimensional form through the use of wire and wood'?

EISNER: That is also a task.

TYLER: These are all tasks. So you haven't really given illustrations of other kinds yet. You know it seemed as though there were going to be several different kinds of expressive objectives. You also say that in the expressive context the teacher hopes to provide a situation in which means become personalized and in which children produce products both theoretical and qualitative. Now in interpreting the meaning of *Paradise Lost*, what's the product in that?

EISNER: The product probably would be something in the way of a written or verbal statement. But the point is that the way in which the poem gets interpreted, the specific characteristics that the product is going to have, if you want to conceive of it in terms of the product, is not something which the teacher necessarily has in her mind or on paper beforehand. The utility, the import, the significance of that kind of an activity (or product of that kind of an activity) is appraised after it is made in much the same way that a critic will look at a painting or a poem and make some appraisal of it. That is, if you use an analogy in the arts, art does not develop by having critics describe the principles, or the characteristics that art forms should have, and then having artists use these principles to produce products which meet those characteristics. On the contrary, criticism has as its subject matter the work of artists, what they paint, sculpt, and write. What the critics do is to try to illuminate what has been done, and when a creative contribution is made through the arts, or I would even argue through the sciences, the critic's function is one of illuminating certain characteristics which were not previously formulated. In other words, the creative contribution is a function of what people produce which has not been preconceived but, upon analysis, is judged to be valuable. So when you have a situation in a classroom where youngsters are asked to discuss or explore a problem, for example, the significance of the learning is, I believe, determined afterward. What the teacher will do is to reflect upon, with the youngster perhaps, what has been done. I think that this is a different kind of situation from looking at the relationship between a product and some previously conceived specifications.

SULLIVAN: But, Elliot, aren't you saying that you are just using a different criterion for evaluating it? Now you are evaluating it in terms of its effects rather than in terms of specific, intrinsic characteristics, such as color or form. You could, in fact, describe at some point or other the effects that it would have on individuals, whether those be effects that please them in some aesthetic way or effects that may have some significance for health purposes.

EISNER: Yes, I think you could, Howard. But if you want to use that kind of criterion, that is, that the product shall be such as to move people aesthetically, it would not meet the standards that many of those who advocate behavioral objectives specify as being necessary in order to have an acceptable criterion.

TYLER: You've lost me, Elliot. You've got to interpret the meaning of *Paradise Lost*. Now you say that is an expressive objective. Partially what bothers me is that this sounds almost like a behavioral objective. Now I don't know whether Jim or Howard would agree that it sounds rather like a behavioral objective, to interpret the meaning of *Paradise Lost*.

POPHAM: No.

TYLER: You'd say 'no,' all right. Are you saying, Elliot, you have no idea what a youngster needs to say about the meaning of *Paradise Lost*?

EISNER: Oh, I might have some general idea.

TYLER: Aren't there some ideas about *Paradise Lost* that you think anybody who can interpret the meaning of it would come out with?

EISNER: Surely, there are some general ideas, but those don't relate to the specific characteristics of the interpretation. If you have 30 different youngsters, it could be, in principle, interpreted 30 different ways, and you might have only 20 models of an adequate interpretation. But upon analysis you might conclude that the 10 which were not a part of your original 20 models were also adequate. It seems to me that this kind of appraisal is terribly important because it opens up the opportunity for the teacher to discover *ex post facto* outcomes of an educational encounter which are also important. I think that the kind of criteria that Howard and Jim formulate with respect to instructional objectives are highly consistent and I would classify them in the instructional area. I'm not arguing that we shouldn't have instructional objectives, but I think that there are differences between these and other kinds of objectives. I'm trying to explicate what I see as some of the differences.

POPHAM: With respect to expressive objectives and the instructional objectives, I see a fairly clear difference, using simple terms, between what a teacher, for example, wants to have happen to the kids and what a teacher decides to do in order to have it happen. Now in the first case you have intents regarding the behavioral changes that will occur in learners. In the second case you have procedures that you're selecting for which you have some hunch that consequences will emerge. It seems to me what you're saying with respect to expressive objectives is that they are the encounters which I might call 'learning activities.' I'm almost sure that when you select them you implicitly ascribe to them probable kinds of outcomes, classes of outcomes, which, let's say particularly in your field of art, we would be less willing to supply preconceived criteria for. But I'm afraid, Elliot, that if we also start calling these activities 'objectives,' then considerable confusion emerges.

EISNER: This is a very important point that you're making and it's one I've thought about. I have no way of specifying the nature of the expressive objective as an outcome because I can't anticipate it. So what I'm taking is the next step down, specifying the kind of encounter which is likely to yield it. But I do think that there is an important difference between formulating objectives which are to yield prescribed outcomes – prescribed in the terms which you, Howard, and other people in the field would like to see them – and looking at the outcomes as a result of educational encounter. I think that a great many educationally important consequences ensue from having such opportunities in the classroom. I would want a school curriculum to provide not only for those things which are of an instructionally objective nature but those things which potentially will yield something of educational value even though the precise dimensions of the outcomes cannot be specified to the level of clarity or specificity that instructional objectives ought to have.

POPHAM: I see the distinction that you are making. On one hand, you have precisely prescribed criteria by which you judge the adequacy of a learner's behavior, and on the other, you don't really know the criteria, or let's say you don't know them as well. Now the danger I see in this is that to the extent to which an instructor is unclear regarding the criteria he will use, he may select instructional means erroneously because he doesn't have a clear idea of what might happen at the end of instruction. This is why I've always liked Munro's statement when he says that art educators have to specify 'tentative but clearly defined criteria.' Now take your example of having thirty students and twenty satisfactory ways to interpret a literary selection. Certainly the tentative criteria would handle the twenty, but they wouldn't handle the new ten. But one can revise the criteria. It seems to me that an instructor who thinks clearly about the tentative criteria is in a more rational position than the instructor who only focuses on the encounter and says, in essence, 'We'll worry about results later.'

EISNER: I think that if you characterize it in terms of what it could lead to negatively, I would have the same concern. But by the same token you can characterize an unfortunate use of instructional objectives. What we're trying to do is to make some theoretical distinctions with respect to curriculum goals that might have pay-offs. I'm not prepared to say that the whole answer resides in the formulation of instructional objectives for every curriculum activity in which students engage in the school. Although many people in the field have talked about the virtues of instructional objectives and their assets, there have been relatively few who have examined the other side of the coin, something I'm attempting to do.

TYLER: I'm still not clear about expressive objectives. Again I'll go back. You say it describes an educational encounter, and you also say it provides both the teacher and the student with an invitation to explore. I don't see that the teacher is doing anything, and this doesn't sound like a description of an educational encounter. I would have expected to have something with an encounter involve at least two people or a person and a product. I don't see a real *encounter* here.

EISNER: That section might have been elaborated more, but a teacher, for example, might want to take a group of kids to a slum area. Maybe these kids live in a lily white suburb and they haven't seen slums except through TV or the movies, and the teacher makes arrangements to take them there. She might not be either able or willing to formulate specific behavioral outcomes for the multiplicity of potential learning experiences that those youngsters will undergo. But after she takes them through the slums they go back to class, they talk about what they've learned. In the course of that discussion and dialogue she finds out, as they do through their own articulation, and this is quite important.

Let me make an aside here. Take, for example, a person like Collingwood who talks about the fact (or at least to him it's a fact as a philosopher and an aesthetician) that a person really doesn't know what he knows until he has expressed it. Then, in the course of discussion about their experience things come to light both to them and to the teacher which the teacher had not preconceived. The diversity of learning for the thirty kids who went to that slum is exceedingly wide. I want to provide in a theoretical conception of curriculum some handles for organizing such activities without making the teacher feel guilty if she does not formulate instructional objectives for what those kids are going to get out of that particular situation.

POPHAM: I'd almost prefer to make the teacher feel a little guilty, as you probably can guess. I have no trouble, I think, understanding what you mean by expressive objectives as you described them. The encounter idea is pretty clear to me. You mean, as you just suggested, that something is done without necessarily preconceived outcomes in mind. An anecdote occurred to me just as you were talking. My first teaching job was in a little town in eastern Oregon. I was teaching a class in American Government and I had been told, I suppose during teacher training days, that 'field experiences' were good. I thought that the idea of an encounter, that is, field experience, was a good thing. We were studying a unit on Municipal Government and I wanted to take my class on a field experience. I didn't know why really, but it did seem like a good encounter. The only thing that seemed worth studying in this little town was that they had a new municipal sewage disposal plant. So I took my class, with no clear conception of outcomes, out to the sewage disposal plant. I think what emerged from this encounter was a more diverse vocabulary to describe the primary product of sewage disposal plants, because some of my students used fairly vivid language throughout the tour. At the end of it, well, I'd taken the class on a field trip. But, in retrospect, I'd never do it again that way, because I didn't have any clear conception of what I wanted to emerge from the encounter. As a consequence, I think I selected a poor encounter. I *should* have felt guilty.

EISNER: I suppose this relates to how one thinks education ought to proceed, and this would be an indication of, you might say, the philosophic difference with respect to the ways in which schools operate. We have places like Summerhill in England and the Oak-leaf School which operate quite differently.

SULLIVAN: I think even your teacher, Elliot, who took the kids on the field trip to the slums would have a number of preconceived ideas about attitudes that she would like them to acquire – attitudes that may or may not ever be expressed naturally in overt behavior other than paper and pencil behavior, or something like that if the teacher attempts to measure it. I think that this could become a very bad encounter for the teacher if they did in fact acquire attitudes that were at odds with those that she had intended. I just can't conceive of her not having some preconceived objectives. I think that's a good example in that a number of other outcomes that she may not have originally anticipated are more likely to accrue, I would guess, on a trip like that other than in direct instructional situations.

EISNER: I think, Howard, that teachers might do what you suggested, that is, have a general idea of the thing that might occur. But surely, those general notions about what she hopes might occur will not meet the specifications that people who are fairly consistent about instructional objectives would have.

SULLIVAN: You know, it seems to me that for her own instructional purposes she might want to evaluate the effects of that trip in such a way that she would recognize that she had, in advance, certain identified attitudes (maybe for her own purposes only measurable through paper and pencil means at that time). She ought to have even written down, or certainly have firmly fixed in her head in some way, what that particular activity and the discussion relating to it was supposed to produce. She would then evaluate whether or not these had been attained and use this to improve her future *encounters* with the class. If she found that their attitudes were more negative than they had been before, she would presumably either change the experience somewhat or drop it altogether for subsequent groups.

TYLER: I was trying to find whether you said anything in here about why you prefer the kind of philosophy you prefer?

EISNER: No, I didn't say anything about that and, as I indicated a couple of times in our discussion. I'm not trying to characterize the men in the white hats and the men in the black hats. I think, as I said at the end of my chapter, that there are certain things that kids *must learn* in school. You don't want 'creative' spellers in school. There are things that you know are going to look a certain way because that's the way we spell and multiply and so forth. On the other hand, we need to provide in school for the development of these modes of behavior which are unique and creative in character, so that this kind of opportunity for production can become, if you will, a part of the repertoire of the youngster, so that culture can remain viable. As I see the curriculum, I want to provide for both kinds of opportunities.

TYLER: So you're saying if you have instructional objectives it's going to close down this possibility?

EISNER: No, we use what we've learned through instructional objectives and the activities which they prescribe, hopefully, in some way that will enable us to develop those things which are not prescribable. In other words, the person needs to learn mathematics in order to eventually use it in some way which has personal significance and maybe even social significance. But there is one thing I'd like to indicate. If you tell a youngster that these are the kinds of things you ought to be getting out of this book or these are the questions that you ought to address yourself to when you read this book, you may indeed help him to be more efficient in extracting the things you've asked for. But you may also be closing off, by doing that, other possibilities in which he discovers or relates meanings that he might not otherwise discover. That is, when you provide a window for looking at something, you also, if I can use the analogy, provide something in the way of a wall. It's not a matter of being against instructional objectives, it's a matter of some kind of appropriate balance and, again, this is what I'm trying to provide. The kind of school that I would like, if you want to characterize it, would be one in which as youngsters move through they would have increasing opportunities to deal more with the expressive than with the systematic and instructional.

SULLIVAN: I think I would like to go back to your remarks regarding the people who are now advocating the use of behavioral objectives. We were talking about art and I suggested that a criterion you might set for it was that it must be given a certain rating (judged as acceptable or outstanding) by a group of observers whether they be experts or other teachers. I think you're right in that people writing objectives generally have not written well about this point. On the other hand, I think that may be the limitation of the state of the technology rather than a limitation of the objectives themselves. I can think of cases in which we have done this very same thing in writing objectives for classes so that you do, in fact, set the criterion as being the judgment of some other group of individuals rather than that the learner's product itself has certain characteristics.

POPHAM: You might, let's say, set up an instructional experience (or encounter, using Elliot's terminology) so that the products produced would be satisfactory to a competent observer and you might even get close to describing the criteria they would use. That would be good enough for you.

SULLIVAN: That's right – that it's described in terms of its effects on others rather than in terms of its own physical characteristics.

POPHAM: I suppose what this gets at is why your particular terminology bothers me. I'm not quibbling about terminology, but I think the idea of talking about an encounter as an objective may actually do a disservice to the cause you want to promote. And I agree with the cause you want to promote. I think the essence of the distinction between things you would call instructional objectives and things you would call expressive objectives is the following: In the case of instructional objectives, you know how to judge what emerges, in the case of expressive objectives you don't know how. Why isn't it better to say for some instructional objectives you have rather clear criteria already in mind. For other instructional objectives you don't have clear criteria in mind, and yet, you want to work toward clarity.

EISNER: I think you want to have your cake and eat it too. What you'd like is to have it both ways, Jim, and I'm more or less taking you, in the plural, at your word in terms of the specifications. Now, if you want to expand the conception of instructional objectives so that it has another dimension to it, then the terminology can go by the boards.

SULLIVAN: You know, this also relates to the point you raised in your chapter about the individuals in the studio and the research laboratory who are engaging in particular endeavors. I pick up the implication from your remarks that they are really not working for the particular objectives or they were not sure of the objectives for which they were working. Again, I feel that they are. In our laboratory we are attempting to produce some reading materials which have specified effects upon other individuals. Now, we are not specifically defining, at this point, the characteristics of those materials because we are unable to state what properties will bring about the particular effects that we want. But we are able to describe them in terms of the effects that they will have and it just seems to me that it's a somewhat different way of looking at the characteristics of a product.

EISNER: I think that is a different kettle of fish. Suppose you take three or four judges and ask them to appraise a product and then you get some kind of consensus with respect to its value. Now that's different from describing the characteristics of the behavior or product that the learner is trying to produce in the first place. I think that's the distinction we need to make. I think it is an important one, Howard, and I don't think we have made that kind of distinction. In the process of writing, in the process of painting, and in the process of researching, ideas emerge which become leading ideas which then direct the course of action. Sometimes these ideas you know are accidental, they are unanticipated. You write yourself clear. You see what you said. This is goal-seeking behavior. In a much vaguer sense it's 'muddling through,' and it's an important kind of activity which I think is very characteristic of people at the cutting edge of enquiry, and the cutting edge of enquiry need not be at the adult level.

Inquiry can be contextually defined so that the youngster can be at the cutting edge of inquiry for him. I would like to see us provide situations in a school where that cutting edge experience can be undergone because in a very important sense you might say that the ultimate criterion of education is an aesthetic criterion rather than a product criterion. It may be that the most important goal of education is to enable people to think in such a way that the kind of experience they undergo is a feelingful experience, is an aesthetic experience. If we enable them to have that kind of experience in school, then maybe they would be more likely to derive that experience subsequently. Unfortunately, I think, too often in school the activities that youngsters engage in are neither instrumental nor consummatory for them.

As I think about people who are doing research or painting, one reason that they do it is because they like the interior excitement that they undergo when they're doing it, and this excitement emanates in large measure from things which they come upon in the course of their muddling through. The process is not as neat, it is not as linear, it is not as systematic as I think the general implications are of many of the things that I read with respect to the specification of instructional objectives and the kind of linear organization of learning activities that should follow from them. And I'm not saying that we don't need some of those. I'm saying that we need to have both dimensions.

POPHAM: I would like to raise one point with respect to the instructional objectives you think we should have. When you observed that if the teacher were to have precise instructional objectives, you ended up with 25,000 objectives pretty fast there. Now, many people have observed that if we do get this precise about objectives then we will run the risk of having too many. Adopting your white hat, that is, the one concerning instructional objectives, how would you suggest that the teacher can keep a manageable number of objectives?

EISNER: I don't know. That's one of the questions I was going to ask you, Jim. Namely, what is the educational unit for which instructional objectives should be formulated? Can we defer that until the discussion of your chapter?

POPHAM: Agreed. Shall we turn to the next chapter then?

Notes

1. TYLER, R. (1950) *Basic Principles of Curriculum and Instruction* Chicago, University of Chicago Press.
2. GAGNÉ, R. (1967) 'Curriculum research and the promotion of learning' in TYLER, R., GAGNÉ, R. and SCRIVEN, M. *Perspectives of Curriculum Evaluation*, AERA Monograph 1, Chicago, Rand McNally, pp. 21–22.
3. CALLAHAN, R.E. (1962) *Education and the Cult of Efficiency* Chicago, University of Chicago Press, pp. 246–47.
4. THORNDIKE, E.L. (1921) *Educational Psychology, Vol. 1, The Original Nature of Man* New York, Teachers College, Columbia Univesity, pp. 11–12.
5. BILLINGS, N.A. (1929) *A Determination of Generalizations Basic to the Social Studies Curriculum* Baltimore, Warwick and York.
6. DEWEY, J. and DEWEY, E. (1915) *Schools of Tomorrow* New York, Dutton, pp. 137–38.

7. HARAP, H. (Ed.) (1937) *The Changing Curriculum* New York, Appleton-Century.
8. MECHNER, F. 'Science education and behavioural technology' in GLASER, R. (Ed.) (1965) *Teaching Machines and Programmed Learning II: Data and Directions* Washington, Department of Audio Visual Instruction, NEA, pp. 443–44.
9. OLIVER, D. (1967) 'The education industries' in *Harvard Educational Review*, 37, 1, p. 111.
10. AMMONS, M. (1964) 'An empirical study of progress and product in curriculum development' in *Journal of Educational Research*, 27, 9, pp. 451–57.
11. EISNER, E.W. (1965) 'Curriculum ideas in time of crises' in *Art Education* 18, 7.

References

BLOOM, B.S., ENGELHART, M.D., FAUST, E.J., HILL, W.H., and KRATHWOHL, D.R. (1956) *Taxonomy of Educational Objectives: Handbook I, The Cognitive Domain.* New York, Longmans, Green (David McKay).

DEWEY, J. (1934) 'Criticism and perception,' *In Art as Experience* New York, Minton, Balch, pp. 298–325.

EISNER, E.W. (1967a) Educational objectives: Help or hindrance? in *School Review*, 75, 3, pp. 250–266. (a)

EISNER, E.W. (1967b) 'A response to my critics' in *School Review* 75, 3, pp. 277–282.

GAGNÉ, R. (1965) 'The analysis of instructional objectives for the design of instruction' In GLASER, R. (Ed.) *Teaching Machines and Programmed Learning, II: Data and Directions* Washington, Department of Audio Visual Instruction, N.E.A., pp. 21–65.

GOODLAD, J.I. (1960) 'Curriculum: The state of the field' in *Review of Educational Research*, 20, 3, p. 192.

KRATHWOHL, D.R., BLOOM, B.S., and MASIA, B.B. (1964) *Taxonomy of Educational Objectives: Handbook II, The Affective Domain* New York, David McKay.

MAGER, R.F. (1962) *Preparing Objectives for Programmed Instruction.* Palo Alto, Fearon.

NERBOVIG, M.H. (1956) 'Teachers perceptions of the function of objectives' doctoral thesis, University of Wisconsin, Dissertation Abstracts, 16, 12, pp. 2406–2407.

NEWMANN, F.M. and OLIVER, D.W. (1967) 'Education and community' in *Harvard Educational Review* 37, 1, pp. 61–106.

POPHAM, W.J., and BAKER, E.L. (1965) 'The instructional objectives preference test' in *Journal of Educational Measurement* UCLA, 2, p. 186.

THORNDIKE, E.L., and WOODWORTH, R.S. (1901) 'The influence of improvement in one mental function upon the efficiency of other functions' in *Psychological Review*, May.

WATSON, J.B. (1919) *Psychology from the Standpoint of a Behaviorist* Philadelphia, Lippincott, pp. 1–2.

Epilogue

After having read the discussion of my paper it is clear to me that the major object of attention was the distinction between instructional and expressive objectives. It is clear also that this distinction needs further elaboration. In this brief epilogue I would like to clarify that distinction and to deal with a few other points in the discussion as well.

The concept 'instructional objectives' is not new to educational literature and I will not elaborate its characteristics here except to identify again the form that statements of instructional objectives are to have in order to be useful. First, they should describe what the student, not the teacher, is to be able to do. Second, both the behavior of the student and the content in which it is to be displayed are to be identified. Third, the context for assessing the behavior is to be described. Fourth, instructional objectives should be sufficiently specific to refer to observable behavior and not to non-empirical mentalistic events. There appears to be little disagreement regarding these specifications of instructional objectives. But, of course, their history is a long one. Bobbitt, Charters, Tyler, Bloom, Gagné, and Mager have all written about them at one time or another.

'Expressive objectives' is a new concept and needs clarification. In my paper I described expressive objectives in terms of encounters that students were to have in an educational setting. This was done in order to provide some type of description of the expressive objective. But I see now what I didn't anticipate at the time I wrote the paper that describing expressive objectives this way tends to confuse them with learning activities. There is enough confusion in the field of curriculum without my contributing more.

What I would like to describe as an expressive objective is the *outcome* of an encounter or learning activity which is planned to provide the student with an opportunity to personalize learning. It is precisely because of the richness of these encounters or activities and the unique character of the outcome that the expressive objective becomes so difficult to describe in advance. To avoid attempting to do the impossible, I shifted to a description of the encounter.

I believe that a large percentage – perhaps the overwhelming majority – of teachers from kindergarten through college tend to think of objectives in these terms. Teachers at all levels, but especially at the elementary level, tend to appraise their own teaching by the extent to which students appear engaged, immersed, caught up, and interested in the activities of the classroom. Engagement, I believe, is a fundamental criterion used by teachers to select learning activities and to appraise their consequences. The reason for using this criterion rather than instructional objectives is because, as I view the situation, teachers believe that engagement, intellectual and emotional immersion, is a better indicator of educational value than achievement test scores.

The risk, therefore, of describing expressive objectives in terms of encounters is one of confounding them with learning activities. One must therefore either be content with taking the risk or not describing the objective at all *before* the encounter or activity but waiting until *after* the encounter to describe what has occurred.

Another point raised in the discussion about the relationship between instructional and expressive objectives was that they might refer to means primarily rather than to ends. Wasn't I really taking issue with the means of education suggested by instructional objectives rather than with the ends to which they were directed?

In my paper I have tried to indicate that the means one uses to educate human beings have bearing upon the ends one achieves. Prescribing to teachers a necessity to have instructional objectives for each learning activity planned is likely to affect the way in which the teacher works and is likely to affect the pervasive quality of the classroom and school. These in turn are likely to affect the quality of the educational experience and the results of that experience. It is this concern rather than a mere concern with how objectives should be stated that rankles those holding fluid, holistic, dynamic conceptions of the educational process. The controversy in the field concerning objectives is not essentially technical but philosophic. It is precisely for this reason that the discussion of objectives is so important, for in their analysis we might unpack the normative premises that have given rise to technical recommendations that have been made by writers in the field.

This monograph had its birth with the suggestion that a handbook be prepared containing technical recommendations on how instructional objectives should be written. At that time the full implications of such a technical codification were not fully understood. I believe we are beginning to recognize that in the area of educational objectives – as with other important educational concerns – the problem is more complex than recognized initially.

4   Emerging Models for Educational Evaluation[1]

In this chapter I will develop three ideas that seem to me to hold promise for improving the process of educational evaluation. These ideas deal with some of the issues surrounding the character and functions of educational objectives, the variety of outcomes that one might reasonably expect schooling to yield, and a set of methods that appear useful for evaluating the character and effects of school programs. That the relationship between objectives and evaluation is, at least theoretically, an intimate one is clear. Almost all writers on education generally and curriculum theory particularly emphasize the point that evaluation procedures should be related to the objectives one has formulated. Thus, any modification in either the content or the form of objectives can have important implications for the method and goals of evaluation. This paper describes some ways in which objectives can be conceived and provides the conditions necessary for expanding modes of educational evaluation.

I would like to say at the outset that the ideas I will develop here are in their infancy. I have not written about them in detail in professional journals; they are glimmers that the task of writing this paper has brightened. They are collectively, as Joseph Schwab might say, an invitation to inquiry rather than a rhetoric of conclusions.[2]

In many ways, the development of new and better ways to evaluate is counter to at least one of the major developments on the educational scene. I am of course referring to the rash of books and articles that have recently appeared chastizing the schools for being test ridden, impersonal, oppressive, indifferent to students as people, bureaucratic, and mindless. *How Children Fail, Compulsory Miseducation, The Open Classroom, The Lives of Children,* and *The Way It's Spozed to Be* are only a few of these books. And their diagnoses of the ills of schooling are antithetical to those found in the books published one and two decades ago, which in their own way also chastized the schools. *Retreat from Learning, Quackery in the Public School, Why Swiss Schools Are Better Than Ours, Educational Wastelands*: the titles tell their stories. The schools, those who run them, those who prepare teachers for them, and those who work in them have borne the brunt of the attacks.

Yet it is because of these attacks and the kind of passionate reform they urge that the need for more adequate methods of educational evaluation becomes even more important. The educational conservatives of the late forties and early fifties introduced the theme that was to herald the curriculum reform movement. That movement, developed with the help of the National Science Foundation and the U.S. Office of Education, provided what some of the conservative critics wanted.[3] It provided a no-nonsense curriculum developed by scholars, implemented by teachers, and geared, at least initially, to the production of young scientists and mathematicians. Educational reform in the mid-fifties was seen primarily as curriculum reform.

That educational reform could be achieved merely through curriculum reform is a seductive aspiration. I wish it were that easy. If we have learned anything from the curriculum reform movement, it is that the problems that pervade our schools go well beyond problems of curriculum. This is not to say that the curriculum of a school, by which I mean the program it provides to students, is unimportant. School programs are important. But one must also realize, as the Holts, Friedenbergs, Dennisons, Goodmans, and Kohls have brought to our attention, that other aspects of the school are also important and, some claim, much more important than the formal curriculum.[4]

The radical critics have made salient the idea that the type of relationship existing between teacher and student is critical. They have pointed out that the organizational structure of the school teaches as surely as the lesson in a workbook or test. The reward system of the school – the covert, muted one – speaks loudly. In short, they have injected a dimension that was generally neglected in the cool, cognitive approach taken by curriculum reformers during the fifties and sixties.

The language and the perceptiveness of some of the reformers are persuasive and in many parts of the country are being heeded. In California, the free schools have become a movement. While their lives are short – their average tenure is about a year and a half – people continue to establish schools that are intended to provide radical alternatives to the public schools. New journals concerned with free schools are being published. And in Berkeley, California, free-school people have elected a candidate for the school board.

Yet it is precisely because the language of the radical reformers is persuasive and because the movement for alternative schools is growing that the need for sound and careful evaluation is important. There is no virtue climbing aboard alluring bandwagons only to find after some pain and dismay that we have indeed been taken for a ride. Rhetoric is not enough when the policies that such rhetoric yields can affect millions of students and teachers.

In calling attention to the growing dissatisfaction with American public schools and the alternatives that are being created, I do not wish to imply that my concern with developing more adequate models for evaluation rests solely upon the desire to assess the consequences of these so-called free schools. That task is important, but it is only a part of the problem. The school programs to which 52 million children are exposed annually are the prime subject that warrants attention. The need for more adequate methods of evaluation is surely as great for this population as it is for that segment of the school population attending free schools.

There is no doubt in my mind that the evaluation movement in education, especially as fostered by the efforts of those who worked on school surveys during the period from 1910 to 1920 and in psychometrics and test development during the First World War, made important contributions to the scientific study of education.[5] At a time when there was a need for more precise and sophisticated conceptions of schooling and teacher training, statistics and other quantitative methods were appropriate and useful tools. One should not forget that the first department of education in an American university was established in 1873; in 1920, education as a formal field of study and practice was still in its childhood. Through the efforts of such men as E.L. Thorndike, John Watson, Harold Rugg, and Charles Hubbard Judd,[6] the tools of research and, more importantly, the conceptions underlying research became a part of the armamentarium of the evaluator. Educational evaluation has grown up within the general field of educational research, and it is only recently that efforts have been made to distinguish between the two.

There was a period in the development of education when the family resemblance between educational research and educational evaluation was a virtue, but educational evaluation employing the premises and practices of educational research has some important limitations. I would like to identify a few of these limitations in order to provide a context for the ideas I will develop later.

First, in the efforts that are made to evaluate the effects of a new program or method of teaching, inadequate attention is often given to distinguishing between findings that are statistically significant and those that are educationally significant. Differences between experimental and control groups can have no educational significance in spite of the fact that the differences are not random ones.[7]

Second, there has been a tendency to reduce educational problems into forms that fit research paradigms instead of finding research and evaluation procedures that fit the problems. The power of the ideas of correlation, analysis of variance, and random selection and assignment is enormous. But there is a tendency to conceive of research questions within the parameters such ideas provide instead of raising interesting questions and inventing fresh ways to answer them.

Third, there has been an overwhelming tendency to attempt to evaluate the effects of programs on student behavior, with very little attention paid to the assessment and description of the environment which creates such effects. This observation has been made most cogently by Lee Shulman in a recent issue of the *Review of Educational Research*:

> The language of education and the behavioral sciences is in need of a set of terms for describing environments that is as articulated, specific and functional as those already possessed for characterizing individuals.
>
> An example that is familiar to all educators is the continued use of such gross terms as 'deprived' or 'disadvantaged' to characterize the environments of many minority-group children. Labeling the setting as 'disadvantaged,' of course, communicates little that is meaningful about the characteristics of that environment. Educators seem unable to progress beyond such a simple dichotomy as 'advantaged-disadvantaged,' Reviewers and critics of research have long realized that even those few categories which attempt to describe environments, such as social class, have been remarkably ineffectual in pinpointing the educationally relevant differences in the backgrounds of individuals.[8]

Not only do I agree with Shulman's observations, but a review I did of the last two years of the *American Educational Research Association [AERA] Journal* indicated that experimental studies reported in those volumes provide about three and a half to four times as much space to reporting the findings of the studies as they do to describing the treatment. Somewhere between one and a half and two and a half inches of copy is devoted to describing what it was that the experimenter manipulated. How can one be expected to replicate experimental studies when such a paucity of information concerning the characteristics of the treatment is provided?

A fourth characteristic of many of the efforts to evaluate the effects of schooling is the failure to recognize the difference between what students will do and what they can do. For example, achievement tests are given in contexts in which students know they must perform well. The set that is induced by the test administrator, the form the test takes, and the setting in which it is administered tend to elicit not what students will do in typical situations in their lives but how they can perform under artificial; circumstances. One revealing example of such a situation occurred annually during my years in elementary school. When I was a student at Lawson Elementary School during the 1940s I was expected, as were all of my classmates, to take a handwriting test on a yearly basis. Each year from grade 3 on the teacher would write on the blackboard in her finest cursive form the following: 'This is a sample of my handwriting on January 24, 1943. If it is not as good as it should be for a student of my age and grade, I will try with my teacher's help to improve by this time next year.'

I remember vividly sitting on the hard oak seat attached to a desk screwed into the floor, eight deep in rows of six. The white, slick, lined paper was before me with the blue-black watery ink at my right as I sat with scratchy pen in hand. Oh, how I worked! To copy those two sentences in my best hand was a venture as difficult as crossing the Niagara on a high wire. After twenty minutes of pain I was through – in my best hand. But what I turned in to the teacher was no more a sample of my handwriting than it was of the man in the moon's. If my teachers wanted to know how I wrote, all they had to do was to look at what I was writing on any school day.

All too many achievement tests have similar characteristics: concurrent or predictive validity is too often a neglected consideration. We ought to be concerned not only with immediate effects, but with long-term effects. What the child will be like a year after the course is over is a far more telling question than how he behaves on the final exam.

In this sense it might be more reasonable to conceive of dependent variables as independent variables. After all, what we want to predict is surely more than test performance. Test performance can be, and in my opinion ought to be, looked upon as a predictor of the future. Using the standard conception, the dependent measure tells you whether the treatment has been effective during the treatment period. *Now* the educational question emerges. Given that it has been effective during the treatment period, does it last? Is it used? Does it make a difference in how people function? There is no doubt in my mind that such questions will be difficult to answer, but there is also no doubt that these questions must be addressed if we are to know if schooling is more than a game.

A fifth characteristic of experimental research which filters into evaluation practices is the extreme brevity of the treatment that is provided. Making important and enduring differences in people requires either a great deal of time or a very powerful treatment, something in the form of a peak experience or one that is traumatic. Neither peak experiences nor traumas are typical of our experimental efforts; thus, time is required to bring about changes of a significant and enduring variety. Yet the average duration of experimental treatment time per subject in experimental studies reported in the last two volumes of the *AERA Journal* is about forty minutes – forty minutes to bring about a change that is to have educational significance! (Everyone, I am sure, realizes that such changes require at least an hour!)

Now there is a good reason for the brevity of experimental treatments. Short treatments increase control, and control reduces confounding. When confounding occurs, the ability to explain is reduced. Yet paradoxically, the more controlled the experiment the more difficult it might be to generalize it to classroom practice, for it is precisely the lack of tight control that characterizes most classrooms. It seems to me we need longer treatment periods as well as more sensitive instruments with which to evaluate the programs that are provided in schools.

Yet despite the caveats I have enumerated, there is interesting work taking place in the field of educational evaluation. The development of criterion-referenced testing is useful even though several of Professor Ebel's[9] reservations are well grounded. The aptitude-treatment-interaction work by Professors Cronbach and Snow[10] also holds promise even though consistent interactions have not been found. The idea of aptitude-treatment-interaction is persuasive and makes psychological sense. Daniel Stufflebeam's[11] context, input, process, and product model is a more comprehensive conception of the loci for evaluation than has been previously articulated. Michael

Scriven's[12] contributions are important new ideas in the evaluation field. In short, good work is being done. I would like now to contribute to that work by explicating the three ideas I identified at the beginning of this paper.

Many of you are familiar with prescriptions concerning the use of instructional objectives in curriculum planning and evaluation. The rationale for their use is straightforward: one must know what it is that a student is able to do in order to determine the effectiveness of the curriculum. This idea was developed in prototype by Franklin Bobbitt in 1924, refined by Henry Harap in the late twenties, rationalized by Ralph Tyler in his famous curriculum syllabus in the early fifties, exemplified in the cognitive domain by Benjamin Bloom in the middle fifties, extended into the affective domain by David Krathwohl, and given extremely precise meaning by Robert Mager in the early sixties. I will not reiterate the limitations that such a concept has as a comprehensive view of educational planning. Many readers are familiar with the views I have expressed in various journals and monographs on the subject.[13] My effort to conceptualize the expressive objective was intended to provide some balance to what I consider to be an extremely narrow vision of what education is and how planning for it should occur. The expressive objective is an outcome of an activity planned by the teacher or the student which is designed not to lead the student to a particular goal or form of behavior but, rather, to forms of thinking-feeling-acting that are his own making. The expressive curriculum activity is evocative rather than prescriptive and is intended to yield outcomes which, although educationally valuable, are not prescribed or defined beforehand. The task of the teacher is to look back, as it were, to evaluate what happened to the student rather than to ask whether the student achieved '90 percent mastery of a set of items placed before him during a forty-minute period.' The expressive activity is one in which the creative personalistic use of skills gained in instructional activities can be employed, developed, and refined. The expressive objective is the outcome of such activities.·

These ideas are not new. I have written about them before. Why then do I reiterate them here? Only to refresh your memory so that the distinction between the instructional and the expressive objective can be seen more clearly as I describe a third type of objective that I believe to be logically distinct from the latter two.

As I thought about instructional and expressive objectives, it occurred to me that neither of these types adequately fits the kind of tasks given to designers, architects, engineers, and commercial artists.

Product designers, for example, work for a client who generally has a problem – a specific problem – that he wants the designer to solve. He might say to the designer, 'I need a device that can be marketed for under fifty cents, which can be made on a vacuum press, and which ladies can use to carry cosmetics.' The problem that the designer has is to take the specifications that are provided by the client, specifications which define function but which do not provide a solution, and to invent an image that provides a solution within the parameters set by the client. In such a situation, the problem is highly delineated but the range of potential solutions is, in principle, infinite. Furthermore, there is generally little difficulty in determining the success of the solution. In this Type III objective – I do not have an appropriate name for it yet – the designer, or architect, or engineer must bring his imaginative resources to bear upon a highly specific problem but one that makes possible a wide variety of solutions. In distinction, the instructional objective provides the solution; what the student is to be able to do is specified in advance, and the objective and the student's behavior or product at the end of an instructional sequence are ideally isomorphic. In spelling or mathematics, for example, instructional objectives describe answers that are known in advance. In Type III objectives, although the problem is known the solutions are not. Ingenuity of solution, appraised on the basis of the parameters or specifications of the problem, is the ideal.

An example might make the use of Type III objectives clear in curriculum planning. Let us assume that a teacher or curriculum development group is working in the area of the social studies and is attempting to develop objectives and learning activities for children around 10 or 11 years of age. The topic being dealt with is the way in which the community handles the movement of people within its boundaries. The curriculum writers are interested in helping children understand that population density affects the type of controls imposed and that optimal solutions to movement need to be appraised by a variety of criteria, time, cost, aesthetic considerations, and so forth. To help children appreciate and understand the dimensions of such a problem, the curriculum writers decide to deal with problems of traffic control and traffic flow and formulate a Type III objective which asks children to improve the flow of traffic by modifying in some way the current traffic patterns near the school. These modifications should make auto traffic more efficient and time saving and should make it safer for students. No new streets can be built; changes must come about by modifying traffic flow on existing streets. A classroom teacher using such an objective would, if he desired, set up teams of students to study this problem and to formulate potential solutions. Each team's solution will be presented and considered by the class as a whole. What the teacher looks for in evaluating achievement is not a preconceived fit between a known objective and a known solution but an appraisal, after an inquiry of the relative merit of solution to the objective formulated, in this case solving problems of traffic control.

With the expressive objective, neither the parameters nor the specifications are given. The student can define his own problem or task and create his own solution. Thus, of the three, the expressive is the most open, the Type III objective is less open, and the instructional objective is least open. But the distinctions between the three types of objectives are not, I believe, matters of degree but matters of kind. Type III objectives encourage the teacher to provide high degrees of structure in setting the problem but also encourage him to leave the avenues for potential solutions wide open. Within the specifications provided, anything that works well, works.

One can legitimately ask whether the distinctions between the three types of objectives I have described are simply an exercise in analysis or whether they have any practical utility for educational planning. I believe these concepts are heuristic, that is, they lead one to view curriculum decision making and evaluation in unconventional ways. They lead to fresh questions. With the three types of objectives, we can now examine a curriculum, one developed either nationally or by the classroom teacher, to determine the extent to which objectives of each type are provided and the degree of emphasis devoted to each. We can compare curricula in different subject matters to determine their use of such objectives.

Furthermore, we can now begin to examine evaluation tools such as standardized tests to determine the extent to which they provide for items or tasks related to these objectives, and if they do not, we can build instruments appropriate for such objectives. Finally, we can consciously begin to design learning activities within the parameters suggested by these types of objectives.

In addition to these tasks, we can enquire whether there is an appropriate rhythm among the types of learning activities implied by the three types of objectives and whether principles can be formulated that teachers might use to decide when to emphasize each type. In short, the distinctions I have drawn indicate more acute directions that can be taken in the construction and evaluation of educational programs. When we recognize that we do not need, indeed cannot successfully have, a single, monolithic conception of educational objectives, we are in a position to generate alternatives in curriculum development and educational evaluation that a single view will not permit. Type III objectives, for want of a better name, can, I believe, provide a wider scope for such enquiries.

A second idea that I would like to discuss deals with an image of the types of outcomes that it seems reasonable to assume are the products of teaching. The dominant, if not exclusive, orientation toward evaluating the effects of instruction is one which is aimed at determining the extent to which objectives are attained. Objectives in turn are usually couched within some subject matter field, especially when it comes to the evaluation of academic achievement. Such a vision or model of evaluation fails, I believe, to attend to other, perhaps equally important, consequences of instruction. For example, it is part of educational lore that a teacher not only teaches a subject matter, but he also teaches himself. Those of us who have had the good fortune to have studied under great teachers know this in acute terms, but even lesser teachers teach themselves. How teachers attack a problem, what their standards of excellence are, their sense of excitement or boredom when they encounter a new idea, their expectations for deportment, their tolerance for ambiguity, their need for precision: these are all teachable characteristics that teachers inevitably convey to students during the course of their work. These effects one might call teacher-specific outcomes. Outcomes dealing with subject matter achievement are content specific.

Teacher-specific and content-specific outcomes are not the only ones that arise in the course of instruction. The student makes his own outcomes. As a result of his previous life history, his particular interests, his turn of mind, the angle at which he comes at things, the student, like all of us, makes his own meaning. Although a substantial portion of the meanings made during a course will be common to virtually all students in that course, each student will develop meanings that are unique. Each is likely to construct from that course ideas which are peculiarly his own. These outcomes are student specific. Seen in the image of a triadically divided circle (see fig. 1), one-third of that circle represents *content-specific outcomes*, a second third represents *teacher-specific outcomes*, and a final third represents *student-specific outcomes*. Content-specific and teacher-specific outcomes are likely to be homogeneous in character across students. That is, the characteristics and values that teachers teach by virtue of what they are, are in large measure common to most, if not all, students in class. Especially in

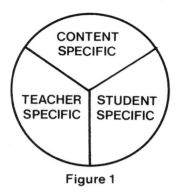

Figure 1

mastery learning are such common outcomes desired.[14] But along with the common inevitably comes the unique. The way a student personalizes meanings – the ideas he creates that are spin-offs from the content of the course or from the musings of the teacher – is also important. Indeed, in the long run they might be among the most important contributions of schooling. This dimension as well as the contributions that the teacher makes to students because he is a particular type of human being have been neglected aspects of educational evaluation. Yet if we are to understand the effects of the programs that are provided, surely these outcomes too must be examined. Thus, this triadic image of outcomes, bounded by a circle representing their unity, discloses the second idea of the three that I mentioned earlier.

Finally, I want to suggest a set of methods that I consider promising as a complement to the quantitative procedures now used so widely for educational evaluation. That set is the procedures and techniques of art criticism. The criticism of art is the use of methods designed to heighten one's perception of the qualities that constitute the work. The end of criticism as Dewey observed is the re-education of the perception of the work of art.[15] To achieve this end, the critic must bring two kinds of skills to his work. First, he must have developed highly refined visual sensibilities; that is, he must be able to see the elements that constitute a whole and their interplay. Second, he must be capable of rendering his perceptions into a language that makes it possible for others less perceptive than he to see qualities and aspects of the work that they would otherwise overlook. The critic, like a good teacher or book, directs attention to the subtle, he points out and articulates, he vivifies perception.

This vivification of perception which it is the critic's office to further is carried out by a particular use of language. It is quite clear that our discourse is not as differentiated as our sensibilities. We experience more than we can describe.[16] Thus, what the critic must do is not to attempt to replicate the visual, dramatic, or musical work verbally, but to provide a rendering of them through the use of poetic language. The vehicles the critic employs are suggestion, simile, and metaphor. These poetic vehicles carry the viewer to a heightened perception of the phenomena.

An example of the use of such linguistic resources can be found in art critic Max Kozloff's description of a painting by Robert Motherwell:

> As an example, let me take a 1962 canvas, 'Chi Ama, Crede' (Who Loves, Trusts), in which a recurring flaw, a disproportion of the generalized over the particular, is held at bay. It is a twelve-foot frieze of wandering tan zones, surrounding two utterly eccentric, squirming turpentine blots of cool rusts, all this laid on in very close values. Basically the picture posits a contrast between restful, opaque fields that hold the surface and uneven strains that, with their shifting shadows, open up a translucent space and suggest a watery, organic agitation. But these rather hormonal blots are hemmed or even locked in by the ground at every stop of their fading perimeters. Here the artist reveals an overloaded liquidity that had dried up and been absorbed, and a mat, diffident facade that discloses an unsuspected strength. But suddenly, at one point, he withholds the paint tissue and, in an irregular glimpse of white canvas, flicks a whip of splatters that are almost electric under the murky circumstances. The whole thing glows as a vicarious pageant of his psyche.[17]

What Kozloff is doing here is using the connotative aspects of language to disclose the 'ineffable' content of visual-emotional experience. Kozloff writes of his efforts as a critic:

> For this, the most appropriate devices at my disposal have been innuendo, nuance, and hypothesis, because what is peripheral to direct statement in language is often central to a pictorial encounter or its memory. The more willingly this condition is acknowledged, the more readily is it possible to avoid the imputation of fact to something which is not 'factual,' while remaining faithful to that catalyst of our aesthetic life — credulity.[18]

Much of what goes on in schools can be illuminated by the tools of criticism. As a generic method, criticism is especially suited to articulating the unique and the personalistic outcomes that are so highly prized by those who complain of the school's impersonality. The reason criticism is so suited is because it does not depend upon the conventional application of class concepts for description and because it does not restrict itself to the primary surface of a situation; the secondary surface, that is, the situation's expressive and underlying qualities, is also a candidate for description and interpretation. Such a mode of evaluation has not, as far as I know, been employed in its full-blown form (although one of my students is using such a method to examine teaching as an art form). There are in the literature examples that approximate such an approach to evaluation:

> I see again in mind my rickety raftered rocky prefab that split the melting frost in the spring. With Sammy Snail wandering down upon us from the rafters, the sun thick tangible bars across the rising dust from the bare floor boards, the loud ever-moving, ever-talking life of the New Race, from corner to corner, from wall to wall, both on the floor and upon the desks. Tall towers rocking precariously, fantastic shapes in colour leaping from the ten-child easel, Little Ones in eddying figures dancing, the clay-births, the sand turning into a graveyard under passionate brown fingers, the water through with one-pint building wharves, bombers zooming on the blackboards, outrageous statements in funnily spelt words on the low wall blackboards, children singing, quarrelling magnificently, laughing for nothing, infectiously, crying for nothing infectiously, Waiwini's Little Brother wailing to me that somebodies they broked his castle for notheen. Bleeding Heart laughing his head off, the Tamatis' dog snuggling about for a cuddle, Pussy insinuating herself fastidiously, the Ginger Rooster scratching about ambitiously for culture, pictures of the meeting house and pa and the Ghost and of big-footed people kissing and words like shearing shed and beer and graveyard and wild piggy and lollies, tongues patrolling Maori lips over intensely personal writing, voices raised in exuberance, in argument, in reading, laughter, singing and crying and How-do-you-spell-Nanny. And our *floor*! You should see our floor! Round about the ten-child easel where the colour drips, it's prettier than the face of the countryside itself. You'd think Autumn himself had

passed this way with his careless brush; slinging his paint about
in his extravagant way. And noise ... noise! And the whole
show rocking like an overcrowded dinghy on high seas.[19]

Although autobiographical, such an account of classroom life
gives the reader a vivid picture of its qualities and of Sylvia Ashton-
Warner's attitude toward it.

But one might ask, 'Isn't such a method merely subjective?' Can
nonquantified description using poetic devices be anything more than
the expression of taste and liable to the grossest forms of unreliability?
Not necessarily. In a very important sense, criticism is an empirical
method. The adequacy of criticism is tested on the work itself. If what
the critic describes cannot be seen in the work, his criticism fails to
perform its function. In short, what he points out must be capable of
being seen. Such a test is easier to apply to non-ephemeral works such
as visual art and music than to the qualities that constitute classroom
life, but such qualities are surely not so fugitive that their existence lasts
only for a moment. Much of what is important in teaching and in
learning is recurrent and regular. Criticism as a set of methods for
analysis and disclosure can, I believe, make them vivid.

As a *complement* to the quantitative procedures we now use, such
methods hold much promise. Their realization will require the creation
of programs designed to prepare individuals with such skills. In a
venture of this kind, departments of art, English, drama, and anthropology might be called upon for assistance. The promise of such
procedures for dealing incisively with educational programs that might
in the future become much more individualized than they are now is
persuasive.

Notes

1. This paper was originally prepared for presentation at the Distinguished
   Visiting Scholars Program. Department of Educational Psychology.
   Michigan State University. I wish to express my gratitude to the students
   and faculty of that institution for their incisive and stimulating comments
   and critique of this paper.
2. SCHWAB. J.J. (1961) 'The Teaching of Science as Enquiry,' in *The Teaching
   of Science* Cambridge, Mass., Harvard University Press.
3. It is estimated that the National Science Foundation and the U.S. Office of
   Education have allocated well over $100 million for teacher training and
   curriculum development in sciences and in mathematics over the past
   ten-year period.

4. See JACKSON, P.W. (1968) *Life in Classrooms*, New York, Holt, Rinehart and Winston.
5. For a lucid account of the psychometric work during the First World War, see JONCICH, G. (1968) *The Sane Positivist: A Biography of Edward L. Thorndike* Middletown, Conn., Wesleyan University Press, pp. 356–82.
6. CREMIN, L.A. (1961) *The Transformation of the School* New York, Alfred A. Knopf. Inc., passim.
7. The notion that scientific enquiry is value neutral has been disputed by numerous students of science. For two cogent accounts of this problem, see BRONOWSKI, J. (1959) *Science and Human Values* New York, Harper and Row; and KUHN, T. (1962) *The Structure of Scientific Revolutions* Chicago, University of Chicago Press.
8. SHULMAN, L. (1970) 'Reconstruction of Educational Research,' in *Review of Educational Research* 40, no. 3, June, pp. 374–75.
9. EBEL, R. (1971) 'Criterion-referenced Measurements: Limitations,' in *School Review* 79, no. 2, February, pp. 282–88.
10. CRONBACH, L.J. and SNOW, R. (1969) *Individual Differences in Learning Ability* Washington, U.S. Office of Education.
11. STUFFLEBEAM, D. (1967) 'The Use and Abuse of Evaluation in Title III,' in *Theory into Practice* 6, no. 3 June, pp. 126–33.
12. SCRIVEN, M. 'Education for Survival.' mimeographed, available from author, 57 pp.
13. EISNER, E.W. (1967) 'Educational Objectives: Help or Hindrance?' *School Review* 75, no. 3, Autumn; pp. 250–60; and 'Instructional and Expressive Objectives: Their Formulation and Use in Curriculum', in POPHAM, W.J. et al. (ed.) (1969) *Instructional Objectives* American Educational Research Association Monograph no. 3, Chicago, Rand McNally and Co, pp. 1–18.
14. BLOOM, B. 'Mastery Learning and Its Implications for Curriculum Development,' in EISNER, E.W. (Ed.) (1971) *Confronting Curriculum Reform*, Boston Little, Brown and Co., pp. 17–49.
15. DEWEY, J. (1934) *Art as Experience* New York, Minton, Balch and Co., p. 324.
16. For a brilliant discussion of the relationship of experience to discourse, see POLANYI, M. (1966) *The Tacit Dimension* New York, Doubleday and Co.
17. KOZLOFF, M. (1969) *Renderings* New York, Simon and Schuster, pp. 169–70.
18. *Ibid.*, p. 10.
19. ASHTON-WARNER, S. (1963) *Teacher* New York, Simon and Schuster, pp. 220–21.

5   Educational Connoisseurship and Educational Criticism: Their Form and Functions in Educational Evaluation

The major thesis of this chapter is that the forms that are used in conventional approaches to educational evaluation have a profound set of consequences on the conduct and character of schooling in the United States. Unless those forms can be expanded so that they attend to qualities of educational life relevant to the arts, it is not likely that the arts will secure a meaningful place in American schools. To understand why we evaluate the way that we do, it is important to examine the sources through which evaluation became a kind of field within American education. If we examine the past we will find that since the turn of the century, since the early work of Edward L Thorndike, there has been a strong aspiration among psychologists to create a science of education that would provide educational practitioners and administrators, as well as teachers, with the kind of knowledge that would allow them to systematically predict, through their ability to control the process and consequences of schooling. The search for educational laws, laws that would do for educational practitioners what the work of Einstein, Maxwell and Bohr have done for physicists was the object of the educational scientists dream. This yearning for prediction through control was, of course, reflected in the desire to make schools more efficient and presumably more effective. Educational research was to discover the laws of learning that would replace intuition and artistry with knowledge and prescribed method. The hunt was on for the one best method to teach the various fields of study that constituted the curriculum. This aspiration to discover the laws of learning was allied with the efficiency movement in education that sought to install scientific management procedures in schools through time and motion study of teaching practice.[1] It reflected then, as it does today, the need to discover the principles and practices that would give us efficient and effective schools.

This desire was, of course, based upon a particular view of the world and of man's position within it. That view was scientific in character. The task of educational research was to treat educational practice as a nomothetic activity, one controlled by laws rather than an ideographic activity, one which was guided by the unique characteristics of the particular situation. Describing the philosophic differences between the nomothetic and the ideographic George Henrik Von Wright writes:

> All these thinkers [Droysen, Dilthey, Simmel, Max Weber, Windelband, Rickert, Croce and Collingwood] reject the methodological monism of positivism and refuse to view the pattern set by the exact natural sciences as the sole and supreme ideal for a rational understanding of reality. Many of them emphasize a contrast between those sciences which, like physics or chemistry or physiology, aim at generalizations about reproducible and predictable phenomena, and those which, like history, want to grasp the individual and unique features of their objects. Windelband coined the label 'nomothetic' for sciences which search for laws, and 'ideographic' for the descriptive study of individuality.[2]

As for evaluation practices, they were to be objective, that is, they were to describe in quantitative, empirical terms whether or not the goals of the curriculum were achieved.

If I dwell upon these matters of the past it is because I believe they are crucial for understanding what we do today and why. Arts education might not be possible except in the skimpiest sense in institutions that are controlled by unexamined assumptions which create a climate, establish a tone, foster a set of priorities that are inhospitable to the kind of life that work in the arts might yield. Although scientific and technological approaches to the methods of schooling have made some important contributions, I believe they have had at least four major deleterious consequences. Let me identify these.

First, because scientific assumptions and scientifically-oriented inquiry aim at the search for laws or lawlike generalizations, such inquiry tends to treat qualities of particular situations as instrumentalities. The uniqueness of the particular is considered 'noise' in the search for general tendencies and main effects. This, in turn, leads to the oversimplification of the particular through a process of reductionism that aspires toward the characterization of complexity by a single set of scores. Quality becomes converted to quantity and then summed and averaged as a way of standing for the particular quality from which the quantities were initially derived. For the evaluation of educational practice and its consequences, the single numerical test score is used to symbolize a universe of particulars, in spite of the fact that the number symbol itself possesses no inherent quality that expresses the quality of the particular it is intended to represent.

The distinction between symbols that possess in their form the expressive content to which they are related and those symbols which through associative learning we relate to certain ideas is an extremely important one. The art symbol exemplified the former while the word or number exemplified the latter. Scientific activity yields propositions so that truth can be determined in relation to its instrumental value, a value dependent upon its predictive or explanatory accuracy. Artistic activity creates symbolic forms which themselves present directly an idea, image, or feeling which resides within, rather than outside of the symbol.

Second, the technological orientation to practice tends to encourage a primary focus of the achievement of some future state and in the process tends to undermine the significance of the present. Take, as an example, the concern in recent years with the formulation of behavioral objectives. Objectives are things that are always out of reach. They are goals toward which one works, targets we are urged to keep our eyes upon. Objectives are future-oriented, and when the future becomes increasingly important to us, we sacrifice the present in order to achieve it. In elementary schools both teachers and students are beleaguered by extrinsic rewards such as token economies. Children are rewarded for the achievement of objectives that themselves have little intrinsic appeal, and teachers may one day be paid in relation to their ability to produce certain measurable outcomes. When the future becomes all-important, it must be achieved at all costs. At the secondary level it leads to the pursuit of high scores on scholastic achievement tests and at the university level to the destruction of experiments and the stealing of books in pre-med programs. Not only must objectives be achieved, but one must also be sure that others do not achieve them. The present is sacrificed on the altar of tomorrow.

Third, scientific and technological approaches to schooling lead, as I have already said, to the attempt to 'objectify' knowledge. Objectification almost always requires that at least two conditions be met. First, the qualities to which one attends must be empirically manifest, and second, they must be convertible to quantity. In this way both reliability and precision can be assured, hence conclusions about a state of affairs can be verified.

That these procedures themselves rest upon certain beliefs that cannot themselves be verified by the procedures that the beliefs espouse does not seem to pose a problem for those who espouse them. But, in addition, these procedures, based as they are on a particular conception of truth, also bring with them some negative injunctions. For example, one must not emotionalize one's language when talking about children, educational practice, or educational goals. Intimation, metaphor, analogy, poetic insight have little place in such a view. For example, instead of talking about children, we are urged to talk about subjects. Instead of talking about teaching we must talk about treatments. Instead of talking about aims and aspirations, we must talk about dependent variables, performance objectives or competencies. And to increase 'objectivity', instead of talking in the first person singular, the third person singular or first person plural is a better form. Somehow, if 'the author', or 'we' conclude something, it is more objective than if 'I' do.

This shift in language, if it only represented a shift in language would not present much of a problem, but the problem exceeds the matter of language per se. The shift in language is a symptom of a larger difficulty when it comes to the understanding of human beings. That problem is that in de-emotionalizing expression and proscribing suggestive language, the opportunity to understand empathetically and to communicate the quality of human experience diminishes. As long as manifest behavior is our exclusive referent – and those forms of manifest behavior that are measurable, at that – the quality of experience will be neglected. Inference about experience has little place in radical behaviorism, but radical behaviorism, exemplified in the work of Thorndike, Watson, Hull and Skinner, has held a central place in American educational psychology. To know what people feel, to know what behavior *means*, we must go beyond behavior.[3]

Fourth, when one seeks laws governing the control of human behavior, it is not surprising that one would also seek the achievement of a common set of goals for that behavior. When one combines this with the need to quantitatively operationalize such goals, the use of standardized tests become understandable. The standardized test *is* standard; it is the same for all students. It not only standardizes the tasks students will confront, but it also standardizes the goals against which they shall be judged. These tests, de facto, become the goals. When this happens, uniformity becomes an aspiration; effectiveness means in practice that all students will achieve the same ends. Individualization, regardless of what it might mean, becomes defined in terms of providing for differences in rate; differentiation in pace, rather than in goal, content, or mode of expression is the general meaning of individualization. Standardized achievement tests do not now provide the means for assessing the significant personalization of teaching and learning. The cultivation of productive idiosyncracy – one of the prime consequences of work in the arts – becomes a problem in a technological orientation to educational practice.

The major points that I have been trying to make thus far are two. First, the forms of evaluation that are now employed to assess the effectiveness of school programs have a profound set of consequences upon the character of teaching, the content of curriculum, and the kinds of goals that schools seek to attain. Evaluation procedures, more than a reasoned philosophy of education influence the educational priorities at work within the schools. Second, these evaluation procedures rest upon largely unexamined assumptions that are basically scientific in their epistemology, technological in their application, and have consequences that are often limited and at time inhospital to the kinds of aspirations that the arts can achieve.

Recognition of the assumptions, character and consequences of conventional forms of educational evaluation are insufficient to bring about change in the ways in which we evaluate. Something more must be provided. That something more is an alternative or a complement to what now prevails, and it is in the articulation and testing of this alternative at which my present work aims.

I have chosen to start with a set of premises about education that are quite different from those underlying conventionally dominant approaches to educational evaluation and to the study of educational practice. I do not believe that education as a process, or schooling as an institution designed to foster that process, or teaching as an activity that most directly mediates that process is likely to be controlled by a set of laws that can be transformed into a prescription or recipe for teaching. I do not believe we will ever have a 'Betty Crocker' theory of education. Teaching is an activity that requires artistry, schooling itself is a cultural artifact, and education is a process whose features may differ from individual to individual, context to context. Therefore what I believe we need to do with respect to educational evaluation is not to seek recipes to control and measure practice, but rather to enhance whatever artistry the teacher can achieve. Theory plays a role in the cultivation of artistry, but its role is not prescriptive, it is diagnostic. Good theory in education, as in art, helps us see more. It helps us think about more of the qualities that constitute a set of phenomena; theory does not replace intelligence and perception and action, it provides some of the windows through which intelligence can look out into the world. Thus one of the functions that theory might serve in educational evaluation is in the cultivation of educational *connoisseurship*.[4]

Educational connoisseurship, about which I will have more to say momentarily, is but half of a pair of concepts that I believe to be particularly promising for thinking about the conduct of educational evaluation. The other half of this pair is the concept of educational criticism. Each of these concepts, educational connoisseurship and educational criticism, have their roots in the arts and for good reason. Because I believe teaching in classrooms is ideographic in character, that is, because I believe the features of classroom life are not likely to be explained or controlled by behavioral laws, I conceive the major contribution of evaluation as contributing to a heightened awareness of the qualities of that life so that teachers and students can become more intelligent within it. Connoisseurship plays an important role toward this end by refining the levels of apprehension of the qualities that pervade classrooms. To be a connoisseur of wine, bicycles or graphic arts is to be informed about their qualities, to be able to discriminate the subtleties among types of wine, bicycles and graphic arts by drawing upon a gustatory, visual and kinesthetic memory against which the particulars of the present may be placed for purposes of comparison and contrast. The connoisseur of anything – and one can have connoisseurship about anything – appreciates what he or she encounters in the proper meaning of that word. Appreciation does not mean necessarily liking something, although one might like what one experiences. Appreciation here means an awareness and an understanding of what one has experienced. Such an awareness provides the basis for judgment.

If connoisseurship is the art of appreciation, criticism is the art of disclosure. Criticism, as Dewey pointed out in *Art as Experience*, has at its end the re-education of perception.[5] What the critic strives for is to articulate or render those ineffable qualities constituting art in a language that makes them vivid. In doing this something of a paradox exists. How is it that what is ineffable can be articulated? How do words express what words can never express? The task of the critic is to adumbrate, suggest, imply, connote, render, rather than to attempt to translate.[6] In this task, metaphor and analogy, suggestion and implication are major tools. The language of criticism, indeed, its success as criticism, is measured by the brightness of its illumination. The task of the critic is to help us to see.

Thus, from what I have said, one can see that connoisseurship provides criticism with its subject matter. Connoisseurship is private, but criticism is public. Connoisseurs simply need to appreciate what they encounter. Critics, however, must render these qualities vivid by the artful use of critical disclosure. Effective criticism requires the use of connoisseurship, but connoisseurship does not require the use of criticism.

What is also clear, when one thinks about it, is that education as a field of study does not have, as do literature, music, the visual arts, drama, and film, a branch called educational criticism. Yet educational practice and the outcomes of such practice are subject to critical techniques. We do not have, for example, journals of educational criticism, or critical theory. We do not have programs in universities that prepare educational critics. We do not have a tradition of thought dealing with the formal, systematic, scholarly study and practice of educational criticism. My work at Stanford is aimed at precisely these goals. With a group of doctoral students I have, over the past two years, been attempting to flesh out the issues, the concepts, the criteria, the techniques, and the prototypes of educational connoisseurship and educational criticism. To do this we have been visiting schools around Stanford to study classrooms and to create criticism, and we have been creating educational criticism within the University itself by critically describing the classrooms and courses offered within the School of Education at Stanford. In addition, we have been making videotapes of classrooms and have been using these as a basis for our own education and the testing of our own criticism. Thus far two doctoral dissertations[7] have been completed in which educational criticism is the major conceptual tool. And two more doctoral students will receive their degrees in June of 1978 whose dissertations also employ educational criticism as a dominant mode of inquiry. In short, we have been working at the task of creating a new way of looking at the phenomena that constitute educational life within classrooms.

In pursuing these aims we have engaged in a kind of dialetic between the conceptualization of educational connoisseurship and educational criticism as theoretical categories and the actual writing of criticism and its attendant problems, such as what the role of the educational critic is when that person is in a classroom. This dialetic has informed both aspects of our work, the theoretical and the practical. Before I share with you an example of our work, let me say a few words about three major aspects of educational criticism.

What is it that one does when one writes educational criticism of a classroom, or a set of curriculum materials, or a school? There are three things that one does. One describes, one interprets, and one evaluates or appraises what one sees.

The descriptive aspect of educational criticism (and these three distinctions are not intended to suggest that they are independent or sequential) is an effort to characterize or render the pervasive and sheerly descriptive aspects of the phenomena one attends to. For example, critical description might tell the reader about the number or type of questions that were raised in a class, the amount of time that was spent in discussion, or the kind of image or impression the teacher or the room gives to visitors. Descriptive educational criticism is a type of portrayal of the qualities that one encounters without getting into – very deeply, at least – what they signify. Following Clifford Geertz, the descriptive aspect of criticism is thinner than it is thick, although we recognize that all description has some degree of thickness to it. Let me give you an example of what is largely descriptive educational criticism written by one of my students.

> Last Thursday morning I visited the auditorium of San Francisco's James Lick Junior High School. I had already stood in this room many times, for many years, in many schools. Recent visits remind me how my body has grown taller and heavier. The scuffed floorboards' squeak feels less congenial. The looming balcony now appears less exotic. My eyes no longer trace geometric patterns in the familiar tan ceiling.
>
> Although I lean on the rear wall, I feel close up to the stage. Between it and me wait twin sections of permanent wooden seats, each twelve across and maybe twenty-five rows deep. In front of the first row I watch the busy pit area, where several adults, some with flash cameras, mingle purposefully amid a baby grand piano, a drum set, several stools and benches, three conga drums, a folding table holding a tenor saxophone in its open case, and two microphone stands. Dark curtains close the raised stages.
>
> About half the seats, those in the rear, are empty. The front half of the auditorium contains an exquisite kaleidoscope of

several hundred junior high kids – standing, sitting, turning, squirming, tugging, slapping, squealing, calling, talking, clapping, laughing, waving. A few stare silent and motionless. Most smile. They make a multicultural mix, of obscure proportions. Here and there an adult, probably a teacher, joins the crowd or stands back to oversee.

Their combined voices swell ceaselessly, like the ocean's face, as though smiling in rhythm with the crowd's surging spirit. Occasionally a single voice calls or whistles to jar this bussing blanket's penetrating caress.

From behind the curtain, a grinning, slim, grey-haired man in a dark blue suit walks down to the audience, talks briefly with someone, picks up the tenor sax, and returns backstage. He leaves the curtains parted about a foot, revealing there people hurrying across the bright stage in last-minute urgency. Indistinct musical sounds from backstage join the audience's hum.

Small groups of kids from nearby schools file in quickly, filling all the remaining seats.

A man carrying a guitar peers out through the curtain, and then walks down to the pit, followed by the tenor sax man. They greet several adults already standing there in the right-hand corner.

A spotlight focuses several different size circles on the curtain. The lights onstage darken. The kids quiet, and their adults come to stand along the walls.

A serious-looking man of average build with thin, straight grey hair, wearing dark slacks, a dark brown turtleneck shirt, and a beige sportcoat, strides directly to the microphone in the center of the pit. In the next ten minutes he and two other adults greet the audience and progressively, systematically introduce the morning's program and their guest, Mr. John Birks Gillespie. The last speaker – Mr. Smith, the school's music director – is the tenor sax player. His final words succumb to the kids' impatient applause.

Now, from the right corner, Dizzy Gillespie struts playfully across to the microphone – a middle-aged Tom Sawyer in a bulky, white, knit cap that hints broadly toward mischief. A brash musical rebel and innovator thirty-five years ago, now Dizzy is a jovial, stocky, black man, with faint white hairs on his chin. Clutching his spangled trumpet against a black-and-white checked sportcoat which reveals his dazzling red shirt, he thanks Mr. Smith and greets his audience.

Hearing his first words, I expect to see Louis Armstrong's eyes and Bill Cosby's grin. Dizzy savors his voice; it flows gently – slow-paced and melodic. His audience sits rapt. Their posture shifts with his frequent vocal pitch and tempo modulations. I can barely recall the kids' homogenized chatter from a few minutes earlier.

For about ten minutes he shares comfortable, chuckly stories about his trumpet and his own music education. Everyone seems to be listening, alert and smiling, and commenting with commotion, which Dizzy encourages.

Abruptly, he announces 'What we're gonna do now is play for you', and with one foot he taps 1–, 2–, 1,2,3,4. The drummer and two guitar players, who followed his entrance, now lean into a comfortable number which Dizzy leads in a moderate tempo. The piece seems unfamiliar to the kids, and they respond to the contrast between its tasty, pattering verse and the soaring chorus. All through the tune, the kids focus their attention on Dizzy, himself. Perhaps sensing this, he plays with their enthusiasm, making games for all to share. For example, turning to face the lead guitar player toward the end of the tune, he dances and sways while the guitar solos a chorus. Simultaneously, many kids are bouncing in their seats.

As the applause following this number dwindles, Dizzy cries out 'Como estas usted?' and, responding to the kids' shouted replies, he announces that the next selection will be Latin. As though addressing a favorite toy, he sits behind the conga drums, develops a minute-long monologue about rhythm in jazz, and clowns with his face and voice while adjusting the microphone stand.

He describes a call-and-response routine for the song, demonstrates the kids' part (they fling their right fists while shouting 'Oh!') and its cue (he sings a call), and drills them in the routine a few times. The kids conclude each practice with applause, laughter, and chatter, and they seem eager for more. Continuing, Dizzy announces that many people clap their hands on the wrong beats. They should clap on '. . . two and four, as in "oom-*cha*, oom-*cha*, oom-*cha*". . . .' By now the kids are clapping solidly on the off-beats. Dizzy lets them take a few more measures and, with the other three musicians, begins the song.

He arches over the three congas with eyes closed, eyebrows raised, mouth slack open, and head pointing up to the right corner of the balcony. As though keeping six apples submerged in three pails of water, he moves his hands intently, rapidly, and gracefully. The kids find themselves creating part of the music they hear. Many clap, smile, talk, watch, and listen. Few are quiet. No one seems bored. Everyone seems involved.

Leaning toward the mike, Dizzy leads several repetitions of the kids' call-and-response routine. He returns briefly to the congas, before stepping up with his trumpet, which he plays, eyes closed, pointing the horn's bell to the same corner of the balcony. Returning to the mike, he chants a hushed 'Swing low, sweet chariot, . . .' Opening his eyes and raising his hands, he replied '. . . coming for to carry me home.' The kids join this response, and continue singing these familiar lyrics to their conclusion. Now standing upright, Dizzy sings a series of scat breaks – bursts of explosive syllables cogently declaring an impromptu rhythmic notion. Many kids answer each break by singing back its echo. Finally, he surprises us with an extended, complicated break. The kids respond with applause and laughter, and Dizzy ends the number here, laughing himself.[8]

The interpretative aspect of educational criticism represents an effort to understand the meaning and significance that various forms of action have for those in a social setting. For example, just what do the extrinsic rewards for reading mean to the third graders who keep charts of the number of books that they have read? What do the eager, outstretched, waving arms and hands signify to both teacher and students when students compete for the opportunity to provide the teacher with the right answer? What kinds of messages are being given to students by the allocation of time and its location in the school day to the various subject matters that constitute the curriculum? To answer these questions requires a journey into interpretation, an ability to empathetically participate in the life of another, to appreciate the meanings of such cultural symbols as lists of books read, handwaving, and time allocation. The interpretative aspect of educational criticism requires the judicious and informed use of a variety of social sciences and the practical wisdom born of experience in schools.

The third aspect of criticism is evaluative. It asks, 'What is the *educational* import or value of what is going on?' To deal with the educational import of classroom life is, of course, to do more than to describe or to interpret it; it is to make some value judgments about it with respect to its educational significance. It is this aspect of educational criticism that most sharply differentiates the work of the educational critic from the work of an ethnographer, psychologist, or sociologist. Educational critics ultimately appraise what they encounter with a set of educational criteria; they judge the educational value of what they see. To make educational value judgments requires not only the ability to see educational subtleties occurring in the classroom and to be able to interpret their meaning or explain the functions they serve, it is also to have a background sufficiently rich in educational theory, educational philosophy and educational history to be able to understand the values implied by the ongoing activities and the alternatives that might have otherwise been employed.

This latter aspect of the evaluative character of educational criticism – to be able to consider the alternatives that might have been employed – requires also a sense of the practical realities of classroom life. Each of us undoubtedly holds some pristine vision of educational virtue that we would like to see schools display, yet most of us realize that these images of educational virtue are seldom fully realized. Practical contingencies keep intruding. Lest we come down too hard on situations that do not live up to our highest hopes, it is important to recognize what is, and what is not, possible in the course of daily educational life.

Thus the ultimate consequence of educational criticism is evaluative in the sense that something must be made of what has been described and interpreted. The task of the critic is not simply one of neutral observer (an impossible position in any case) nor is it one of disinterested interpretation. The critic uses what he or she sees and interprets in order to arrive at some conclusions about the character of educational practice and to its improvement.

Although I have said that educational connoisseurship can have as its subject matter anything that can be perceived or experienced and, by implication, that educational criticism can describe what connoisseurship provides, it is time now to be more specific about what can be attended to in educational practice. What are the potential candidates for critical attention? Obviously the particular functions criticism is to serve and the particular audience to which it is directed will influence, if not determine, what is criticized and how it is shared. Yet, in general one can focus upon the qualities of the relationship that exists between teacher and student and the kinds of devices that the teacher employs to stimulate interest, to reward, to explain, and to manage. Teachers seldom have the opportunity to get informed feedback on their teaching. How they are doing they read in the reflections found in the eyes of children. Although this is a relevant source of information, it is neither an exhaustive nor an adequate one. Informed educational criticism may give a teacher a view of his or her own teaching that he simply would never otherwise possess.

The character of the discourse within the classroom is another candidate for critical attention. How do the children participate? What is the quality of what they and the teacher have to say? To what extent do they participate both psychologically and verbally in what transpires? Is their enthusiasm feigned or real? Is what they are learning worth their time and effort? And just what are they learning? Is it what is being taught, or are they learning other things that are carried by the manner of teaching and the organization and structure of the school day? What about the materials they use, the textbooks, the learning kits, the visuals with which they come in contact? What do these materials teach? How are they laid out? What does their format convey? What messages are held between the lines of textbooks that for so many children occupy central roles in their school experience?

What about the relationships among the children themselves? Is it competitive or cooperative? Is the class a collection of individuals or a community? What is the pervasive quality of educational life that children in this particular classroom lead? How is time allocated within the school day? How are the various subjects taught? What values are conveyed by the ways in which time and space decisions have been made?

What is the quality of the work that children create? What is the character of their expression, verbal, written, visual, or musical? Over time, what kind of development is evident? In what ways is the development of intellectual curiosity and autonomy displayed? In what ways are they treated when they are expressed?

These questions represent some of the potential candidates for attention in the effort to create telling educational criticism. To be sure, these very questions reflect a conception of educational value. Only a fool would choose to attend to the trivial.

Finally, I wish to say a few words about the problems of validity, or, put another way, can educational criticism be trusted?

In determining whether the validity of educational criticism, that is whether what the critic says is happening, what it means, and what its educational worth is, is justified, there are three possible sources of disagreement between two or more critics. You will recall that I said that educational criticism has three aspects to it: descriptive, interpretive, and evaluative. Two critics, for example, might agree on what is occurring, agree on what it signifies, but disagree on what its educational value is. Or two critics might agree on what is occurring, disagree on what it signifies, but agree on its educational value. This occurs when two people like what they see, but for different reasons. Still another source of disagreement is when two critics see two different things, but agree upon their significance and agree on their educational value. I am sure you can play out the rest of the hand, but the point is that the reasons critics might agree or disagree in their critical disclosures are several. One cannot know without analyzing the grounds or basis of what they have to say.

Although these conditions make the problems of validating educational criticism complex, there are still some useful criteria to apply. One of these criteria deals with determining the extent of structural corroboration within the criticism itself, and another deals with the criticism's referential adequacy.

Structural corroboration is a process that seeks to validate or support one's conclusions about a set of phenomena by demonstrating how a variety of facts or conditions· within the phenomena support the conclusions drawn. It is a process of demonstrating that the story hangs together, that the pieces fit. One of the best examples of structural corroboration can be found in Agatha Christie's *Murder on the Orient Express*. What the inspector did to solve the puzzling crime was to gradually piece the puzzle together so that the conclusion that all of the passengers on the train had a hand in the murder was cogent. The evidence was persuasive because each component corroborated the other. In the end a structure was created whose parts held together.

American jurisprudence is largely based upon a combination of structural corroboration and multiplicative corroboration. Structural corroboration is sought as two lawyers present the facts of the case to prove or disprove the innocence or guilt of their client, and multiplicative corroboration is practiced when twelve members of a jury concur or fail to concur that the evidence is sufficiently coherent and cohesive to remove any reasonable doubt.

But one of the liabilities of structural corroboration, as Geertz has pointed out, is that nothing can be so persuasive and coherent as a swindler's story. Something more must be added.

It's here that referential adequacy comes into play. Since criticism's aim is the re-education of perception, good educational criticism, like good criticism of anything else, should help the reader or listener see more than he or she would without the benefit of the criticism. In this sense, the test of criticism is empirical, more empirical than numbers usually signify. The test of criticism is empirical in the sense that one asks of the criticism whether the referents it claims to describe, interpret and evaluate can be found in the phenomena to which it attends. Is the teacher's enthusiasm really infectious? Do the children really support each other? Is the room really a celebration of the senses? The referential adequacy of educational criticism is determined by looking at the phenomena with the aid of the criticism. If the criticism is referentially adequate one will find what the critic has described. To the extent that it is effective it should illuminate qualities of teaching and learning that would otherwise go unseen. By making these aspects of educational life visible, the teacher, supervisor, school administrator or school board member is in a position to make judgments about them. Thus, educational policy and the more narrowly defined aspects of educational decision making will have, through educational critic-ism, a wider more complex base of knowledge upon which to deliberate.

I would like to conclude by coming back full circle to the issues with which I began. Educational evaluation has had a particular tradition in this country. It is one that conceives of knowledge as scientific and believes that precision is a function of quantification. This tradition has made important contributions to the conduct of educa-tion, but as an exclusive mode of enquiry it invokes limits that in the long run exclude from our understanding more than they include. The time is ripe for broadening the base upon which enquiry in education can go forward. It is time to make more catholic our sense of possibility; we need, in my opinion, to widen our epistemology. In practice this means recognizing that the forms that humans create, the forms of art, as well as the forms of science, afford unique opportuni-ties for conceptualization and expression, and hence for communica-tion. What we can know is shaped by the intellectual structures we are able to use. Many of those structures are framed in forms of knowledge that are non–discursive. Since educational evaluation has, I assume, as its ultimate objective improving the quality of the educational life students lead, I see no reason why we should not exploit the various forms of understanding that different knowledge structures can pro-vide. Educational connoisseurship and educational criticism represent two modes through which we come to understand and express what we come to know. But those modes themselves represent only a small portion of the possibilities in the conduct of educational evaluation. Some day we will make use not only of criticism in a poetic or artistically discursive mode, we will exploit the possibilities of film, video, photography, graphic displays and the like. But that story will have to wait for another time. What we need today is a breakthrough in conception, a wedge in the door of possibility. Educational connoisseurship and educational criticism, it seems to me, offer some promising possibilities, not only for broadening the base of educational evaluation but for helping those of us in the arts committed to the improvement of the process of education.

Notes

1. CALLAHAN, R. (1962) *Education and the Cult of Efficiency* Chicago, University of Chicago Press, *passim*.
2. VON WRIGHT, G.H. (1971) *Explanation and Understanding* London, Routledge and Kegan Paul, p. 5.
3. GEERTZ, C. (1973) *The Interpretation of Culture* New York, Basic Books Inc.
4. EISNER, E.W. (1975) 'The Perceptive Eye: Toward a Reformation of Educational Evaluation,' Invited Address, Division B, Curriculum and Objectives, American Educational Research Association, Washington, D.C., March.
5. DEWEY, J. (1934) *Art as Experience* New York, Minton, Balch and Company.
6. KOZLOFF, M. (1969) *Renderings* New York, Simon and Schuster.
7. VALLANCE, E. (1974) *Aesthetic Criticism and Curriculum Description* unpublished doctoral dissertation, Stanford University; and GREER, D. (1973) *The Criticism of Teaching* unpublished doctoral dissertation, Stanford University.
8. This descriptive educational criticism was written by one of my doctoral students, Robbie Schlosser. I am grateful for his permission to use his work in this article.

6   On the Uses of Educational Connoisseurship and Criticism for Evaluating Classroom Life

That there is an intimate relationship between the assumptions and procedures employed to assess educational effectiveness and the kinds of programs schools offer is known to all familiar with the forces affecting schools. It is my argument that the assumptions and procedures used in conventional forms of educational evaluation have, in the main, been parochial. They represent an extremely narrow conception of the way in which educational evaluation can be pursued. A wider, more generous conception of educational evaluation is badly needed. This paper defines the contours of such a conception.

Those familiar with the evolution of the evaluation field already know that it has been significantly influenced by the assumptions and procedures employed in doing educational research. And educational research in turn took as its model the natural sciences and had as its aspiration development of theory and methods that would make educational practice scientific. This aspiration is alive and well today. We still aspire to create a scientifically managed form of educational practice.

Yet, scientific procedures are not the only forms through which human understanding is secured and scientific methods are not the only ways through which human influence can be confidently created. What I shall do here is to suggest perhaps not so much an alternative as a needed supplement to the use of scientific procedures for describing, interpreting, and evaluating educational settings. I call this new, non-scientific approach to educational evaluation an approach that requires *educational connoisseurship and educational criticism*.[1] The remainder of what I have to say will be devoted to defining the meaning of these terms and to describing the way in which they can be used to evaluate educational settings.

What is Educational Connoisseurship and Criticism?[2]

What I propose starts not with a scientific paradigm but with an artistic one. I start with the assumption that the improvement of education will result not so much from attempting to discover scientific methods that can be applied universally to classrooms throughout the land, or to individuals possessing particular personality characteristics, or to students coming from specific ethnic or class backgrounds, but rather from enabling teachers and others engaged in education to improve their ability to see and think about what they do. Educational practice as it occurs in schools is an inordinately complicated affair filled with contingencies that are extremely difficult to predict, let alone control. Connoisseurship in education, as in other areas, is that art of perception that makes the appreciation of such complexity possible. Connoisseurship is an appreciative art. Appreciation in this context means not necessarily a liking or preference for what one has encountered, but rather an awareness of its characteristics and qualities.

Take an example of connoisseurship in a realm simpler than education, that of wine. The wine connoisseur has, through long and careful attention to wine, developed a gustatory palate that enables him to discern its most subtle qualities. When he drinks wine it is done with an intention to discern, and with a set of techniques that he employs to examine the range of qualities within the wine upon which he will make his judgments. Body, color, nose, aftertaste, bite, flavor – these are some of the attributes to which the wine connoisseur attends. In addition, he brings to bear upon his present experience a gustatory memory of other wines tasted. These other wines, held in the memory, form the backdrop for his present experience with a particular vintage. It is his refined palate, his knowledge of what to look for, his backlog of previous experience with wines other than those he is presently drinking that differentiate his level of discernment from that of an ordinary drinker of wine. His conclusions about the quality of wines are judgments, not mere preferences. Judgments, unlike preferences which are incorrigible, can be grounded in reasons, reasons that refer back to the wine's qualities and to other wines of the same variety.

Connoisseurship in other fields shares principles similar to those of wine connoisseurship. Connoisseurship in cabinet-making, for example, requires a similar ability to place what one currently examines into a context of cabinets one has already seen. What is the quality of the varnish that has been used? How many coats have been applied? What about the construction? Have the joints been mitered, dovetailed, doweled, finger-lapped, or tenoned? Are the edges banded and so on. Knowing what to look for, being able to recognize skill, form, and imagination are some of the distinguishing traits of connoisseurship.

When it comes to the fine arts, even more is required for connoisseurship to be exercised. Works of art have a history, develop in a social context, and frequently possess a profundity in conception and execution that surpasses wine and cabinets. The poetry of e. e. cummings, the music of Stravinsky, the cinematography of Fellini and Bergman, the plays of Ibsen and Genet, the paintings of Rothko; connoisseurship with respect to these creations goes well beyond the use of awakened sensibility. Such works require an ability to recognize both how and why they depart from conventional modes in their respective art forms. To recognize such departures requires an understanding not only of the forms the various arts have taken in the past but also an understanding of the intentions and leading conceptions underlying such works. The problems the artist formulates differ from period to period: the problems of Cézanne are not those of Duccio or Bellini or Motherwell. To appreciate the work of such men requires, therefore, not only attention to the work's formal qualities, but also an understanding of the ideas that gave rise to the work in the first place. This in turn requires some understanding of the socio-cultural context in which these artists worked, the sources from which they drew, and the influence their work had upon the work of others.

If connoisseurship is the art of appreciation, criticism is the art of disclosure. What the critic aims at is not only to discern the character and qualities constituting the object or event – this is a necessary but insufficient condition for criticism – the critic also aims at providing a rendering in linguistic terms of what it is that he or she has encountered so that others not possessing his level of connoisseurship can also enter into the work. Dewey put it nicely when he said, 'The end of criticism is the reeducation of the perception of the work of art.'[3] Given this view of criticism – a view I share – the function of criticism is educational. Its aim is to lift the veils that keep the eyes from seeing by providing the bridge needed by others to experience the qualities and relationships within some arena of activity. In this sense criticism requires connoisseurship but connoisseurship does not require the skills of criticism. One can function as a connoisseur without uttering a word about what has been experienced. Enjoyments can be private; one can relish or feel disdain in solitude. Criticism, on the contrary, is a public art. The critic must talk or write about what has been encountered; he must, in Kozloff's terms,[4] provide a rendering of the qualities that constitute the work, its significance, and the quality of his experience when he interacts with it.

Let's look at a piece of criticism by Max Kozloff as he describes his visit to an exhibition of paintings by the contemporary British painter Francis Bacon:

> Wandering up and down the ramp of the Francis Bacon exhibition at the Guggenheim Museum on a sunny afternoon is a grisly experience. The joys of painting and the presence of a brilliant mind are not enough to dispel one's morbid embarrassment, as if one had been caught, and had caught oneself, smiling at a hanging.
>
> ... Earlier I was aware of his velvety, featherlike white strokes, which tickle the navy blue ground and form an urgent image all in their own time, only as an irritant. It is irritating, that is, to be cajoled, wheedled and finally seduced into an enjoyment of a painted scene whose nature connotes only horror or repulsion. Such are his various tableaux of crucifixion and murder, although his merely voyeuristic glimpses of male orgies arouse guilt in this same way.[5]

Kozloff's language is notable on several grounds. First, the language itself, independent of its relationship to Bacon's paintings, is sufficiently rich and vivid almost to enable the reader to experience the quality of what Bacon's work must be like even if one had never seen Bacon's paintings. Like a good storyteller, Kozloff himself paints linguistically a visually vivid picture of what he has encountered. Second, Kozloff not only tells us about the quality of the paint, the feathery character of the artist's brush strokes, the quality of the color that the paintings possess, he also attends to his own experience – its quality, its mood, its voyeuristic feelings, 'as if one had been caught smiling at a hanging.' Kozloff lets us in not only on the qualities of the work, but on the qualities of his experience when he interacts with it. Third, notice the kind of language that Kozloff uses to render the work. It is a language filled with metaphor and with unlikely analogies – 'smiling at a hanging.' This use of metaphorical language is at base poetic. Metaphor is the recognition of underlying commonality in what is usually considered discrete and independent. The sudden recognition of such commonalities through the use of metaphor provides a bridge between the critic's language and the work and provides the conditions through which insight is generated.

Both connoisseur and critics use, of course, an array of values that focus their perception. One of the essential characteristics of human perception is that it is selective. One cannot look at everything at once and although characteristics of the perceptual field itself play a role in guiding perception, the leading ideas one holds about the arts, wine, or cabinetmaking also perform a role in focusing attention. These leading ideas and values about what counts grow from tradition and habit as well as from implicit and explicit theories about the nature of artistic virtue. In the fine arts such theories are explicitly created by aestheticians and implicitly by the critics themselves. When Roger Fry lauds 'significant form,' he calls the critics' attention to the formal structure of the work; when Bernard Berenson applauds 'tactile qualities,' he reminds us that solidity and volume are crucial considerations in works of visual art; when Leo Tolstoy tells us that good art is sincere, clear, and that it establishes a communion among men's feelings he draws our attention to moral and ethical considerations that flow from our encounters with art.

The lesson to be learned here is that sheer description unguided by value considerations is rudderless. Seeking and selecting require guideposts. In the arts aesthetic theory provides them.

What is the Relationship of Connoisseurship and Criticism to the Study of Educational Phenomena?

Thus far I have devoted my attention to the concepts of connoisseurship and criticism as applied to the arts. But what is the relationship of these concepts to education? How can practices useful in the arts be usefully employed in studying the conduct of classrooms? It is to these questions that we now turn our attention.

It is an old truism that scientific studies in education are as often defined by the form of research one has learned to use as by the substantive problems one believes to be significant. Becoming familiar with correlation procedures too often leads simply to questions about what one can correlate; the existence of statistically reliable achievement tests too often leads to a conception of achievement that is educationally eviscerated. Our tools, as useful as they might be initially, often become our masters. Indeed, what it means to do any type of research at all in education is defined, stamped, sealed, and approved by utilizing particular premises and procedures. A brief excursion into the pages of the *American Educational Research Journal* will provide living testimony to the range of such premises and procedures.

For example, during the past three volume years the *AERJ* has published over 100 articles. Of these only three were non-statistical in character.

Yet the range, richness, and complexity of educational phenomena occurring within classrooms are wider than can be measured. Some phenomena can only be rendered. It is this richness and this complexity to which educational connoisseurship addresses itself.

Imagine a ninth grade class in algebra. The school, in an upper-middle-class suburb, is one of those single-storey, try-hard modern school buildings that looks like the district ran out of funds before it could be finished. The classroom is a boxlike environment, anonymous except for the sundry array of hand-carved initials that decorate the wooden desks that line it. Not even a nod is given to visual interest. The only visual art in it is a dog-eared poster of Smokey the Bear, reminding students to put out their campfires. The rest is blackboard, light green plaster walls, and small windows well above the level through which students can look out onto the world. Suddenly the buzzer pierces the atmosphere with a baritone voice that startles even the geraniums. To the students it is only a familiar reminder that class is ready to begin.

How do these tightly zipped, vivacious youths enter the room? What expressions do they wear on their faces? What do their posture, their pace, their eyes say about Algebra I to which they return each day at 10:05? How does the class begin? Is the procession of discourse one that stimulates, satisfies? Is it one of dutiful routine, one of feigned enthusiasm that so many students of the well-to-do do so well?

How does the teacher respond to students? What does the tone of his voice say to those who do not understand? Do you detect the tinge of impatience that humiliates?

How is the class paced? Does it have a sense of movement and closure? Is competitiveness engendered by the subtle but pointed reminders of extra credit, of the quiz the day after tomorrow, and of grades for college? What is the quality of the ideas and the analyses with which the students venture forth into the life of the mind? What is this teacher, in this setting, saying about algebra *and* about education to the students who meet him every day at 10:05?

These are some of the qualities, ideas, and practices to which an educational connoisseur might attend. But educational connoisseurship is not reserved for those outside of the teaching profession. Educational connoisseurship is to some degree practiced daily by educational practitioners. The teacher's ability, for example, to judge when children have had enough of art, maths, reading, or 'free time' is a judgment made not by applying a theory of motivation or attention, but by recognizing the wide range of qualities that the children themselves display to those who have learned to see. Walk down any school corridor and peek through a window; an educational connoisseur can quickly discern important things about life in that classroom. Of course judgments, especially those made through windows from hallways, can be faulty. Yet the point remains. If one knows how to see what one looks at, a great deal of information – what Stephen Pepper refers to as 'danda' in contrast to 'data'[6] – can be secured. The teacher who cannot distinguish between the noise of children working and just plain noise has not yet developed a basic level of educational connoisseurship.

Listen to the shop talk of teachers, the kind of discourse they carry on in the lounge; their shop talk reveals the application of their own levels of connoisseurship to the settings in which they work. If teachers and school administrators already possess educational connoisseurship, then why try to foster it? There are several reasons. In the first place connoisseurship, like any art, is capable of refinement. Teachers on their own – like all of us – develop whatever connoisseurship they can or need. What is obvious, by definition, we learn to recognize easily and early. What is subtle and complex we might never perceive. As Ryle[7] has pointed out, seeing is not simply an act, but an achievement. Seeing is a realization secured. Unfortunately, one of the consequences of familiarity is the development of obliviousness. We learn not to see; we turn off what we have become accustomed to. Thus, a teacher with years of experience in the classroom or a school administrator with a decade behind the desk might develop only enough educational connoisseurship to enable them to cope at minimal levels within the classroom and school in which they work. Being oblivious to a large portion of their environment they are in no position to bring about change, to rectify eductional ills they cannot see, or to alter their own behavior. What is even worse, the conditions and qualities they do see they might believe to be natural rather than artifactual. We often come to believe, because of habit reinforced by convention, that the way things are is the way they *must* be. More refined levels of educational connoisseurship could militate against such seductive comforts.

In the second place connoisseurship when developed to a high degree provides a level of consciousness that makes intellectual clarity possible. Many teachers are confronted daily with prescriptions and demands from individuals outside the teaching profession – demands that are intended to improve the quality of education within the schools. Many of these the teachers feel in their gut to be misguided or wrong-headed; the demands somehow fly in the face of what they feel to be possible in a classroom or in the best interests of children. Two examples should suffice. The pressures toward accountability defined in terms of specific operational objectives and precise measurement of outcomes are pressures that many teachers dislike. Their distaste for these pressures is not due to professional laziness, recalcitrance, or stupidity, but is due to the uneasy feeling that as rational as a means-ends concept of accountability appears to be, it doesn't quite fit the educational facts with which they live and work. Many teachers, if you ask them, are unable to state why they feel uneasy. They have a difficult time articulating what the flaws are in the often glib prescriptions that issue from state capitols and from major universities. Yet the uneasiness is often – not always but often – justified. Some objectives one cannot articulate, some goals one does not achieve by the end of the academic year, some insights are not measurable, some ends are not known until after the fact, some models of educational practice violate some visions of the learner and the classroom. Many teachers have developed sufficient connoisseurship to feel that something is awry but have insufficient connoisseurship to provide a more adequate conceptualization of just what it is.

In the third place the development of higher levels of connoisseurship that we have in general at present might provide new subject matters not only for theoretical attention, but for conventional empirical research. Of what use is it to test a new method for the teaching of spelling to third graders if 15 per cent of the children, because of where their desks are placed, cannot see the blackboard? Significant effects in schooling might be the result of factors that experimenters do not see and cannot, therefore, control. Jackson notes,[8] for example, that in elementary school classrooms when students come up to the teacher's desk for help, the teacher visually scans the classroom every forty seconds or so. He also notes that children seated on the periphery of the room tend to withdraw more – out the window as it were – than children seated up front or in the middle of the room. What do such behaviors mean for teaching and learning? What do they reveal about how children and teachers cope with the demands made upon them? These questions and others that could be raised grow out of the perceptive, critical observations that Jackson was able to make. These variables and others like them could provide new and productive leads for educational research. Such leads depend for their existence on the realizations that educational connoisseurship provides.

The end of criticism, unlike connoisseurship, is that of disclosure. Criticism applied to classroom phenomena is the art of saying just what it is that is going on in that setting. Take, for example, that mode of human performance called teaching. What is it that teachers do when they teach? How do they use themselves? How do they move? What level of tension, of affect, of spontaneity do they display? To what extent do they reveal themselves as persons to the students with whom they work? Are they approachable? In what ways? What kinds of values, ideas, and covert messages do they emphasize? How, given questions such as these, can the qualities to which such questions guide us be disclosed? How can they be disclosed in a way that does not rob them of their vitality as experienced? Here the educational critic has a task similar to his counterpart dealing with live theater. The critic's task in each case is to provide a vivid rendering so that others might learn to see what transpires in that beehive of activity called the classroom. What the educational critic employs is a form of linguistic artistry replete with metaphor, contrast, redundancy, and emphasis that captures some aspect of the quality and character of educational life.

In this task the educational critic does far more than describe behavior. A strictly behavioral description of what teachers do would not only avoid dealing with the intentions of the teacher, it would also describe in quantitative terms the number of behavioral moves made by the teacher. One such description goes like this:

> Launching is primarily the function of the teacher rather than the pupil. The teacher speaks 85.2 per cent of all structuring components; in contrast, the pupil speaks only 10.2 per cent. The range for the teacher is from a high of 96.8 per cent in Class 6 to a low of 73.5 per cent in Class 13, with a median of 86.2 per cent. The range for the pupil, on the other hand, is from 23.6 per cent in Class 13 to zero in Classes 9 and 10, with a median percentage of 11.8 per cent.
>
> Halting-excluding is strictly a function of the teacher; in no class does the pupil perform this function. When the teacher does halt or exclude a subgame, he usually does so in a multiple component move in which he also launches a new sub-game. More frequently, however, the teacher does not explicitly halt or exclude sub-games; rather, he signals the end of one sub-game by launching a new sub-game.
>
> Speakers perform the function of launching by using one of three methods: announcing, stating propositions or announcing

and stating propositions. As shown in Table 17, the most frequent method is announcing; that is, giving public notice about one or more dimensions of the game or sub-game. Speakers launch by announcing in 45.2 per cent of all structuring components, by announcing and stating propositions in 34.1 per cent and by stating propositions in only 16.1 per cent.

Such a description is, of course, useful for some purposes, but it is not likely to capture the meaning or character of the teaching that has occurred. Such a description of behavior is 'thin' and can be contrasted to what Geertz[9] refers to as 'thick' description. Thick description aims at describing the meaning or significance of behavior as it occurs in a cultural network saturated with meaning. For example, a behavioral description of an eyelid closing on the left eye at the rate of two closures per second could be described in just that way. But a thick description of such behaviors within the context of a cultural subsystem could be described as a wink. The meaning of a wink, especially if the person at the other end is someone of the opposite sex, is entirely different from a description of eyelid closures at the rate of two closures per second. To fail to recognize the difference in the critical description of behavior is the same as neglecting the iconography used in works of visual art. The splash in the ocean in Breughel's painting *The Fall of Icarus* can be critically described only if one knows the story of Icarus. Once aware of the story, the significance of the painting and the meaning of the splash become clear.

It is obvious that the creation of effective criticism requires the artful use of language. Good critics use language in a way that requires a certain poetic and fluid range of words and phrases. Since the artful use of language is so important in the creation of criticism, wouldn't it be reasonable to use professional writers or critics in fields other than education to create educational criticism? The answer to that question is no. While it must have a sense of linguistic fluency and imagination, good criticism requires more than simply using language artfully. In all fields, but especially in education, the need to understand the values and history beneath practices being employed is crucial. In educational settings the critic must be in a position not only to perceive the superficial and apparent but the subtle and covert. What is subtle and covert in classrooms is not by definition visible to an educationally naive eye. But even more, the educational critic needs to know what form of educational practice the particular practice he encounters represents so that the criteria he employs in describing that practice are appropriate to it. One does not give low marks to a cubist painting because of a paucity of color; one does not condemn Monteverdi because his music does not have the melodic line of the romantics. Each form of an art needs to be appraised by the style it represents and the criteria appropriate to it. A lecture is not intrinsically bad and a discussion intrinsically good, regardless of the number and types of interactions in a discussion. There are many types of educational excellence and an educational critic should be familiar with them.

In addition to these competences of the creation of adequate educational criticism, the educational critic needs to be able to recognize what was neglected or rejected as well as what was accepted when a teacher uses a particular approach in a classroom. What values are being embraced? What values are being rejected when one decides to use particular educational procedures? Given the values that appear to animate classroom practices, how might they have been employed? In short, competent educational criticism requires far more than the writing skills possessed by a good novelist or journalist. It requires a broad grasp of educational theory and educational history and it would be a distinct advantage for critics to have had experience as classroom teachers.

It is instructive to note that the type of connoisseurship and particularly the type of criticism I am describing does not have a firm or well-developed tradition in schools of education. Such traditions do of course exist in highly sophisticated forms in literature, drama, the visual arts, poetry and music. And cinematography, the art form of the twentieth century, is rapidly developing a tradition of criticism. The study of education in this country has evolved from different roots, those of the natural and social sciences. To do research in education has meant to.do scientific work. To have evidence regarding educational practice has meant to have scientific evidence. Those whose interests and aptitudes for studying educational phenomena veered toward the humanistic or artistic modes of conception and expression have, unfortunately, too often been thought of as woolly headed, impressionistic romantics. Educational connoisseurship and criticism have not been encouraged. An ounce of data, it seems, has been worth a pound of insight.

Can Educational Criticism be Trusted?

One of the persistent concerns of those who do conventional forms of educational research and evaluation centers around the reliability of the instruments used. How can one be confident that the performance of individuals or groups being sampled is representative or consistent? How can one be sure that the judgments made by experts are reliable? The question of the dependability of criticism is, too, a concern of those doing criticism. How can we be sure that what educational critics say about educational phenomena is not a figment of their imagination? How can we know what confidence we can place in the critic's description, interpretation, and evaluation of classroom life?

The problem of determining the reliability of the critic's language is addressed by judging the referential adequacy of what he has to say. This is done by empirically testing his remarks against the phenomena he attempts to describe. Criticism has as its major aim the re-education of perception. Therefore, the language used to describe educational phenomena, such as teaching, should disclose aspects of that performance that might otherwise not be seen. The critic's language is referentially adequate when its referents can be found in the work or event itself. If a group of readers cannot find these referents in what has transpired, it may be due to (a) poor critical talk; (b) critical talk that is inappropriate for the competencies of the audience listening to it or reading it; or (c) an audience so unprepared to perceive that a much more powerful educational program for that audience is needed. Poor critical language or inappropriate language for a given audience can be problems from which any type of study can suffer. Conventional forms of educational research might also be so poorly articulated that they become incomprehensible. The technical level of the discourse of conventional research might, similarly, be inappropriately sophisticated or prosaic for a given audience. Insofar as the products of man are to have educational consequences, the fit between the audience and the message needs to be taken into account.

It is possible for critics to bring such bias to an encounter that they misread the situation. Their prior commitments function under exceptional circumstances as blinders rather than guides for seeing what is happening. But this liability, too, is not absent from conventional research. Theoretical convictions can lead one to gross misinterpretations of classroom life, and biases toward particular modes of statistical analyses or forms of testing can also create distortions in the state of affairs encountered. The tools we use are not simply neutral entities but have distinctive effects on the quality of our perceptions and upon our understanding.

When one deals with works of visual art and works of literature, there exists a certain stability in the material studied. But what do we do with things and events that change over time – classrooms, for instance? How can something as fluid as a classroom be critically described and how can such descriptions be tested for their referential adequacy? It should be noted that stage plays and orchestra performances, too, share some of the fluidity of the classroom or school, yet these art forms have a long critical history. What I believe must be done to fairly test the referential adequacy of critical discourse is two-fold. First, the classroom being studied needs to be visited with sufficient persistency to enable the critic to locate its pervasive qualities, those qualities through which aspects of its life can be characterized. Classrooms or schools are not so fugitive that their pervasive qualities change on a daily basis. What is enduring in a classroom is more likely to be educationally significant than what is evanescent. These enduring or pervasive qualities can become objects of critical attention. An educational connoisseur should be able to perceive what the critic has described when given the opportunity to do so.

Second, the availability of videotape recordings and cinematography now make it possible to capture and hold episodes of classroom life that can be critically described. Such videotaped episodes can then be compared with the criticism created and their referential adequacy determined. In addition, playback features of videotape make it possible to scrutinize expression, tempo, explanation, and movement in ways that live situations will not permit. Disputes about the adequacy of the criticism can be resolved, at least in principle, by re-examining particular segments of the tape. The technology now available lends itself exceedingly well to the work to be done.

One might well ask whether educational connoisseurship and criticism are likely to lead to useful generalizations about educational practice. Can the study of a handful of non-randomly selected classrooms yield conclusions that apply to classrooms other than the ones studied? The answer to these questions is complex. Insofar as the application of critical procedures discloses subtle but important phenomena that other classrooms and teachers share, then of course the gist of critical disclosure is applicable. But the only way to know that is to be able to learn from critical discourse what might be worth looking for in other educational situations. In other words, if it is true that the universal does indeed reside in the particulars which artistic activity constructs, the renderings of those constructions in critical language should open up aspects of classroom life that participate in such universals. To know that requires itself a sense of connoisseurship. Unlike the automatic application of a standard, what one learns from effective criticism is both a content within a particular classroom and a refined sensibility concerning classrooms that are useful for studying other educational situations.

There is another way in which effective connoisseurship and criticism might yield warranted generalizations and that is as cues useful for locating phenomena that might be subsequently pursued through conventional educational research. Creative scientific work in any field depends upon new realizations, new models, or new methods to guide inquiry. Insofar as effective criticism reveals aspects of educational phenomena that were previously unnoticed or under estimated, a fresh focus for conventional scientific study could be provided.

Thus far I have emphasized the similarities between criticism in the arts and criticism in education. But the fine arts are not identical with educational settings and the extent to which criticism in the arts can also be applied to education is something that needs to be determined. For example, art critics deal with completed works of art, not work in progress. The art critic looks at a completed painting, the music critic a finished symphony, and so forth. An educational critic has no such complete whole. Classroom activities flow into one another; seldom do classroom events form a completed whole. If this is true, what bearing does it have upon the doing of educational criticism?

Critics in the arts work within a long tradition;[10] they have at their disposal a tradition of critical writing, a language that is sharable, and a set of terms that have conventional meaning within the arts: impressionism, surrealism, constructivism, baroque, line, color, value, composition are conventional signs that those working in the arts understand. To what extent do we in education have similar terms and a comparable tradition? Is such a tradition possible and desirable in describing educational settings? Why hasn't one comparable to the arts been created? Are there differences between the criticism of the arts and of classrooms that make such a tradition unlikely?

In the world of the arts, critics have established themselves as inhabitants; art critics and art criticism are expected. Will teachers, school administrators, parents, educational theoreticians, and educational researchers accept educational criticism and educational critics? Will commitment to scientific objectivity lead to a rejection of criticism as a method of studying in education? Will teachers be able to use what critics provide? To what extent can educational criticism contribute to more effective teaching? What hampers critics from doing effective criticism when they have the opportunity to observe classrooms?

Summary

What are the major points I have tried to make? First, I have pointed out that the methodology of educational evaluation has been dominated by scientific assumptions. These assumptions and the methods they yield, I have argued, do not exhaust the ways in which men come to know. Their exclusive use has led to a limited and parochial conception of how educational evaluation can proceed.

Second, I have described two concepts – educational connoisseurship and educational criticism – concepts embedded not in a scientific tradition, but an artistic one. I have argued that these concepts yield procedures that could provide a needed complement to the scientific approaches to evaluation used today.

Third, I have described the ways in which these concepts might be applied to describe, interpret, and evaluate educational settings, and I have identified some of the unanswered questions and potential problems that flow from their use.

But most importantly, I have tried to open up a new window through which educational practice might be studied and described. My hope is that the vision you secured through that window looks attractive and promising.

These are the things I have said. I would like to conclude by identifying some of the things I neglected saying. I have not talked about the possibility of creating courses in schools of education devoted to educational connoisseurship and criticism. I have not described the ways in which these concepts might be used to evaluate the products children create in schools. I have not discussed the training of educational connoisseurs and critics, nor have I mentioned the possibility of developing journals and books in education that present and analyze critical descriptions of educational settings. I have totally neglected talking about new forms through which the results of educational evaluations can be reported, forms that rely on film, videotape, taped interviews, logs, visual displays, and the like. I have not suggested the possibility that doctoral dissertations might someday not need to be bound in book form for library shelves, but shown on film with an accompanying perceptive narrative. I have not talked about what the promise of such dissertations might mean for that proportion of doctoral students who now feel compelled to be junior psychologists in order to do studies they do not believe in so that they can get their PhDs. I haven't talked about the potential long term political consequences that might flow from opening up a new and legitimate approach to the study of education.

I have neglected talking about these things, and more. Yet all of them are possible. Whether they will be realized will depend upon the extent to which educational connoisseurship and criticism as concepts can capture the imagination of the field. It will also depend upon the usefulness of their application in practice. That application, it seems to me, is an appropriate agenda not only for those concerned with educational evaluation, but for anyone concerned with the design and improvement of educational programs.

Notes

1. The term connoisseurship has some unfortunate connotations that I would like to dispel within the context of the work proposed. One such connotation is that of effete, elite consumerism or snob; something belonging to the upper classes. Connoisseurship, as I use the term, relates to any form of expertise in any area of human endeavor and is as germane to the problems involved in purse snatching as it is in the appreciation of fine needlepoint.

   Similarly, criticism suggests to some people a harping, hacking, negativistic attitude toward something. This is not the way in which the term is used here. Criticism is conceived of as a generic process aimed at revealing the characteristics and qualities that constitute any human product. Its major aim is to enable individuals to recognize qualities and characteristics of a work or event that might have gone unnoticed and therefore unappreciated.

2. The concepts of educational connoisseurship and educational criticism have evolved from conceptual work extending over the past decade. Those interested in this work might refer to: EISNER, E.W. (1963) 'Qualitative Intelligence and the Act of Teaching,' in *Elementary School Journal*, Vol. 73, No. 6, March; EISNER, E.W. 'Instructional and Expressive Objectives: Their Formulation and Use in Curriculum,' in POPHAM, W.J. et al. (1969) *Instructional Objectives*, American Educational Research Association Monograph No. 3. Chicago, Ill., Rand McNally; EISNER, E.W. (1972) 'Emerging Models for Educational Evaluation,' in *School Review*, Vol. 80, No. 4, August; EISNER, E.W. (1974) *English Primary Schools: Some Observations and Assessments* Washington, D.C., National Association for the Education of Young Children; and EISNER, E.W. (1975) 'The Future of the Secondary Schools: A Viewpoint,' in *Curriculum Theory Network*, Vol. 5, No. 3. These concepts are being operationalized by my students and me at Stanford University in the study of elementary and secondary school classrooms.

3. DEWEY, J. (1934) *Art as Experience* New York, Milton Balch and Co.

4. KOZLOFF, M. (1969) *Renderings* New York, Simon and Schuster.

5. *Ibid.*
6. PEPPER, S. (1945) *The Basis of Criticism in the Arts* Cambridge, Mass., Harvard University Press.
7. RYLE, G. (1949) *The Concept of Mind* New York, Barnes and Noble.
8. JACKSON, P. (1968) *Life in Classrooms* New York, Holt, Rinehart and Winston.
9. I first encountered the concepts of 'thick' and 'thin' description in listening to a paper by Clifford Geertz given at Stanford University in 1974.
10. The study of symbols as used in the arts is called iconography and is perhaps best exemplified in the work of PANOFSKY, E. (1974) *Meaning in the Visual Arts* New York, Overlook Press.

7   *The Impoverished Mind*

There is a problem that is receiving little attention today, the demise of the balanced curriculum. Amidst the demands for a return to the educational virtues of the past, curricular balance seems to be an abandoned idea, a romantic notion, appropriate perhaps during an era of greater educational latitude, but not particularly appropriate for today's educational world.

The Unbalanced Curriculum

My thesis is simple and straightforward. I believe the current emphasis on the production of measurable competencies in the three Rs is creating an unbalanced curriculum that will, in the long run, weaken rather than strengthen the quality of children's education. This chapter aims to provide the grounds for this belief and to lay a foundation upon which a balanced curriculum can be built.

If one reviews the research that has been done on methods of teaching, on forms of grouping students, and on teacher personality and their effects, one will find that one of the most important variables that has been discovered that influences what students learn in school is what students are given an opportunity to learn.[1] This mind-shattering generalization (long known by anyone free from the blinders of much professional socialization) has profound implications for curriculum decision-making. From it one can infer that one of the most important curriculum decisions that can be made is deciding what to teach. Content inclusion and content exclusion decisions define the parameters within which a great deal of what students learn is to be found.

Decisions about what the curriculum shall consist of with respect to content are important, not only because such decisions define the opportunities students will have for learning that content, but because they also define for students what is regarded as important in school.

Time is one of our most precious resources. Once it is used, it is gone, never to return again. It is, in this sense, a limited and exhaustible commodity. Thus, what we choose to 'spend' time on says something about what we value. Decisions about curriculum content and the amount of time devoted to given content areas therefore not only influence the opportunities children have to learn, but they also influence what children perceive to be of value in the school and in the culture-at-large.

If one wanted to secure an operational definition of what is valued in school, one could do little better than to calculate the amount of instructional time devoted to the teaching of content areas within the curriculum. If this calculation is made, it will become quickly apparent that some areas receive a great deal more attention than others. For example, at the elementary level about 60–70 per cent of all formal teaching is devoted to the language arts and arithmetic. If we calculate the amount of time devoted to, say, music or art, it turns out that about three per cent of school time each week is devoted to these fields. On the average, art and music are taught about one half-hour to about one hour per week. Thus, children spend more time at recess than they do studying either art or music in the schools.

I use art and music only as examples. The social studies, the sciences, field trips, and other activities in content areas once believed important for children are also casualties of current educational priorities. Increasingly, more and more teachers are having less and less time to devote to the social studies, science, or drama, or to take field trips and the like.

Although the amount of time devoted to different content areas is a powerful index of what we value in schools, the amount of time devoted to various fields of study is not the only cue that teaches youngsters what is valued. Consider, for example, the location of time. When a subject is taught also says something about what is important. Art and music are taught in the afternoon, not in the morning. In the morning, children need to think; thus reading and arithmetic are taught in this part of the day. When youngsters do not have to think, or when they do not have to think as clearly, the 'noncognitive' fields can be attended to. Thus, mornings are for cognition and afternoons for affect.

Consider further which afternoons the arts are taught. Very often they are taught on Thursday, or, more likely, on Friday. Again, the point here is not specific to art or music, but rather to the means through which the use of time teaches children what schools value. The amount of time and the location of time are two such means.

Well, what does this all have to do with balance in the curriculum? What is the relationship between time spent and children's opportunities to learn? In the simplest terms, it is not possible to have any semblance of curriculum balance whatsoever if the content areas needed for such balance are absent from the curriculum or given so little time that their effectiveness is neutralized. If one of the most significant factors influencing learning in school is the opportunity to learn, then the lack of opportunity to deal with particular content fields vitiates the child's opportunity to learn what those fields have to provide. A decision to teach X in a program that has time constraints is also a decision not to teach Y.[2] Current pressures upon teachers, supervisors, and school administrators are leading to an ill-conceived use of school time that may have short-term gains, but will have, I believe, long-term costs. It is to the grounds for curriculum balance and the costs of its neglect that I now turn.

Symbol Systems and Modes of Consciousness

Human beings possess the capacity to contact and construe reality in a variety of ways. The sensory and symbol systems that humans have invented to express what they have come to know create different forms of awareness and make different modes of understanding possible. With our sensory systems, we experience various aspects of a multidimensional reality. This is what I mean. Consider autumn. Recollect what it means. Conjure up an image of its features. Autumn for some is the last three months of the Julian calendar. For others, it is the period in the second half of the year when light and darkness are of equal proportion. Autumn for others still is the end of summer, and for teachers, autumn is the psychological start of a new year.

But autumn can also mean the crunch of leaves as you trample through a favorite forest. It might mean the crackle and snap of burning branches, or their special aroma wafting from the flames. For some, autumn might mean the blaze of orange, yellow, and light green leaves that stand crisply against a clear and bright blue sky. For others, autumn is a special feel to the breeze, a kind of soft chill that heralds the coming of winter. Which one is the real autumn? Autumn is not one thing, it is many. We have the capacity to know autumn in the various ways in which it can be known, and we have the ability to conceptualize, to conjure in the mind's eye images of sound, sight, smell, and touch to help us recall the ways in which autumn is known to us.

Now the ability to use these sensory systems is to some degree an automatic consequence of maturation. Humans are born with the capacity to see and to hear, to taste and to feel, but the development of these capacities to a point beyond their uses for survival is a cultural achievement. We do not, simply as a result of maturation, develop highly refined forms of intelligence in their use. The ability to see what is subtle, to taste what is delicate, to hear what is muted, and to feel what is fleeting, is a result of learning. Culture provides for the development of some of these abilities, but neglects others.[3]

The cultivation of sensory systems requires the development of intelligence in those modes of perception in which the systems function. But the ability to transform what those systems provide into a public form requires an ability to use the symbol systems that pervade the culture.[4] Each symbol system – mathematics, the sciences, art, music, literature, poetry, and the like – functions as a means for both the conceptualization of ideas about aspects of reality and as a means for conveying what one knows to others. Each symbol system has unique capabilities. Each symbol system sets parameters upon what can be conceived and what can be expressed. Thus, through painting we are able to know autumn in ways that only the visual arts make possible. Through poetry we can know autumn in ways that only poems can provide. Through botany we are able to know autumn in ways that only botanists can convey. How autumn is conceived and, hence, what we know about it depends upon the symbol systems we use or choose to use.

Are some symbol systems better than others? Are some more rigorous or more precise? What do different symbol systems do that others do not? What are the particular strengths and weaknesses that different symbol systems have for portraying or communicating aspects of reality? Consider for example the sense of life we call 'suspense.' To most adults the meaning of the word suspense is not particularly obscure. If it is used in a sentence, it is likely to be understood. Now suppose that someone wanted to convey that sense of life called suspense, not by words, but by music. We can readily imagine what the music might be like, and we have little difficulty recognizing that suspense can be expressed in music as well as in discursive language; people who listen to music can experience that quality of life we call suspense if the composer and the musician are competent to write and to play it.

Compare this scenario with a situation in which suspense is to be created through sculpture. Here the problems become formidable. It becomes difficult even to conceive of the ways in which such a concept might be conveyed through sculpture, a symbol system that is spatial rather than temporal. Suspense is a temporal phenomenon as are music and language. These symbol systems lend themselves better to the expression of what is a temporal experience than a symbol system that is spatial.[5]

Consider another example. Suppose for a moment that you were moving to another part of the country and that you asked a friend to look around for an apartment for you. Your friend writes back and says that he or she has found an apartment, but that it will need new carpeting since the existing carpeting is badly worn. What kind of additional information would you want from your friend? More than likely you would want to know how much carpeting is needed, and, for that kind of knowledge, the appropriate symbol system is arithmetic. If you wanted to know how much carpeting is needed, you would not want a picture of the living room, you would want a set of numbers. But, if you wanted to know what the living room looked like, you would not want a set of numbers, you would want a set of pictures. A particular symbol system is useful for some types of information, but not for others, and vice versa. Thus, when we choose to become 'literate' in the use of particular symbol systems, we also begin to define for ourselves what we are capable of conceiving and how we can convey what we have conceived to others.

Learning to Write Means Learning to See

The relationship between a symbol system as a mode of conception and its public manifestation in, say, mathematics, literature, or art is not simply a one-way street. That is, it is not simply the case that the mode in which conceptualization takes place is the form in which expression must occur. Put another way, because I am able to visualize certain features of a reality does not mean that that reality must be symbolized visually. One can conceptualize in one mode and express in another. In this sense, there is a rich and productive interaction between modes of conceptualization (which, incidentally, are themselves symbolic since all aspects of reality are abstracted for conception) and the form one chooses to use to publicly render what one has conceptualized. Perhaps the most vivid example of this is to be found in literature. Consider the following passage from Annie Dillard's book *Pilgrim at Tinker Creek:*[6]

> The shadow's the thing. Outside shadows are blue, I read, because they are lighted by the blue sky and not the yellow sun. Their blueness bespeaks infinitesimal particles scattered down inestimable distance. Muslims, whose religion bans representational art as idolatrous, don't observe the rule strictly; but they do forbid sculpture, because it casts a shadow. So shadows define the real. If I no longer see shadows as 'dark marks,' as do the newly sighted, then I see them as making some sort of sense of the light. They give the light distance; they put it in its place. They inform my eyes of my location here, here O Israel, here in the world's flawed sculpture, here in the flickering shade of the nothingness between me and the light.
>
> Now that shadow has dissolved the heavens' blue dome, I can see Andromeda again; I stand pressed to the window, rapt and shrunk in the galaxy's chill glare. 'Nostalgia of the Infinite,' Chirico; cast shadows stream across the sunlit courtyard, gouging canyons. There is a sense in which shadows are actually cast, hurled with a power, cast as Ishmael was cast, out, with a flinging force. This is the blue strip running through creation, the icy roadside stream on whose banks the mantis mates, in whose unweighted waters the giant water bud sips frogs. Shadow Creek is the blue subterranean stream that chills Carvin's Creek and Tinker Creek; it cuts like ice under the ribs of the mountains, Tinker and Dead Man. Shadow Creek storms through limestone vaults under forests, or surfaces anywhere, damp, on the underside of a leaf. I wring it from rocks; it seeps into my cup. Chasms open at the glance of an eye; the ground parts like a wind-rent cloud over stars. Shadow Creek: on my last walk to the mailbox I may find myself knee-deep in its sucking, frigid pools. I must either wear rubber boots, or dance to keep warm.[7]

What is perfectly apparent from this passage is that Annie Dillard had to be able to see in order to write. She had to be able to visualize, to form concepts of the reality to which she previously had attended. Out of this ability developed the experiential content for her literature. What made her book possible was not so-called 'writing skills,' it surely wasn't the rote application of the rules of grammar or punctuation, it was first the capacity to see, second the ability to conceptualize what had been seen, and third, the ability to transform those conceptions into a form that rendered them vivid. Her eyes, which are a part of the mind, provided the content that made her writing possible.[8]

But the influence does not stop there. What Annie Dillard has given us is literature, but what her literature helps us do is to see. Once having read her book, we can never see a creek or a shadow in quite the same way as we once did. Her writing becomes a means for guiding our attention by making vivid what was previously ignored. Thus, Annie Dillard's eyes make her literature possible, and her literature gives vision to our eyes. The circle is completed.

This relationship between seeing and writing, and writing and seeing holds, a *fortiori*, in all of the modes through which human conception and expression occur. The concepts we learn in mathematics facilitate forms of cognition that can have their expression in music. Pythagoras is perhaps the most stunning example. What we are able to understand through poetry can contribute to the creation of penetrating theory in the social sciences. The mind draws upon a variety of forms of knowing to give birth to ideas and these ideas, I am arguing, need not be expressed in the modes within which the conceptualization has occurred. Consider what Einstein had to say about the role of visualization in his own work in mathematics.

> The words or the language, as they are written or spoken, do not seem to play any role in my mechanism of thought. The psychical entities which seem to serve as elements in thought are certain signs and more or less clear images which can be 'voluntarily' reproduced or combined.... But taken from a psychological viewpoint, this combinatory play seems to be the essential feature in productive thought – before there is any connection with logical construction in words or other kinds of signs which can be communicated to others. The above-mentioned elements are, in my case, of visual and some of muscular type. Conventional words or other signs have to be sought for laboriously only in a secondary stage, when the mentioned associative play is sufficiently established and can be reproduced at will.[9]

Einstein was, of course, a genius. But the processes he identified are not unique to geniuses.

What does all of this mean for a rationale for curriculum? Simply this, if the ability to use symbol systems for purposes of conceptualization and expression are, at least in part, a result of cultivation, then it would seem to follow that programs that deny students opportunities to learn to use such systems of thought and expression deprive them of the kinds of meaning that they can learn to create.

Put in terms of a value statement, we can now state: If education has as one of its major aims the development of each child's ability to create meaning from experience, and if the construction of meaning requires the use of skills applied within a symbol system, then the absence of such systems within the curriculum is an impoverishment of the quality of education children receive.

Viewed from this perspective, balance in the curriculum is not simply a plea for the equal representation of cultural artifacts, but rather an imperative for helping students learn how to expand their modes of consciousness. Balance in the curriculum in this view is a conception rooted in an understanding of the nature and scope of cognition. It is not the case that certain cultural forms, such as the arts, to name but one example, are affective and mathematics cognitive. It is the case that each of the major cultural forms we call the arts and the sciences, the social studies and the humanities are symbol systems that humans use in order to know. They are all cognitive. Symbolic processes are the means through which consciousness is articulated, and they are also the means through which what has become conscious can be publicly shared.

The structure or syntax of such public forms are often subtle and technical: They are encoded forms that one must learn to 'read' if meaning is to be secured. A school curriculum that neglects attention to these publicly coded symbolic forms diminishes the child's opportunities to think in the modes these forms make possible. Such a curriculum restricts the child's opportunity to refine incipient skills of visual perception. It diminishes the child's chances to employ the modes of imagination that poetry and drama can engender. It withholds from the children the opportunity to cultivate their capacities to hear what is subtle. These forms of educational deprivation exact a price, I have argued, not only in those spheres of human activity in which the skills function directly, but also in those other spheres in which sensitivity to the visual world, to the auditory, and to the imaginative are crucial. Cognitive forms of deprivation cannot be isolated to a compartmentalized conception of mind that often serves as a convenient but misleading fiction for justifying an impoverished view of education. The mind is of a piece.

At present, the development of the forms of consciousness that a balanced curriculum makes possible is not a high priority in American schooling. The public has been told that children no longer read as well as they once did, that they have difficulty spelling, that their writing skills are less than they ought to be. We have developed and used various kinds of tests to provide 'scientific' evidence of the decline in students' ability, and the public now expects these matters to be remedied. For classrooms throughout the nation, this has resulted in a return to the so-called basics and to a neglect of other forms of understanding that a balanced curriculum represents. Even university professors of education who ought to know better use extraordinarily limited data to support beliefs about educational decline and suggest or imply that the appropriate remedy is to do more of the same. In short, we have coped with the pressures put upon the schools by looking for short-term gains in the 'basics' at a cost of neglecting what tests like the *California Test of Basic Skills* do not measure.

It is not likely, in my view, that devoting more time to what now already consumes 60 to 70 per cent of instructional time in school is the way to improve what we are doing. The fact of the matter is, that if there is a serious problem regarding reading, writing, and arithmetic, we don't know what the nature of the problem is. We don't know because we haven't looked. Measuring symptoms is not an adequate way to locate causes, and testing, whether norm or criterion referenced, will not provide the kind of information teachers need to improve what they do. What is needed is attention to the processes of classroom life and the use of forms of disclosure that can capture and convey what goes on in those settings we call classrooms and schools. I have suggested in this paper that the kind of symbol systems one chooses to use sets parameters on what one can say. The form influences the message. If this is true, then it follows that numbers are but one symbol system for describing reality, and it is one that provides useful information for some things, but not for everything. Unfortunately, we in our educational culture have used this form as the *sine qua non* of objective assessment and have therefore limited, inadvertently, what we can know about what we are doing. In education, we need to catch many fish, but we have used nets that let many of the most interesting ones slip through.

Toward Balance in Educational Evaluation

What I am suggesting is that the line of argument I have advanced with respect to a balanced curriculum has direct implications for the way in which we conceive of evaluation. If balance in curriculum is needed to help children learn to experience the world widely, so too must be the approaches we use to evaluate. One symbol system cannot provide the richness of view that we need. Ironically, the aspiration to provide an unbiased, objective description of what students learn and how teachers teach by measuring the extent to which objectives have been reached and by counting the moves or utterances teachers make in the classroom often distorts the very reality such procedures aim to describe. The limited perspective our present methods of evaluation employ too frequently leads us to accept the part for the whole.

A balanced curriculum needs to be complemented by a balanced approach to evaluation. To do the latter will require a radically new basis for work in this field. This new work will require a model of inquiry that includes not only scientific premises and procedures, but artistic ones as well. It will be qualitative as well as quantitative. We need first of all to visit classrooms and observe with a sensitive and informed eye what the processes are that occur in such settings. We need, in my view, to see at least as much as we need to count. We need, I believe, to develop what I have called *educational connoisseurship*,[10] an art that is concerned essentially with the appreciation of what one attends to. In the arts, connoisseurship has a long tradition. Those who appreciate music, the visual arts, theatre, ballet, and those who have taken the time, expended the energy, and who have learned to appreciate the important subtleties of these art forms have developed high degrees of connoisseurship. We need the analogue to this mode in the appreciation of classroom life.

To some extent we already have educational connoisseurs in each school. I am speaking here of teachers. I would like one day to see schools in which teachers can function as professional colleagues, where a part of their professional role was to visit the classrooms of their colleagues, and to observe and share with them in a supportive, informed, and useful way what they have seen. Less professional isolation and more professional communication might go a long way to help all teachers secure more distance and hence to better understand their own teaching.

But to share what one has seen requires the ability to communicate in a way that does justice to the qualities observed. This process is one of criticism, but not criticism in a negative sense; rather, criticism in the sense in which it is used in literature, film, and the arts. I have called this form of criticism *educational criticism*. The end of criticism, wrote Dewey, is the re-education of perception.[11] The critic's function is to serve as a midwife to perception. The educational critic provides a description, interpretation, and evaluation of the classrooms he or she has seen, and through that process raises the level of awareness that a teacher can secure. Simply knowing the final score of the game after it is over is not very useful. What we need is a vivid rendering of how that game is being played. Educational connoisseurs who can function as educational critics can render that service and make it vivid. At Stanford, seven doctoral dissertations have been completed that do just that.[12]

We also need to use symbol systems that are employed in film, that use teacher logs and student interviews, and that employ graphic visual analysis of the work students create. We need slides of classroom activity and photos of work in progress. In short, we need to use an approach to educational evaluation that capitalizes on our human capacity to come to know reality in its multidimensional richness. The reduction of this richness of a single symbol system is an impoverishment of our ability to understand its multiple features. I am happy to say that the foundations for the work I have just described are well underway. Such work is being done not only in the United States, but in England and in Europe. I speak here of the work of Phillip Jackson of the University of Chicago, whose book *Life in Classrooms*[13] did so much to demonstrate the power of critical description. I speak of the work of Robert Stake at the University of Illinois, whose 'responsive evaluation'[14] advocates the use of a wide variety of data and methods for evaluating educational practice. I speak of the work of Parlett and Hamilton in England and their concern with 'illuminative evaluation,'[15] and the work of Hamilton, Jenkins, King, McDonald, and Parlett represented in their recent book, *Beyond the Numbers Game*,[16] a book, like George Willis' new book, *Qualitative Evaluation*,[17] that emphasizes non-conventional approaches to evaluation. And I speak of Fred Erickson's educational ethnographic work at Harvard that attempts to describe in fine detail what happens in classrooms.[18] These scholars are swimming against the current tide, but, nevertheless, contributing to the development of an approach to evaluation that will complement the conventional forms of evaluation that have dominated our thinking since the turn of the century.

In the long run, we need a curriculum for children that does justice to the scope of their minds, and we need evaluation practices that do justice to the lives that students and teachers lead in classrooms. Even though the current educational climate adumbrates another image, I believe we are at the threshold of realizing these new-found aspirations for education. Someday I believe we shall see school curricula that make wide forms of knowing possible and modes of evaluation that can capture the richness of their consequences. When that day arrives, educational inquiry as it occurs in teaching, evaluation, and research, will be recognized as both art and science, and the appreciation of Man's capacity to understand will provide the grounds for what we teach and how we come to know our achievements.

Notes

1. ROSENSHEIN, B. (1976) 'Classroom Instruction' in *The Psychology of Teaching Methods* National Society for the Study of Education Yearbook; 1976, Chicago, University of Chicago Press; and WALKER, D. and SCHAFFARZICK, J. (1974) 'Comparing Curricula' in *Review of Educational Research* 44(1) Winter.
2. I have called this absent curriculum the 'null curriculum.' For a discussion of these concepts see my book (1979) *The Educational Imagination: On the Design and Evaluation of School Programs* New York, Macmillan and Co.
3. EISNER, E.W. 'What Do Children Learn When They Paint,' in *Art Education.*
4. The discussion of symbol systems has been informed by my colleagues Richard Snow of the Stanford School of Education and Gavriel Solomon of Hebrew University, Jerusalem.
5. This example is taken from a lecture by Rudolph Arnheim, delivered at Stanford University in March 1977.
6. DILLARD, A. (1974) *Pilgrim at Tinker Creek* New York, Harpers Magazine Press.
7. *Ibid.*, pp. 62–63.
8. For a discussion of the eye as a part of the mind see STEINBERG, L. (1972) 'The Eye Is a Part of the Mind' *Other Criteria* New York, Oxford University Press.
9. HOLTON, G. (1967–68) 'Influences on Einstein's Early Work in Relativity Theory' in *The American Scholar* 37(1) Winter.
10. See the following for a discussion of this concept: EISNER, E.W. (1977) 'On the Uses of Educational Connoisseurship and Criticism for Evaluating Classroom Life,' in *Teachers College Record* 78(3), February; EISNER, E.W. (1977) 'Educational Connoisseurship and Educational Criticism: Their Forms and Functions in Educational Evaluation' in *Journal of Aesthetic Education*, Bicentennial Issue.
11. DEWEY, J. (1934) 'Criticism and Perception' in *Art as Experience* New York, Minton, Balch and Co.
12. These dissertations are: GREER, W.D. (1973) *The Criticism of Teaching* Stanford, Calif. Stanford University; VALLANCE, E.J. (1975) *Aesthetic Criticism and Curriculum Description* School of Education, Stanford University; McCUTCHEON, G. (1976) *The Disclosure of Classroom Life* School

of Education, Stanford University; DAVIDMAN, L. (1976) *The Formative Evaluation of the Unified Science and Mathematics in the Elementary Schools Curriculum* School of Education, Stanford University; ALEXANDER, R.R. (1977) *Educational Criticism of Three Art History Classes* School of Education, Stanford University; STERNBERG, B.J. (1977) *What Do Tokens and Trophies Teach?* School of Education, Stanford University; BERK, L.M. (1977) *Education in Lives: An Application of Biographic Narrative to the Study of Educational Outcomes* School of Education, Stanford University.

13. JACKSON, P. (1968) *Life in Classrooms* New York, Holt, Rinehart and Winston.

14. STAKE, R. (1975) *Evaluating the Arts in Education* Columbus, Ohio, Charles E. Merrill Pub. Co.

15. PARLETT, M. and HAMILTON, D. (1972) *Evaluation as Illumination: A New Approach to the Study of Innovative Programs* Center for Research in Educational Sciences, University of Edinburgh, Occasional Paper 9.

16. HAMILTON, D. *et al.* (1978) *Beyond the Numbers Game* London; Macmillan Education, Ltd.

17. WILLIS, G. (1978) *Qualitative Evaluation* Berkeley; Calif., McCutchan Publishing Co.

18. ERICKSON, F. (1976) 'Some Approaches to Inquiry in School Community Ethnography' Workshop Exploring Qualitative/Quantitative Research Methodologies in Education, Far West Laboratory for Educational Research and Development, in cooperation with the National Institute of Education and the Council on Anthropology and Education, July.

8   *Humanistic Trends and the Curriculum Field*

At present a major anomaly exists in the field of education both in England and in the United States. The anomaly I speak of is the growing concern among lay people and professionals alike that schools are not doing as well as they once were and that if the educational quality of the past is to be recaptured we must emphasize the 'basics', we must return to what is truly fundamental in schooling, namely, teaching children to read, to write and to compute. This concern with the basics is exacerbated by information given to the public that test scores are slipping and have been for quite a few years. Since 1970 in the United States the drop in Scholastic Aptitude Test Scores has been 30 points in the verbal and 50 points in the mathematical sections of the test. To ensure that appropriate efforts are made to pay attention to these areas of performance, proficiency tests are being mandated by the States and minimum performance levels are being established that must be met by any student seeking a graduation diploma.[1] 'Back to basics' and 'minimum standards' are the watchwords.

These concerns are not limited to the United States. In Calgary, Canada, recent headlines read: 'Education Report: Go Back to 3Rs'.[2] And in England a national project has been undertaken by the Department of Education and Science that would provide for the English what the National Assessment Program has provided for Americans: quantitative indices of the educational health of the nation.[3]

While this concern with the so-called basics and their assessment is going on, there is another movement developing simultaneously. That movement is concerned with the creation of a fundamentally different conception of education, in particular educational evaluation. It is this new movement, born and nurtured within the university that serves as the conceptual and philosophic antithesis to a conception of education limited to the three Rs and to a form of evaluation limited to quantitative description.

The movement I speak of is the growing interest among academics in the use of qualitative forms of inquiry in education. Like the so-called 'back to basics' movement, this interest is not limited to the United States. In England it is represented in the work of Barry MacDonald, Lawrence Stenhouse and Malcolm Parlett; in Scotland by David Hamilton; in Norway by Torsten Harbo; in Germany by Hartmut von Hentig; and in the United States by Stake, Jackson, Eisner, Willis, Mann, Walker, Huebner, and a host of others. What we see emerging in the university is the epistemological and methodological opposite of what is being advocated as desirable for the schools. It is this new movement, this growing interest in the exploration of qualitative forms of inquiry in education that I wish to discuss in this chapter. To my mind this growing interest represents one of the most radical and promising developments in education since the turn of the century, since it aims to explore and exploit a fundamentally different set of assumptions about the nature of knowledge than the view that has dominated education since 1900, at least in the United States.

By qualitative forms of inquiry I mean that form of inquiry that seeks the creation of qualities that are expressively patterned, that seeks the explication of wholes as a primary aim, that emphasizes the study of configurations rather than isolated entities, that regards expressive narratives and visuals as appropriate vehicles for communication. Qualitative methods tend to emphasize the importance of context in understanding, they tend to place great emphasis on the historical conditions within which events and situations occur, and they tend to argue that pieces cannot be understood aside from their relationship to the whole in which they participate. To understand an event or situation one must perceive it as an aspect of a larger pattern, rather than as an entity whose characteristics can be isolated and reduced to quantities.

To emphasize, as I have just done, the distinctive characteristics of qualitative inquiry is not to suggest that those who use such methods reject quantitative procedures. They do not. What they do reject is the assumption that objectivity can only be secured through quantitative or scientific methods. They reject the claim – implicit or explicit – that rigour in educational inquiry *requires* the use of methods that result in conclusions that can be stated in terms of probabilities. Let the problem determine the method, not vice versa.[4] Thus what we find are arguments for a multiple set of approaches to the ways in which educational inquiry can be pursued. The methods must be broadened.

As I see it, the motives for the development of qualitative methods in education emanate from three major sources. First, there are those whose interest stems from political motives. These individuals view the schools as an institutionalized conspiracy to keep children dependent, ill-informed and tolerant of mindless tasks so that when they become adults they will fit into the existing social order. To such individuals the feckless character of schools is not indicative of failure but of success. Schools, they believe, were and are intended to be a mindless experience for the young. Because the research establishment and the testing industry participate in this subterfuge, they are important targets to attack. Critical methods, particularly those that illuminate the kinds of experience that teachers and students have in schools, hold promise for raising the public's level of critical awareness. In addition, such methods have a kind of emotional impact in revealing what really goes on in schools, and thus might lead the public to seek significant changes in the structure and goals of schooling. For many of those politically motivated the use of qualitative methods is more compatible with a socialistic society or a Marxist-socialistic philosophy. Qualitative methods of evaluation, they believe, might make a significant contribution to the realization of such ends.

The second motive for the development of qualitative approaches to educational inquiry is methodological. Many of those interested in the uses of such methods regard laboratory research procedures associated with educational psychology as inappropriate for the study of classroom life and desire a more flexible and naturalistic approach to inquiry. For such individuals, ethnography, for example, provides a more desirable and more appropriate alternative. By attending to the context as a whole and by observing what naturally transpires without intervention by experimenters, a more valid picture of educational life can be secured. With more valid data, the likelihood of developing theory that is useful for understanding classrooms, teaching, and schooling is increased.

It should be noted that the motives here are not necessarily political in character. What those who wish to extend the methods of inquiry in education seek is not necessarily the radical reform of school or society, but the widening of legitimate procedures for research and evaluation. They frequently find the dominant view of research parochial and the methods for evaluating what students learn superficial.

The third motive for the development of qualitative approaches to evaluation is at base epistemological. Those moved by this ideal regard scientific epistemology as inadequate by itself for articulating all that needs to be known about schools, classrooms, teaching, and learning.

Scientific and quantitative methods are important utilities for describing some aspects of educational life and their consequences, but they are far too limited to be the exclusive or even the dominant set of methods. To complement these methods of evaluation, evaluators must look to the qualities that pervade classrooms, the experience that students have in schools, and the character of the work that children produce. To see these qualities requires a perceptive eye, an ability to employ theory in order to understand what is seen and a grounded set of educational values so that an appraisal of the *educational* significance of what has been seen can be determined.

But what is equally as important as perceiving the qualities that constitute classroom life is the ability to convey these qualities to others. For this to occur the methods used must be artistically critical. The educational critic must be able to create, render, portray, and disclose in such a way that the reader will be able to empathetically participate in the events described. The language of the critic using qualitative methods capitalizes on the role of emotion in knowing. Far from the ideal of emotional neutrality so often aspired to in the social sciences, the educational critic exploits the potential of language to further human understanding. The language she or he uses is expressive, so that the kind of understanding the reader can secure is one that reaches into the deeper levels of meaning children secure from school experience. To convey such meaning, the artistic use of language is a necessity.

The import of this orientation for education is significant for several reasons. First, it has long been recognized that the procedures used to evaluate students, teachers and schools have a profound effect on the kinds of priorities that the curriculum reflects.[5] When achievement, defined in terms of standardized forms of performance within specific subject areas becomes salient, it is likely that teachers will devote attention to those areas and in the process place less emphasis or neglect entirely areas that are not defined by test performance. What is counted, counts.

For students the need to do well on the instruments that assess achievement is a necessary condition for upward mobility within the educational system. When school districts develop proficiency tests to ensure school effectiveness, a climate within schools is created that increases pressures upon teachers and students alike to do well on the measures that are used. If students are to succeed within the system, excellence defined in terms of test performance is necessary.

For teachers, the use of achievement and proficiency tests represents a clear articulation of school district priorities. It does not mean much to express a commitment to goals that will not be used to appraise the quality of what has occurred in classrooms. Teachers, like students, know what counts: the use of standardized achievement tests provides vivid testimony. Thus, teachers who are to look effective must do so by having their students do well on the tests that are used. In the process of adaptation many professional values are often compromised. Survival is still a basic biological need.

The criteria that apply to teachers also apply to school administrators. In the United States school principals (headteachers and headmasters) as well as superintendents of local education authorities hold no tenure in their positions.[6] While these administrators cannot be easily fired from the teaching force, their ability to maintain their administrative positions (and the salaries that come with them) is dependent upon having the positive regard of the school board and the community. To have this regard the schools for which they are responsible must provide what lay people regard as quality education. When quality education is defined by test performance, how students do on tests is critically related to how well the public believe administrators are doing. Thus, the circle is completed. Those who design the methods of evaluation have a profound effect on the priorities that are held within schools. The climate, tone, emphasis and allocation of resources are all significantly influenced by the standardized and quantified rites of passage that are becoming increasingly important in the schools.

It is for these reasons that the significance of qualitative approaches to educational inquiry are so important. Schoolmen have been woefully derelict in giving the public anything other than standardized methods for appraising educational quality. There have been few alternatives to highly reductionistic indices of learning available. By developing, not so much alternatives, but complements to the conventional approaches to evaluation and research, the possibility of balance in view, in method and in 'data' can be created – at least in principle.

What is it that qualitative methods of inquiry provide and can they be regarded as humanistic? What is it that such a view illuminates that more conventional methods neglect? What are the potential second-order effects that emanate from the assumptions used in qualitative forms of inquiry in education?

As I have already indicated, qualitative forms of inquiry are typically focused upon patterns of phenomena within a more complex configuration rather than on the experimental isolation of casual variables. This means, in practice, the need to view a situation in a way that seeks meaning in the culture of the situation rather than in the manifest behaviour of individuals. To say this is to embrace a view of enquiry that regards manifest behaviour as meaningless unless it is related to a larger cultural network. The classroom provides that network. To the qualitative inquirer this means that one must try to uncover the meaning of action, moves, behaviours, and not simply the fact that behaviour has occurred.

Now the import of this orientation is critical in a period in which performance standards are sought after regardless of the means used to achieve such standards. The qualitative inquirer in education is likely to be interested in the meaning of the move perhaps even more than the move itself. Thus, he is in a position to explicate the costs as well as the benefits of certain forms of achievement. By attending to meaning rather than to behaviour as such, by relating behaviour to culture, and by paying attention to process as it develops within classrooms and schools, the qualitative inquirer is in a position to secure a much more complex view of educational situations. For many, I suppose, a more complex view might be regarded as somewhat of a liability, but the cost of simplistic conclusions about the quality of education are far greater than most lay people realize. There might not be any adequate way to describe the outcomes of schooling that can be reduced to numerical indices. It is precisely in the illumination of the complexities and richness of educational life that qualitative inquiry in education holds its greatest promise. Rather than reduce the human mind to a single score, qualitative inquirers attempt to adumbrate its complexities, its potential, and its idiosyncracies.

There are other benefits as well. The processes of educational practice – the quality of discourse, the character of explanation, the relationships among students and teachers, the intellectual vitality of discussion – are seldom addressed in conventional modes of evaluation. For the most part conventional evaluation practices address themselves to outcomes rather than to processes. And even when methods are used that focus on, say teaching, the data provided is almost always a very slender slice of the reality that it is supposed to represent. For example, data provided by a Flanders Interaction Analysis or a Bellack-type analysis of classroom discourse is inadequate for mentally reconstructing the events from which those data were secured. The richness and diversity of the classroom that the data represent are virtually impossible to imagine hence, the conclusions derived from such data are in a singificant sense acontextual.

When it comes to the products of achievement testing, the

information provided is even less satisfactory. The measured outcomes that achievement tests provide say nothing about the antecedents of those outcomes; perhaps that is why classroom teachers find them so unhelpful. Knowing the outcome of the game, so to speak, tells you nothing about how it is played, whether the problem – if there is a problem – is with the pitching, the hitting, or the fielding; the lack of an adequate goalie, swift wings, effective strikers, or a smart midfielder. What we have in achievement test data are consequences, and only a small portion of them at that.

Yet it is these outcomes that the public seeks to know more about. And the risk, of course, in acceding to their wishes is one of using whatever means necessary to provide the public with what will make it content. In the process children may be sacrificed educationally for the seductive comforts of high test scores.

Because qualitative methods of evaluation pay special attention to the processes of schooling they have the potential to provide the illumination and insight that will help lay people and educators alike secure a more adequate understanding of what goes on in schools. At present this understanding is minimal. The conventional methods of evaluation, as I have already indicated, have focused on outcomes, not processes. Research in education of an experimental variety has minimized extended contact with classrooms; classrooms are conceptually messy, difficult (even impossible) to control, and confound effects so that the identification of causes is formidable.[7] In the pursuit of precision and generalizability the major subject matters of educational practice have too often fallen by the wayside.

There is another potential value in qualitative forms of inquiry that deserves special mention. That value is in their potential to enable readers to empathetically participate in the events that the writing describes. To be able to use written material this way, the material itself has to be created as an art form. To create such writing requires a willingness and an ability to pay attention to the form of expression, to the use of metaphor, to the tempo and character of language. One must exploit the potential of language as an artistic medium, not merely as a descriptive one. One seeks, at least in part, the creation of an expressive analogue to the qualities of life perceived and appraised within schools and classrooms. The form must speak in a way that is at base non-discursive.[8]

Although this might sound strange to educationalists reared on a strict diet of social science, the means I have described participate in a tradition considerably older than the oldest of the social sciences. I speak here of literature, of history, of poetry, and of drama. Is fiction less true than fact? Where precisely is the line between a false fact and a truthful fiction? I play here – but only partly – for educators have much to learn from the traditions of inquiry that too seldom have entered schools and departments of education. The humanities have much to provide, both theoretical and practical, that can help us understand what goes on in the minds and hearts of men and women. It is our professional socialization that keeps us from this tradition; the tinge of embarrassment about the use of metaphor, allusion, expressive language. Yet I believe that this neglected tradition has the potential to provide the depth that knowing perception must have. Monocular vision is shallow.

What then can we say about the potential contributions of humanistic, or as I have preferred to call them, qualitative forms of inquiry in education? Their contributions to education are several. I will cite them here.

First, qualitative forms of inquiry in education hold promise for providing a more complex and complete picture of educational practice and its consequences. By illuminating patterns and by portraying relationships that go unnoticed in conventional approaches to evaluation a more complex image of classroom life is secured. Such an image can serve as an antidote to highly simplistic indices of classroom interaction and educational achievement. When educational policy is based on the information such indices provide it is likely to neglect what is important, be wrong-headed and have a tendency to embrace Utopian bandwagons to solve educational problems that require serious and sustained deliberation.

Second, qualitative forms of inquiry have the potential to expand our conception of the ways in which we come to know. Because qualitative forms of inquiry utilize modes of conception and disclosure that exploit the expressive powers of language, they have the potential to help individuals secure a feel for the reality they are trying to understand. To be able to put yourself in the place of another is crucial for understanding how others feel. This requires both an act of imagination and a form that can engender the appropriate feeling – to the extent to which qualitative forms of inquiry create such forms, to that extent they make it possible to vicariously participate in events of situations in which one was not actually present. Through such vicarious participation we come to understand through the life of feeling what straightforward prose cannot convey.

This contribution to human understanding through the creation of expressive form also has the potential for expanding our view of the variety of content areas or disciplines to which students could be exposed. If non-discursive forms of understanding are regarded as third-rate types of knowledge, schools are likely to continue to give them a marginal place in the curriculum. But if the value of non-discursive forms of understanding is recognized, the possibility that more attention will be given to them is increased. This is not to say that understanding will secure their position, it is only to say that the appreciation of their value provides a firmer grounding for deciding what is taught than does ignorance.

Third, because qualitative forms of inquiry tend to focus on processes that animate classroom life, the possibility of locating the antecedents to educational success and failure is more likely. At present teachers have little opportunity to secure feedback on what they do in classrooms. Achievement testing, whether standardized or not, is a form of summative evaluation. Why what happened did happen is something achievement test scores fail to describe. This lack of information makes it virtually impossible for teachers to use test results to intelligently alter or sustain what they are doing. Furthermore, there has been an overwhelming tendency in conventional forms of educational research to enter classrooms for the briefest periods of time, to collect the data and to leave. Such visits are the equivalent of educational commando raids. One can only wonder what the researcher has seen, how representative the experiment was with respect to the usual conditions of classroom life, and what kinds of feedback the researcher is able to provide to the teacher. Because qualitative forms of evaluation are largely process-oriented the possibility of being helpful to teachers and others concerned with the quality of those processes is increased.

Fourth, one of the most significant potential contributions of qualitative forms of inquiry is something that it least aims to achieve. Through the development of a complementary set of assumptions and methods to those that are used in scientific approaches to educational inquiry in general and educational evaluation in particular, those using conventional methods and assumptions are more likely to appreciate their particular strengths and limitations. Without a lusty complement, the unique characteristics of method are often overlooked since no alternative frame of reference is available with which to compare. As Goethe said, 'A person who knows only one language does not know his own'. The monopoly of social-science methodology in educational inquiry has been a conceptual liability, not only for those seeking other ways, but for those using such methods themselves. Qualitative methods and artistic or humanistic assumptions complement quantitative and scientific ones to the benefit of both.

Finally, the fifth potential contribution of qualitative inquiry in education is the intellectual equity it provides to those whose aptitudes reside in qualitative and artistic forms of expression in contrast to quantitative or scientific ones. For many individuals, particularly graduate students, there have been few options aside from the social sciences that have been legitimate to use to pursue educational problems in scholarly ways. The advent and growing legitimation of qualitative methods is providing the intellectual permission for them to use aptitudes that play to their strengths rather than to feel compelled to do work for which they have little aptitude or interest. In the process surely higher quality work in education will result.

To be sure, qualitative forms of inquiry offer no panaceas for educational problems. Their methods are demanding, the time it takes to use them exceptionally long, the questions of generalizability difficult, and the verification of their conclusions complex. Yet, because they do provide another view, because they do provide another peak upon which to stand, they promise a great deal. In the last analysis their utilities still need demonstration, but what we have is the advent of a tradition long absent in educational discourse and not merely a refinement of the existing conversation. Given the resistance of our problems to our usual methods and assumptions, this newcomer to education should be given a warm welcome.

Notes

1. At the end of 1976 seven States enacted legislation dealing with required competencies.
2. *The Calgary Herald* (4 October 1977).
3. The project I speak of is the Assessment of Performance Unit under the direction of the Department of Education and Science.
4. It should be noted that in a deep sense, method always has some influence on the character of problem formation since problems cannot be formed outside of some method. It is the extreme sense of using only method to define problems that is intended by these remarks.
5. The use of Scholastic Aptitude Tests are a prime example of the influence testing has upon school priorities. When scores on such tests decline – even though they claim to assess aptitude rather than achievement – schools are regarded as failing and are urged to emphasize areas of performance that will increase scholastic aptitude scores. Indeed, some secondary schools offer courses specifically designed to help students achieve high scores on such tests.

6. It should be noted that although the vast majority of school administrators hold no tenure as administrators, in some school districts they do.

7. The tendency to minimize contact with classrooms in experimental research is reflected in the fact that in 1974–76 the modal amount of treatment time per subject in experimental studies reported in the American Educational Research Journal was about 45 minutes.

8. For a discussion of the application of non-discursive modes of learning and expression see EISNER, E.W. (1977) 'On the use of educational connoisseurship and criticism for evaluating classroom life' in *Teachers College Record* Vol. 78, No. 7, February; (1976) 'The forms and functions of educational connoisseurship and educational criticism' in *Journal of Aesthetic Education*, Bicentennial Issue; and *The Educational Imagination: On the Design and Evaluation of School Programs* New York, Macmillan.

9 The Use of Qualitative Forms of Evaluation for Improving Educational Practice

During the past five years my students at Stanford and I have been attempting to develop and articulate, both theoretically and practically, a qualitative, artistically grounded approach to educational evaluation. My interest in such an approach has developed out of an uneasiness that I have long felt with the tacit assumptions and explicit procedures embedded in conventional methods of evaluation. These methods participate in a tradition that has occupied a commanding position, not only in the field of evaluation, but in educational research as well. That tradition, as is well-known, is rooted in the aspiration to apply the methods of science to the study and explanation of social phenomena. It is a tradition that undergirds most departments of psychology, sociology, and economics. It is a tradition upon which most of the prestigious schools and departments of education in the universities of this country have been built, and it is a tradition into which most aspiring doctoral students are socialized.

Although I feel uneasy about the conventional methods of evaluation, I should say, and hastily, that my uneasiness does not lead me to reject scientific approaches to either evaluation or educational research. Rather, my uneasiness results from the feeling that such approaches, and the methods of inquiry that are regarded as legitimate within their borders, somehow fail to tell the whole story. As a result of the partial view that such methods provide, a biased, even distorted picture of the reality that we are attempting to understand and improve can occur. In some respects this result is paradoxical because the stringent canons of social science methodology are the product of a desire to reduce bias and diminish distortion; the claim that they may in fact contribute to bias and distortion is a severe critique, if true, and a paradox of their intention.

My uneasiness with conventional methods of scientifically

grounded evaluation does not emanate solely from the constraints imposed upon them by their epistemological commitments. It also emanates from the goals and intended functions of such evaluation. These goals and functions have been largely concerned with the measurement of performance. Although in recent years evaluators have become increasingly interested in the process of educational practice, the standardized achievement test, whether norm- or criterion-referenced, is still the paradigmatic tool for educational evaluation. (The works of Hamilton, Jenkins, King, MacDonald, & Parlett [1978], MacDonald & Walker [1976], Stake [1975] exemplify approaches to evaluation that pay attention to the quality of the process of education.) Its primary function is to assess how well a student or a group of students perform.

There is, of course, nothing wrong with knowing how well or how poorly a student performs. Yet schools, insofar as they are educational institutions, should not be content with performance. Education as a process is concerned with the cultivation of intellectual power, and the ability to determine what a student knows is not necessarily useful or sufficient for making that process more effective. Thus, the second source of my uneasiness with conventional approaches to evaluation is that they focus almost exclusively on the products of the enterprise (a narrow slice at that) while they neglect the conditions, context, and interactions that led to these consequences. In practical terms, they provide very little that is of use to the teacher in order to know what to alter or what to maintain in the course of teaching or in the design of the curriculum.

It was these factors, factors that I first felt intuitively rather than explicitly, that motivated the direction which my students and I have taken over the past five years. In the past two years it has become clear to me that the issues I have been attempting to address go far deeper than I had initially realized. Essentially, my concern is a desire to form a conception of mind, to create an image of a person and to learn how that person comes to know. At base, the issues with which I have been concerned reside in grasping the forms of rationality that humans can employ in the course of their lives. (See Langer [1967] and Polyani [1960].) I would like to provide a sketch of these issues and to share some of the theoretical problems with which my students and I are grappling. (Much of the work done at Stanford has been in the form of doctoral dissertations. Some of these dissertations are Alexander [1977], Berk [1977], Davidman [1976], Greer [1973], McCutcheon [1976], Sternberg [1977], and Vallance [1975].) I will then discuss the kinds of evaluation in which we are engaged and the kinds of unresolved difficulties that they pose.

'Man by nature,' remarked Aristotle, 'seeks to know.' Evaluation is also a means for knowing. But the initial problem, at least for those interested in conceptualizing evaluation, is not one of deciding what to evaluate, but rather of elucidating the means through which knowing is made possible. How is it that an individual knows? What forms are employed in order to know? And how does one represent what one knows to others? Perhaps the best place to start is with those aspects of the organism that appear to have obvious functions in cognitive activity. Consider the senses. The human organism, unless congenitally abnormal, is endowed with a variety of sensory systems that make it possible for it to experience the environment in which it functions. Each of these sensory systems provides different kinds of information about the environment: the visual world, the world of sound, of taste, and so on. Without these senses our capacity to know would be radically curtailed. Without the opportunity to use our senses, they could be irrevocably atrophied. In short, the senses function as channels through which we experience. The content for consciousness that they make possible is far wider than words or numbers. Indeed, words and number are cultural devices through which we transform and reduce qualities of experience into those particular forms. Our consciousness, and hence our knowledge of the world, is not limited to either words or numbers. Each of the senses provides an avenue for experience and each provides a means through which the internal and external representation of the world become possible. I will try to illustrate this with an example.

Let me ask you for a moment to recall your mother's face. Think about the face that you have seen so many times. Recall the experiences you have had for so many years. I am willing to predict that there is not a soul among my readers who does not know what his or her mother's face looks like. I am willing to predict that when I ask you to recall your mother's face you conjured up not a set of numbers, not a set of words, but an image, a visual image. You thought in pictures rather than in words. Indeed, there are no numbers that will do justice to your mother's face, yet in principle it is possible to represent that face in centimeters for the length of her nose, mouth, eyes, the circumference of her skull and, I suppose, even to counting the number of hairs on her head. Your knowledge of your mother's face and my knowledge of mine are represented in visual images. What we know in this form is made possible through our sense of sight.

Knowing in this mode has analogues in all of the other senses. Although we secure the image of our mother's face by having the opportunity to empirically encounter it, when she is not present we can reconstruct that image through imagination. Thus, what we know about our mother's face is the result of the way we construe her features in the empirical world. What we can imagine is what we are able to construe in the privacy of our covert imaginative life.

But let us suppose that we now want to help others come to know our mother's face, that we want to enable them to know, as we do, how she appears. Here the problem becomes more complex, for what we must do now is to transform an image held in the imagination into a public form. We can, of course, try to describe her face in words, and if we are skilled in the use of spoken or written language we may be able to generate an image in the mind of another that is similar to the one we hold. But that task would be extremely difficult. If we were skilled at drawing or sculpture we could transform our mental image into a visual one. We could create a public form that presented to the world an image that would enable others to identify our mother from a group of other mothers. If only we knew how to draw or sculpt our task might be somewhat easier. If we knew how to dance we could create a series of movements that attempted to approximate our mother's face, but even if we were a skilled dancer, the special features of our mother's face would not easily be represented in the kind of language that dance can employ. The language of movement is difficult to use to render an image that takes shape in static space.

I believe that what we can learn from this little scenario is that our knowledge of the world takes shapes in different sensory modalities and that these modalities provide the content from which transformation or symbolic representation is made. The extent to which we are literate in the symbol systems appropriate for conveying or making such knowledge public, to that extent we are able to share what we know with others. To the extent that our literacy is limited, to that extent what we know must remain locked in our psyche, a private experience that we are unable to share, and, in a sense, to adequately critique (Eisner, 1978).

What we can also learn is that certain types of knowledge do not lend themselves to transformation into certain symbol systems. Pictures that are painted of our mother's face, even by a semiskilled artist, are likely to provide a closer likeness than a dance performed by the most skilled dancer. Words, too, will fall short. It appears that what we know, the kinds of concepts we can form, are at least as numerous as the sense modalities we possess. The transformation or rendering of these concepts requires skill in a medium, to use Olsen's (Note 1) phrase, and even then some concepts are virtually unrenderable in some languages. Langer (1957) is quite explicit on this point when she discusses the functions of discursive and nondiscursive forms regarding their ability to express human feeling. She writes as follows:

> Such knowledge is not expressible in ordinary discourse. The reason for this ineffability is not that the ideas to be expressed are too high, too spiritual, or too anything else, but that the forms of feeling and the forms of discursive expression are logically incommensurate, so that any exact concepts of feeling and emotion cannot be projected into the logical form of literal language. Verbal statement, which is our normal and most reliable means of communication, is almost useless for conveying knowledge about the precise character of the affective life (p. 91).

I have attempted thus far to identify some of the functions of the sensory systems as vehicles for providing the content for knowing and the relationship between that content and its transformation through a public symbol system. I do not want to give the impression, however, that simple contact with the world is a sensory event that occurs automatically simply because we are sentient beings. The forms our experience takes, and the degree to which it is differentiated, depend upon the existence of what Neisser (1976) calls 'anticipatory schemata,' or what Dewey (1977) refers to more generally as the 'experiential continuum,' or as I have called it in our work on evaluation, 'connoisseurship' (Eisner, 1976a, 1977). These three concepts are not identical, but they do share similarities. Seeing, hearing, tasting, and feeling are, as Ryle (1962) put it so well, not *task* verbs but *achievement* verbs. One can look without seeing, listen without hearing, eat without tasting, and touch without feeling. To have a content for consciousness, an achievement must be won; one must not merely perform a task. The extent to which our achievements are differentiated and diverse, to that extent will imagination have the stuff with which to work. But if, as Neisser says, anticipatory schemata perform a selective function in perception, their absence in our symbolic repertoire creates a kind of self-fulfilling prophecy. What one does not have a schemata for, one is less able to experience; what one does not experience, one is not likely to miss. Where schemata exist, the probability of experience is increased. In short, we tend to experience what we know how to find. Ernst Gombrich put it well when he said that artists do not paint what they can see; they see what they can paint.

Perhaps it would be well to summarize the major points I have tried to make thus far before moving on to a discussion of their meaning for educational evaluation in general and to our work at Stanford in particular. There are four points that are of particular importance.

First, the aspiration to develop a science of education and the influence of positivistic and operationalistic conceptions of knowledge have severely limited our conception of cognition. If meaning is circumscribed only to propositions which can be validated by logical criteria or by measurement, those fields, and therefore those forms of knowing that are neither propositional nor numerical, are, by definition, regarded as noncognitive. This view of knowledge, I believe, has been a major constraint in education, educational research, and educational evaluation.

Second, the sources of knowledge are at least as diverse as the range of information provided by the senses. Each of the senses provides a unique content that is not replicable by other sense modalities.

Third, concepts can be formed in the imagination by using the content provided by each of the sense modalities. Images of reality are therefore made possible by what the visual, auditory, and the other sensory modalities provide. Concept formation is not limited to what will take the impress of linguistic or numerical terms alone.

Fourth, to make public what has been conceptualized in the imagination requires an ability to competently employ the vocabulary and syntax of a symbol system. Each symbol system, like each sensory system, is nonredundant. What one can say for one is not literally translatable for another. If the skills necessary to make this transformation from image to symbolic expression are not available, expression, and hence communication of that content, are not possible.

These considerations regarding the nature of cognition did not precede, but followed from the qualitative approach to evaluation in which my students and I have been engaged over the past five years. Once they became explicit rather than implicit, it became easier for me to understand what accounted for my initial uneasiness with conventional approaches to educational evaluation. To cast a net into the sea that is unintentionally designed to let most of the fish get away, and then to conclude from those that are caught of what the variety of fish in the sea consists is, at the very least, a sampling error of the first order. Then to describe the fish that are caught in terms of their length and weight is to reduce radically what we can know about the qualitative features of the ones that have been caught, not to mention the features of those that the net failed to catch in the first place. In this sense, I suspect, I may be accused of trying to weave new kinds of nets. So be it.

Let me turn now to our work in evaluation. Here two concepts are of particular importance. The first is what we refer to as *educational connoisseurship*, the second *educational criticism*. Educational connoissuership is the art of appreciation. It is the result of having developed a highly differentiated array of anticipatory schemata that enable one to discern qualities and relationships that others, less well differentiated, are less likely to see. In some respects all of us are connoisseurs of a sort. For some of us the subject matter of our connoisseurship resides in the appreciation of golf clubs or greens, for others in Baroque music, for others still in football or French wine. For all of us working in the field of education, I suspect, the subject matters of our connoisseurship are found in the processes of schooling: in the character and quality of teaching, in the interactions of children, in the organization of the school as a whole, and in the use and character of the materials of instruction. The reason connoisseurship is so important is that it provides the content for knowing. It makes possible the stuff we use for reflection.

Connoisseurship, as has been noted, depends upon the differentiated use of anticipatory schemata. These schemata allow one to bracket phenomena so that they become defined and visible. Some of the schemata may take the form of prefigured concepts that have discursive labels. For example, one may intentionally look for manifestations of 'competition' in the classroom and try to determine its sources, but what we decide counts as competition is essentially nondiscursive. We recognize it by a variety of images we hold. It may manifest itself in the tone of voice that one child uses in speaking to another; it may emerge in the particular way in which someone stands, or in what he or she says. All of this occurs in a living context that plays a significant role in the meaning we give to the tone of voice, the posture, and the content of someone's remarks. To know what counts as competition, one must not only have models or schemata or competition to apply; one must also know how those schemata function within a context (Neisser, 1976). Without an appreciation of context conditions the possibility of misinterpreting what one seeks is high.

Although all of this may sound abstract and complex, it should be reassuring to note that what I have described we do in our social relations regularly. Perhaps nowhere is it more vivid than at cocktail parties. All of us know quite well how to perceive and interpret the behavior of others at such events. We understand the context and when someone says to us 'You have never looked better,' we reply in kind. We also know that the question, 'How are you doing?' is neither a request for a dissertation on our recent medical history nor for a report of our bank balance. We have, through acculturation within our social relationships, become connoisseurs of a sort and our connoisseurship enables us to determine how to respond to a polite question, when to bring a conversation to closure, when to initiate one, and when it is time to go home. Our need to survive socially has required us to cultivate high levels of connoisseurship of the social world.

But connoisseurship, as important as it is, is nevertheless a private undertaking. Although we often act upon the information it provides, if we wish to convey what we have come to know to others, we face the problem of transformation. We must find a way of transforming the qualitative aspects of our experience into a form that others can 'read' (Eisner, 1976b). It is in this process that educational criticism is paramount.

Dewey (1934) put it this way: 'The end of criticism' he wrote 'is the re-education of the perception of the work of art' (p. 324). The critic's task is neither to use the work as a stimulus for psychological projection, nor is it to be the subject of judicial pronouncements. The function of the critic is to illuminate, to enable others to experience what they may have missed. To do this, critics use words. They try to say in words what words cannot say. 'It is this paradox,' writes Kozloff (1969), 'that lies at the heart of criticism.' How is it done? Not by simply categorizing events as they occur but by constructing an image of what has occurred, an image related to the events but which gives them in spoken and written form the level of vitality and meaning that they possessed when they emerged. To achieve such an end the educational critic must be able to use language artistically. He or she must not be discouraged from exploiting the power of language to inform in the multiple ways in which it can inform. In short, language must not be restricted to a didactic, expository mode alone, for to do so is not only to limit what can be conveyed, it is to distort the character of the situation one is trying to understand. The 'straight facts,' unencumbered by context, are paradoxically nonfactual.

Thus the task of the educational critic is to write in a way that will enable the reader to vicariously participate in the events that constitute that aspect of classroom life about which the critic speaks (Eisner, 1979). Such participation makes it possible for readers to know that aspect of classroom life emotionally. Through it they are able to know what only the artistic use of language can provide.

Educational criticism, however, is not limited to the artistic description of events. It also includes their interpretation and appraisal. Interpretation as we conceive it is the process of applying theoretical ideas to explain the conditions that have been described. Why is it that this classroom functions in this particular way? Why do these side effects occur? How does the reward structure of this classroom shape the relationships students have with one another? How is time used in this classroom and why does it mean what it means to students? Questions such as these require answers that are more than descriptive, they require the application of relevant theory in the social sciences. The application of such theories to the qualities that have been described constitutes the second important phase or aspect of educational criticism.

The third phase or aspect of educational criticism is concerned with appraisal or evaluation. What is the educational significance of what children have learned? What is the educational import of what has transpired? What are the educational trade-offs among the pedagogical devices that the teacher has used and were there alternatives that could have been selected? Please note that this last question begins to soften the distinction between appraisal and supervision and/or 'coaching.' When an educational critic appraises in a way which is designed to provide constructive feedback to the teacher, evaluation begins to perform its most important function: providing the conditions that lead to the improvement of the educational process. In some respect this function of educational evaluation is analogous to the function the conductor performs when guiding an orchestra in the performance of a symphony. The conductor's task is first to hear what the orchestra is playing and to assess it against the schema of the music that he holds. Second, the conductor must locate the discrepancy between the schema and the performance and then provide feedback or criteria that will enable the orchestra to improve its performance. The process is one of making and matching, or schema and correction. What follows is a description of Zubin Mehta's rehearsal of the New York Philharmonic as it was recently reported in the *New Yorker* (1978):

'Let's get started.' He gave a brisk downbeat for Ravel's 'La Valse,' which begins with a deep murmur of string basses, a whisper of cellos, and a bassoon solo. After a few bars, he stopped, and looked around at the orchestra. 'I would like the first four basses to play pizzicato,' he said, 'Also, basses, the second and third part of the two trills should be softer.' A few minutes later, when the basses were accompanying the violas, Mr. Mehta stopped them again and said, 'Sometimes I've done this with one bass, because if you use too many you get a blur. How many are doing it?' Four bass players raised their hands, and Mr. Mehta looked skeptical. 'Why don't you change the bow on the F,' he said, 'so the accent can make the passage clearer. And then, if you could *all* play also piano ...' The musicians began again, and Mr. Mehta gradually swept them up into the complex patterns of Ravel's mordant apotheosis of the Viennese waltz, pausing from time to time to adjust a transition, correct a dynamic, or redefine an entrance. ('Cellos and basses, that pizzicato chord two bars before thirty-four sounds forced. Maybe we can taper down ... Brass, how staccato can you play those triplets? ... Basses, don't lose the downbeat after thirty-four; it's the only impulse that is carried right through the piece ... Bassoon, more legato after sixty-one; it helps the strings.') As 'La Valse' reached its turbulent climax, Mr. Mehta seemed to become intoxicated by the collective sound of the orchestra. He leaned over the violins, smiling ferociously, his knees bent, his right foot stamping out the rhythm on the podium; whirled in a semi-crouch to encourage the cellos with his mouth open in a silent scream; and flung his body back in an arch, both arms outstretched above his head, to punctuate each shattering crescendo. During these gymnastics, he was also balancing the orchestral voices with great care, giving precise instrumental cues to produce crisp attacks, and maintaining a clear, rapid beat with the baton clenched in his right hand. As we watched and listened, an invisible current seemed suddenly to flow between musicians and conductor. When the orchestra took a break at the end of the piece, most of the tension in the hall had vanished. (pp. 22–23)

What is clear from Mehta's remarks is that he is able to hear music as a connoisseur (someone who knows), that he also knows what he wants to hear, and that his feedback to the symphony is designed to enable it to successfully approximate the musical image or schemata that he holds. It is an example of schema and correction. There are parallels (but only parallels) to teaching. If teachers were regarded as conductors, then supervisors might be regarded as resident educational critics. Teachers might be so close to their classes that they would no longer be able to hear the symphony as clearly as they might, or even as they once did. The critic here would provide a fresh eye, would have the needed distance to hear what the class was playing, and be able to illuminate those qualities to the teacher in a way that would be helpful. In such a context, interpersonal skills and trust between educational critic and teacher is crucial. The teacher must be willing to have a critic in the classroom and must be willing to listen (but not necessarily heed) what the critic says. In this context, criticism often takes the form of a dialogue between the teacher and the critic – not quite coaching and not necessarily a written essay about the classroom. Educational criticism in the context of teaching shares similarities with the kind of counsel that marks the dialogue of friends. Trust is a necessary condition. One makes oneself vulnerable only to those who one believes are not intending to hurt.

The mere mention of such a relationship must dramatically illuminate the distance between such a practice and the ways we typically try to improve teaching. The vast majority of teachers have nothing like such feedback. Most of us try to learn about teaching in the reflections we find in our students' eyes. We sometimes make inferences from their casual remarks or from remarks sometimes made in anger. We reflect on our teaching walking home after class or rehearse before entering it, but basically we conduct our teaching alone. Few of us ever receive reflective, competent educational criticism about that portion of our professional lives in which we engage so often and from which we seek so much satisfaction. As a result, most of us are only partially aware of our strengths as teachers, and perhaps more importantly, what we do that interferes with our teaching. The structure of the institutions in which we work does not make such feedback likely and the supervision that some teachers receive is often perfunctory or in a mode concerned largely with approval/disapproval rather than with the improvement of performance. The once-per-year visit of the principal to the teacher's classroom is primarily intended to meet the requirements for determining tenure, rather than something that one colleague does to be helpful to another. Given the complexity of teaching and our apparent desire to improve it, I believe schools need to develop structures which will make sustained observation and feedback possible. The subtleties that count in teaching are not likely to be mastered or even perceived in pre-service programs of teacher education. The occasional workshops or lectures that characterize in-service education may also be inadequate. We need, I believe, a much more integrated process of professional development, something that becomes a part of the ongoing life of the school, as much as the coffee break or the pledge to the flag.

I would like to conclude my remarks by turning to some of the unresolved theoretical problems that educational criticism poses. I have already argued that what we know takes form in a variety of sense modalities and is distilled and expressed in a variety of symbol systems. To secure knowledge of teaching, one need not limit one's attention to those pedagogical moves that one can count. Indeed, I have suggested that counting, unencumbered by context, can seriously mislead. After all, does it not seem strange to believe that it would be possible to secure meaningful information about teaching through a process that (1) tape-records classroom discourse while neglecting visual cues and context, (2) transcribes such tapes into typescript, thus eliminating the tone and tempo of voice, (3) reduces typescripts to the classification and enumeration of pedagogical moves, while neglecting the meaning expressed by the moves, and (4) further reduces moves into quantities which are then statistically analyzed.[1] The gradual and ineluctable reduction of information leaves precious little with which to form robust generalizations about a complex and subtle enterprise. Yet we have persevered in the use of such methods and with meagre results. As Bronfenbrenner (1976) has said, such research has little or no ecological validity.

Educational criticism, however, is not without its own problems. Every method contains its own strengths and weaknesses. A high level of precision is possible when one counts but is diminished when one is required to judge. Educational criticism relies upon judgment. Still another problem, and one of its most serious ones, is the tension that exists between using language to artistically describe and the fact that the use of such language often leads readers to conclude that the description is biased. If an educational critic creates an artistically expressive rendering of a classroom and through it helps another appreciate its emotional meaning or its 'essential character,' he or she risks being regarded as biased or as having written something which is not factual. The less expressive a description is, the truer it appears to be – at least in our culture. Yet if there is an absence of emotional or qualitative content, the description risks leaving out more of what is important in the classroom. This tension between artistic description and flat reporting is a difficult one to resolve.

Another difficulty centers around our apparent need to draw conclusions that are statable in discursive terms as a summary of our inquiries and the fact that the reduction of an artistically rendered criticism of a classroom to four or five conclusions robs the criticism of what it has to offer in the first place. How does one do justice to Saul Bellow's *Herzog* in a summary of a few sentences? The answer is clear: one does not. Yet we seem to have a need to draw conclusions, to distill what we have learned, to render what we know to the unambiguity of the third decimal place. In conventional approaches to evaluation and research there is a greater possibility that this can be done without doing violence to the subject being evaluated or researched. It is less likely in material that is artistically rendered since the work as a whole is the message, not an artistically eviscerated symbol of it.

Another difficulty with educational criticism is its costliness:[2] it takes a great deal of time and skill to do it well. One does not simply administer a standardized test, analyze the results, and send it back to the school. Educational criticism requires one to invest a great deal of time in the classroom. It is an activity that requires the critic to be the instrument: the application of a standardized observation schedule in order to count the incidence of occurrences simply will not do. Frankly, I do not know whether in the practical world of schooling such an investment can reasonably be expected, and I do not know what proportion of teachers and administrators can develop the level of connoisseurship and the critical writing skills necessary for making educational criticism useful.

Yet educational criticism, and even more, the larger epistemological issues it adumbrates, widen the array of tools that we can legitimately use in order to see, understand, and improve not only the teaching but the educational process generally. If the forms of perception, conception, and expression define the content of what we know, then not only is artistic discourse relevant for revealing the qualities that constitute educational practice, but so too are film, video, and drama. Perhaps the major virtue of educational criticism is that it expands our understanding of how we come to know, and as a consequence it makes new avenues for educational evaluation and research possible. Even if it does not succeed in becoming a major mode of evaluation in American schools, that contribution may be enough to have made the effort worthwhile.

Notes

1. This approach to research on teaching has been characteristic rather than exceptional. Most of the observation schedules that have been developed reduce teaching into the incidence of 'acts.' The 'melody' of the enterprise is simply lost in such procedures.
2. The amount of time that it takes to do adequate educational criticism is considerably larger than the time it takes to use a check-off sheet to describe teaching performance. However, if one compares the utility of the former to the latter, the cost of educational criticism as a means of improving teaching compared to usual descriptive procedures may be smaller than one realizes. The basic question, of course, is a cost-benefit ratio, rather than the determination of cost alone.

References

ALEXANDER, R.R. (1977) *Educational Criticism of Three Art History Classes* doctoral dissertation, Stanford University, University Microfilms No. 78–2125.

BERK, L.M. (1977) *Education In Our Lives: An application in biographic narrative to the study of educational outcomes* doctoral dissertation, Stanford University, University Microfilms No. 78–2132.

BRONFENBRENNER, U. (1976) 'The experimental ecology of education' in *Teachers College Record*, 78(2), pp. 157–204.

DAVIDMAN, L. (1976) *The Formative Evaluation of the Unified Science and Mathematics in the Elementary Schools Curriculum,* doctoral dissertation, Stanford University, University Microfilms No. 76–25987.

DEWEY, J. (1934) *Art as Experience* New York, Minton, Balch and Co.

DEWEY, J. (1977) *Experience and Education* New York, Macmillan.

EISNER, E.W. (1976) 'Educational connoisseurship and educational criticism, their form and function in educational evaluation' in *Journal of Aesthetic Education.* Bicentennial issue, 10(3–4), pp. 135–150. (a)

EISNER, E.W. (1976) Reading and the creation of meaning, *in Claremont Reading Conference, 40th Yearbook, 1,* pp. 1–15. (b)

EISNER, E.W. (1977) 'Use of educational connoisseurship and educational criticism for evaluating classroom life,' in *Teachers College Record*, 78(3), pp. 345–358.

EISNER, E.W. (1978) 'The impoverished mind' in *Educational Leadership*, 35(8), pp. 617–623.

EISNER, E.W. (1979) *The Educational Imagination: On the design and evaluation of school programs*, New York, Macmillan.

GREER, W.D. (1973) *The Criticism of Teaching* doctoral dissertation, Stanford University, University Microfilms No. 74–13632.

HAMILTON, D., JENKINS, D., KING, G., MACDONALD, B. and PARLETT, M. (1978) *Beyond the Numbers Game* London, Macmillan Education.

KOZLOFF, M. (1969) *Renderings: Critical Essays on a Century of Modern Art*, New York, Simon and Schuster.

LANGER, S. (1957) *Problems of Art* New York, Scribner and Sons.

LANGER, S. (1967) *Mind: An essay on human feeling* (Vols. 1 & 2). Baltimore, The Johns Hopkins University Press.

MACDONALD, B. and WALKER, R. (1976) *Changing the Curriculum* London, Open Books Publishing.

McCUTCHEON, G. (1976) *The Disclosure of Classroom Life* doctoral dissertation, Stanford University, University Microfilms No. 76–26037.

NEISSER, U. (1976) *Cognition and Reality* San Francisco, W.H. Freeman.

OLSEN, D. (1978) *The Arts and Education: Three cognitive functions of symbols* paper presented at the Terman Memorial Conference, School of Education, Stanford University, October.

POLANYI, M. (1960) *Personal Knowledge* Chicago, University of Chicago Press.

RYLE, G. (1962) *The Concept of Mind* New York, Barnes and Noble.

STAKE, R. (1975) *Evaluating the Arts in Education* Columbus, Ohio, Charles E. Merrill Pub. Co.

STERNBERG, B.J. (1977) *What do tokens and trophies teach?* doctoral dissertation, Stanford University, University Microfilms No. 78–8851.

THE TALK OF THE TOWN. (1978) *The New Yorker*, September 4, pp. 22–23.

VALLANCE, E.J. (1975) *Aesthetic Criticism and Curriculum Description* doctoral dissertation, Stanford University, University Microfilms No. 76–5820.

10 *Mind as Cultural Achievement*

The Context of American Education Today

The title 'Mind as Cultural Achievement' reflects the belief that what people become is largely a function of what they have an opportunity to experience. In this sense our minds are products of the kinds of tools that are made available to us during the course of maturation. This view of mind as something that is made rather than given is an optimistic one. It implies that those of us who work in the field of education have a special opportunity to influence the ways in which the young can come to regard the world, to influence the kind of sense they make of it, to affect the kinds of categories, attitudes and meaning that they secure from their experience.

The realization of such ambitious possibilities assumes that the form and content of school programs embody the diversity of tools that are available in the culture. It also assumes that once available, the ways in which they are taught are educationally effective. To achieve such an end has never been an easy one, but today it is particularly difficult. The American public – at least as far as schools are concerned – wants attention paid to what it regards as basic to education: competencies in reading, writing and arithmetic. The idea that education can be used to foster the growth of mind is not a salient theme in discourse about the condition of schools today. We seem today to be elsewhere. Just what is the current situation in which education finds itself? What are the conditions with which it has to cope? What is the context that must be considered in any effort to build a conception of educational practice that does justice to the kinds of mind that children can come to own?

From my vantage point, expectations for American schools are consonant with a variety of other expectations that characterize our culture, circa 1979. We are a culture recoiling from the trauma of the Sixties, attempting to mend the breach of broken family life that since the late Fifties has increased in rate each year.[1] We are a culture trying to obtain the kind of security that cults and religious dogmatism make possible, seeking to cleanse the society by demanding that a capital price be paid for a capital offense, trying to reduce our fiscal contributions to those who are unable, unwilling or denied the opportunity to help themselves. Since 1969 the growth of membership in religious fundamentalism has increased about fifteen percent and the trend suggests no immediate decline.[2] The reinstitution of capital punishment has occurred in thirty-five states thus far since 1972.[3] The funds available for education subsequent to the advent of Proposition 13 in California and elsewhere has been substantially reduced.

These developments in the culture at large are quite consistent with the attitudes that are currently being expressed toward schooling, attitudes reflected not only in the reduction of funds available for schools, but in the expectations that the public holds for schools, expectations that manifest themselves in the growing approval of corporal punishment as a means of coping with misbehavior, with the establishment of uniform competency standards for graduation from secondary school, and now, in a growing number of school districts, even for promotion from one grade level to the next. It also expresses itself in the demand for evidence in the form of measured performance on achievement tests that often have little relationship to the curriculum. Indeed, non-promotion in some districts is regarded as a virtue not only because it is believed to motivate pupils but because it provides prima facie evidence that the district has at least a set of standards. One Miami newspaper thinks so highly of the Dade County School District's failure ratio that it listed each of the schools in the district in relation to the percentage of students that it failed in the previous year, this being done as evidence of the return of rigor in schooling. While the stick approach to motivation is employed in the Dade County schools – the eighth largest school district in the United States – the district also recognizes the virtues of the carrot. The same district entices students to return to school by offering them what are called 'attendance incentives.' In a story titled 'Schools Dangle Freebies in Front of Students' the *Miami Herald* describes these incentives as follows:

> Trying to reduce the high absentee rates in the Dade Public Schools, officials have come up with a plan to entice truants into

classrooms with gifts of frisbees, T-shirts, hamburgers, chicken dinners and yo-yos. The first attendance incentives donated by local businessmen will be handed out to students next month with the best attendance record at Brownsville Junior High School and Douglas Elementary School. Teachers with the best attendance rate in those schools will be rewarded with free gasoline, record albums and crab dinners. Robert Davidson, the school community liaison officer instrumental in starting the program said that other schools in the system are being encouraged to adopt similar programs.[4]

I refer to the Dade County Schools not because they are educational aberrations but because they exemplify much of the prevailing climate in schooling. That climate is one that places a very great emphasis on measured forms of educational performance, but tends to neglect attention to the performer himself. It is a climate that places a very high premium on the use of packaged forms of instruction that make it increasingly difficult for teachers to use the classroom as a place for the discovery of outcomes, as well as the achievement of those already part of the packages they are obliged to use. It is a climate that all too often has been aided and abetted by educationists who offer glib prescriptions about how to form meaningful objectives, to diagnose learning difficulties, to prescribe teaching methods, to employ test instruments, and to locate the discrepancies between goals and outcomes. It is a climate that emphasizes the value of time in learning and that measures efficiency by the brevity of time it takes to realize prescribed ends, as if the things that we cherish most we seek to do in the briefest time possible. Perhaps most important it is a climate that provides little space in the curriculum for the development of those forms of thought that lie outside of a narrow view of literacy.

It is this climate, or more generally this cultural context, in which the schools find themselves today. To reiterate, it is a climate that has engendered a limited view of education and in this sense, paradoxically, expects too little of education rather than too much. It is one that has an abiding faith in our ability to measure the significant outcomes of schooling, and therefore neglects, ironically, what might be most educationally enduring. It is a climate that focuses on the behavior of students but which pays little attention to the kind of experience they have. It is a climate that seems to have lost sight of purpose in education by its single-minded attention to the development of competencies in the use of technique, as if technique was itself a virtue.

It is these conditions that provide the background for my remarks. There are, to be sure, among the nearly two million teachers, 100,000 schools, and 16,000 school districts in the United States, places that are educationally excellent in the deepest sense in which education can be excellent. But these places, I submit, exist in spite of the pervasive national climate within which our schools function. It is time, indeed, it is long past the time that we should as students of education ask again about what education as both a process and goal can be. One place to begin such an inquiry is with the examination of the nature of mind and the forms it uses in order to know.

Sensory Systems and the Forms of Representation

Basic to any understanding of mind is the importance of understanding the functions that the sensory systems perform in the realization of consciousness. If to be conscious is to be aware, then it follows that consciousness requires a subject matter. That subject matter is to be found in our ability to experience the qualities that constitute our environment, or to experience those qualities we generate as images in the privacy of our covert mental life. Our sensory system performs an active role in this process by putting us in contact with the world in those realms of the world to which they are sensitive. If the nerve endings in our fingers were severed through an accident or illness, our ability to experience the feel of things and hence to be conscious of them would not be possible. If our optic nerve were cut we would lose the experience of sight. If our inner ear were damaged, our ability to experience sound would be lost. These observations are, in a sense, obvious once we think about them. But their meaning for education and their role in the achievement of mind is not. The sensory systems provide the experiential options that every normal human being can use, but they are options that require more than simple maturation in order to fully function. They require the kind of cultivation that is represented by their highest level of achievement in our culture. The educational development of the sensibilities is not an automatic consequence of maturation.

The child's ability to use the senses as mechanisms for the articulation of thought can be legitimately regarded as a form of literacy. By literacy I do not mean simply being able to read or to write or to cipher, but rather being able to secure or express meaning through what I shall call *forms of representation*. Literacy may be regarded as the generic process of being able to 'decode' or 'encode' the content of these forms. Because conception and expression are as diverse as any of the sensory modalities humans can use, literacy can be employed, developed, and refined within any of the forms of representation the sensory systems make possible.

If my emphasis on the centrality of the senses in the realization of mind appears to suggest that the sentient human is a passive receiver of sensory information, I wish now to disclaim such an implication. What the sensory systems provide are options for experience, avenues for consciousness. There is no guarantee that such options will be taken or that the consciousness they make possible secured. On the contrary, there is much evidence to suggest that most of us are only partially literate, that we do not know how to experience much of what either nature or culture makes possible. Part of the task of education – and I would suggest one of its most important tasks – is to foster such literacy. Without it life is only partially lived. If partially lived, then in one sense it might be said that we are only partially alive.

The failure to develop the forms of literacy the senses make possible can result from two conditions. The most radical and the rarer of the two occurs in drastic forms of sensory deprivation. The realization of what is biologically latent requires, we have learned, an environmental trigger. Without certain nutrients during infancy growth in height will be irreversibly stunted. Without access to light from two to twelve weeks of age in a kitten's life, the kitten will no longer be able to see.[5] Without adequate environmental stimulation during our 'golden years,' the decline of that life is likely to be increased, especially for those men and women who have worked in factories.[6] What this suggests is that humans are not immune to atrophic processes and that the lack of opportunity to use certain capacities increases the likelihood that those capacities will decline.

Although these sources of sensory deprivation as causes of illiteracy are important, perhaps the major source of illiteracy is the failure of schools to provide the kinds of programs that would make such literacy possible in the first place. Sensory qualities are almost always subtly arranged: there is more to see, hear, taste, and feel than meets the unprepared mind. To secure the experience that is potential in the sensory events that constitute the world, we must learn how to have such experience. Even among things natural, trees, mountains, landscapes and the like, qualities do not speak for themselves. One must bring to them, as it were, a receptive attitude and an inquiring mind. One must ask to receive. But when we deal with the products of culture rather than nature the task becomes even more complex because in such forms of representation qualities are intentionally patterned, are a consequence of purpose, possess a past and participate within a tradition. These patterns or configurations constitute the syntaxes through which meanings are conceptualized and shared. Being literate within these forms means being able to perceive their subtle qualities as well as being able to cope with their syntax. The level of subtlety and complexity that such forms of representation possess requires a level of literacy that is equal to them. To put it more simply, great cultural forms in the arts as in the sciences, demand great audiences.

I said that the forms of representation that are available in the culture are not only patterned form, but forms that possess a syntax. The word syntax is derived from the Latin *syntaxis* which means 'to arrange'. The arrangements that forms such as mathematics and formal speech and text take can be distinguished from those that are taken by vernacular speech, poetry, the visual arts, music and dance. One of the major differences is that the use of number, to consider a paradigm case, is controlled by prescriptive rules that are formally codified, while the syntaxes of the arts, to use a contrasting example, have no comparable formal codifications. Room is left for personal ingenuity in arrangement. One of the major pedagogical tasks in the teaching of arithmetic, or spelling, or punctuation, or grammar, is to enable students to learn how to follow the formally codified rules that govern the use of elements within these fields. There are, after all, only two ways to spell a word in the English language and virtually all of mathematics from elementary through secondary school consists of problems whose answers are known and whose procedures are to be learned so that the students' answers and the teacher's will be the same. Isomorphism between teacher expectation and student performance in such fields is a virtue. The teacher who assigns the same maths lesson to all her pupils is successful to the extent that variance in their response is minimized.

The acquisition of those skills that make correct responses possible in such fields has, of course, certain virtues. When rules are codified and explicit as they are in the three Rs ambiguity can be reduced, precision can be increased, and the security of knowing when one is right or wrong obtained. If the syntax of a form of representation is highly rule-governed, it makes it possible to reduce idiosyncratic interpretations, if not to eliminate them altogether.

But while the precision and predictability that rule-governed systems make possible is a virtue for some tasks, it is not a virtue for others. In the arts, for example, rules are not codified, they are seldom explicit, and they admit – indeed they encourage – the pursuit of personal ingenuity. What the arts employ is a syntactical system that encourages the use of imagination, that values productive idiosyncracy. In the arts conventions seldom have the prescriptive explicitness of highly rule-governed forms of representation. In artistic forms of representation cognitive skills different from those used in forms of representation that are rule-governed are cultivated, tolerance for ambiguity is fostered, and the ability to exercise judgment is prize.

To distinguish between the syntactical structures of forms of representation that are highly rule-governed and those that are less so is not to suggest that one is educationally valuable and the other is not. The existence of differing forms of representation in culture testify to their distinctive utility for enabling humans to conceptualize and convey to others the kinds of meanings they wish to express. If we assume that the capacity for meaning is diverse within man and common among men, then it seems reasonable to assume that the forms of representation that man has invented are a product of his need to give expression to what his nature makes possible. In other words, music and mathematics, to take two examples, exist because they are the only vehicles through which the meanings they make possible can be created.

Given this general view of meaning and mind, two specific points need emphasis. First, while the capacities for meaning are a part of the biological constitution of the human organism, the extent to which those capacities are actualized depends upon the forms of representation that humans learn to use. For a great many such forms the opportunities for their use are available as a normal part of socialization. Vernacular speech is the most obvious example. No normal child fails to learn to speak. However, the level of competence with which it is used without special tuition seldom exceeds the level found in the culture at large. And in general these levels are not particularly high. *TV Guide* is a stunning index in this regard. Thus, left on their own children will tend to achieve those level of literacy that are represented in the forms that they find around them. These levels hardly exhaust the potential of either the forms or the children.

Second, the kind of meaning that individuals are able to secure from their experience is directly related to their ability to use the forms of representation that are available. These forms are, as I have suggested, non-redundant. What one can say is that the experience in prose is not possible in poetry, and what is possible in poetry is not possible in mathematics. What is possible in mathematics is not possible in dance. No literal translation from one form of representation to another is possible without some loss of meaning.

Thus far I have described the sensory systems and the forms of representation as if these forms functioned independently. The fact of the matter is that they interact and feed off one another in both our private imaginative life and in the forms we use to make that life public. For example, we have the ability to conceptualize not only in each of the sensory modalities – we can visualize, we can recall and create auditory concepts, we can engender imaginatively taste and touch as well as number and word – but we are also able to experience concepts in these forms simultaneously. It is no great psychological feat to be able to hear a melody while at the same time experiencing a mental image. Indeed, with practice we can hear music, speak sentences and see images all at the same time. Such an ability allows us to rehearse activities mentally prior to acting upon them empirically. I am suggesting that our ability to engage in such rehearsal is educable: we can improve our ability to construe such mental images if we have the opportunity to learn to do so.

But there is a further way in which our ability to form concepts affects the nature and quality of what we can express. I refer here to the fact that the mode in which we conceptualize need not necessarily be the mode in which what we have conceptualized is expressed. Writing is a prime example. For a writer to have a content to express, the writer must first be able to experience the world he intends to write about. This experience is not initially verbal. It is, at first, qualitative. From experience with the qualitative, the content for the expression is born. The task of the writer in part is to make vivid his experience, that is, to accomplish the miracle of transforming qualitative experience existing in one realm into an arrangement of words which succeed in saying what words can never say. The writer starts his writing with vision and ends with words. But the reader, while starting with words, ends with vision. Similarly, visual artists may start with words – a manifesto of political beliefs, as did the futurists, or a theoretical intrigue with the unconscious as did the surrealists – and from words end with visual images. The point here is that the forms through which humans think are not condemned to solitary confinement within their own cells. The mind is a social entity.

Let me restate the argument I have tried to make thus far. It has five parts.

First, the sensory systems make it possible to contact and portray the world in different ways. I have called these modes of portrayal 'forms of representation.'

Second, these forms of representation are available in the culture at large and function as means through which we conceptualize, express and recover meaning.

Third, to become literate in a wide sense means more than to be able to read, write or cipher. It means being able to use a variety of forms of representation for conceptualizing, expressing and recovering meaning.

Fourth, since each form of representation emphasizes the use of different sensory systems and employs a different syntax, the kind of meaning that each provides is unique. What can be expressed in one form is not expressable in another.

Finally, at present, schools neglect the development of literacy in many of the forms of representation that are available in the culture. This neglect denies children access to meanings that are specific to particular forms, and adversely affects the kinds of meanings they can express in the forms that they are taught in schools.

In developing this argument I have taken something for granted that should be confronted directly. I intend to do so now. I refer here to the generally held belief that the concept of literacy can only be applied to what is truly a language and that the only true languages are speech, text and number. Furthermore, thinking itself, it is argued, can only be mediated by language. Thus to talk about thinking within or through forms of representation that are not governed by the rule of logic, is either to speak of language metaphorically or to seriously misunderstand the fundamental nature of thought. One writer, Adam Schaaf, puts the case this way:

> When we adopt the monistic standpoint, we reject the claim that language and thinking can exist separately and independently of one another. Of course, we are talking about specifically *human* thinking, in other words about *conceptual* thinking. Thus we assert that in the process of cognition and communication, thinking and using a language are inseparable elements of one and the same whole. Integration is so perfect and interdependence is so precise that neither element can ever occur independently, in a 'pure' form. That is precisely why the functions of thinking and language may not be treated separately, let alone contrasted with one another.[7]

It seems to me a strange view of thinking to limit thought to verbally or mathematically mediated activity. Such a view implies that the activities of painters, composers, athletes and all others whose medium of expression is non-verbal or non-mathematical first must think in verbal or mathematical forms before they are able to translate them into the qualities and actions that constitute the works that they create. This hardly squares with common experience or with the reports that such individuals make about their own cognitive processes. But perhaps the activities of artists and the like are really not a function of thinking at all. But if this is the case, what are they a function of? Inspiration, perhaps, catharsis, being touched by the Muse. These explanations hardly seem adequate. Even Chomsky, who staunchly advocates the view that the human's capacity for language is a genetic and uniquely human aptitude, suggests that thinking is not limited to language:

> Is it the case, for example, that humans necessarily think in language? Obvious counter-examples immediately come to mind. Our only evidence of any substance is introspective, the introspection surely tells me that when I think about a trip to Paris or a camping expedition in the Rockies, the few scraps of internal monologue that may be detected hardly convey, or even suggest the content of my thought. In struggling with a mathematical problem, one is often aware of the role of a physical, geometrical intuition that is hardly expressible in words, even with effort and attention ...[8]

Thinking, Chomsky suggests, is not only *not* limited to language as it is conventionally defined, but non-linguistic forms of thinking may underlie the activity of those whose work is eventually expressed in words or numbers. Indeed the history of science is filled with individuals whose self-reports indicate that non-verbal thinking was central to the solutions they were seeking. A view that limits thinking to what is verbally or mathematically mediated, it seems to me, must either have a limited view of thinking or must be obliged to use the concept as a special case of a larger more generic cognitive process. Dewey put the issue beautifully when he says in *Art as Experience*:

> Any idea that ignores the necessary role of intelligence in production of works of art is based upon identification of thinking with use of one special kind of material, verbal signs and words. To think effectively in terms of relations of qualities is as severe a demand upon thought as to think in terms of symbols, verbal and mathematical. Indeed, since words are

easily manipulated in mechanical ways, the production of a work of genuine art probably demands more intelligence than does most of the so-called thinking that goes on among those who pride themselves on being 'intellectuals.'[9]

Enough said about thinking, but what about the notion that the concept of language can and ought to be extended so that it includes forms of representation that do not use words or number. Here the problem becomes a bit sticky. The term language is derived from the Latin 'lingua' and is thus etymologically derived from speech or 'tongue.' When people speak of language they typically mean speech or text. Because of the highly rule-governed character of mathematics, it, too, is brought under the umbrella of language. Indeed, to be numerate is to be literate in number. Except for the specialized term semiotics, we do not have in the English language a generic term that includes all forms of patterned expressions that convey thought. And the term semiotic is a technical term that is more prevalent in the fields of linguistics and philosophy than in common discourse. Because of this deprivation in our own discursive language, I wish to extend the concept of language so that it exceeds its conventional meaning. If language is regarded as a vehicle that makes it possible for humans to conceptualize and express what they think, and if through such expression communication occurs, then forms beyond speech, text and number qualify as non-discursive forms of language.

Perhaps the clearest example of this is, paradoxically, located in written language itself. I speak here of literature and poetry. The communicative content of these forms of expression is surely not limited to their literal meaning. Indeed, the literal as contrasted with the figurative reading of literature and poetry is their anathema. And for the figurative, there is no rule-governed syntax comparable to those used in mathematics or formal discursive expression. If a form of representation must use a formal, codified rule-governed syntax in order to qualify as a language, we must either say that literature and poetry are not examples of language and do not communicate, or revise our conception of language so that it recognizes the fact that they do.

Forms of Representation and Their Meaning for Education

My discussion thus far has been largely technical. I have tried to describe the contributions to mind that are made by the forms of representation that are available in the culture, to root these to the sensory systems which have given rise to them, and to expand the concept of literacy so that it includes more than the ability to read and write. Literacy, I have argued, can be regarded as the ability to secure or convey meaning from patterned forms of expression. Much more could be said about these matters. I have not discussed the relationship of technique to expression and the limits it places upon it, nor have I discussed the virtues of chance and error in the process. I have not mentioned the ways in which temporal and spatial forms of representation affect what can be expressed. These issues will have to wait for another occasion. Because readers of this book are interested in the improvement of education, perhaps now it would be well to say something about what the concept of mind as cultural achievement might mean for four of the major subject matters of education: for the goals of education, for the content of the curriculum, for the processes of teaching, and for the ways in which we evaluate.

With respect to the goals of education, let me simply say that I believe that one of education's major aims should be the cultivation of the student's literacy as I have described it. I embrace such an end-in-view for schools because I believe education ought to expand the varieties of meaning students can experience. Many of those meanings are to be found in the great cultural forms of the world. Access to these forms depends upon the student's ability to 'read' their contents.

I value the cultivation of wide forms of literacy not only because I believe the great works of art and science ought to be accessible to students, but because the acquisition of such literacy makes it possible to read the environment at large. Making sense of the world requires an ability to give it form, to perceive and grasp its expressive patterns, in short, to read what it means. One learns how to read phenomena that were never intended to be communicative as well as those forms that were. Indeed, it is the ability to construe meaning from the forms of nature as well as culture that the forms of art and science are made. The forms of representation that people learn to use provide the concepts and schemata for constructing such meaning.

As for the curriculum, if what I have said has merit, it would mean that the schools would allocate time so that students had the opportunity to develop the varieties of literacy I described as important. At present they do not. If one uses time as an index of what is important in school, there is no question where priorities lie. About seventy to eighty-five percent of all of the time allocated for instructional purposes in elementary schools is devoted to the teaching of the three Rs. The arts, by contrast, secure from two to four per cent of instructional time per week, the sciences somewhat more, and the social studies slightly more than the sciences. A curriculum that does not give students the opportunity to become literate in certain forms of representation handicaps their ability to use other forms of representation. As I have suggested, we write as much with our eyes and ears as we do by following the rules of grammar and logic. Children who do not learn to see will not be able to write, not because they cannot spell, but because they will have nothing to say. And if they are unable to hear the cadence, tempo and melody of what they write, it is likely to be mechanical and stilted. At a time in which schools are being asked to narrow their focus, I would urge them to expand their focus. The creation of a balanced curriculum is one of the most pressing curriculum problems of the day.

Regarding teaching, I would suggest that the likelihood of developing broad forms of literacy among students depends upon having teachers who themselves are broadly literate. For teacher preparation this means at least three things. First, during the course of the teacher's general education the skills needed to recover different forms of meaning should be developed. It is not likely that a teacher will be able to be critical or pedagogically helpful in those realms that the teacher himself does not understand. Second, it means that the prospective teacher also needs to understand the nature of the forms of representation that he teaches, that is, to be able to distinguish between the ways in which propositional and non-propositional forms communicate, to grasp the distinctive ways in which time, for example, is used in the novel as compared to the dance, to appreciate the function of color in painting as contrasted to its use in music. What I am suggesting is that teachers not only need to be literate in the fields they teach, but that they be able to rise above those fields to appreciate their distinctive and complementary functions.

Third, in the course of teaching it would be well if teachers developed the skills needed to help students learn how to treat problems using different forms of representation. What can be said about history through drama or through visual images that is not likely to be said in didactic prose and vice versa? The ability to use different forms of representation should broaden the options students have to display what they have learned and it should also allow some youngsters to shine in ways that expression limited to writing might not make possible. If we want to know what children are capable of doing, it seems reasonable to give them a chance to do it. If the mind, for the moment, can be likened to a great supermarket containing wide varieties of food, then does it not seem restrictive to limit the young to two or three aisles. There are foods in other places that are worth tasting.

Finally, with respect to evaluation I would urge that we support and expand the current efforts being made to broaden the ways in which we evaluate. Conventional modes of evaluation, particularly the use of achievement tests, are designed to capture only a slender slice of educational life. Yet, the results of their use have substantial consequences for the schools. To use such devices as the exclusive tools for evaluation is like casting a net into the sea that is intentionally designed to let the most interesting fish get away. To then describe the ones that are caught strictly in terms of their weight and length is to reduce radically what can be known about them. To proceed further to conclude that the content of the sea consists of fish like those that remained in the net is to compound the error even further. There are more kinds of fish than we are able to catch with the nets that we use. There is more to know about the ones that we catch than what we can describe with the forms of representation we typically employ. We need, I believe, to secure the kinds of understanding that different forms of representation make possible. In short, we need new nets. Film, descriptive narrative, artistically rendered prose, graphic displays of children's works, interviews and the like all have something unique to tell us about the processes of education and their consequences. Our understanding of the effects of education should not be limited to what can be revealed by digits carried to the third decimal place.

In this article I have tried to lay out an optimistic view of the mind. Education itself is an optimistic enterprise. We work with others in the belief that what we do contributes to the kind of life that we and our students are able to lead. I have suggested that these achievements are the result of newly-acquired forms of literacy, new forms of representation through which our minds can function. Although culture provides these forms, the effects of their use exceeds what we typically mean by the transmission of culture. Transmission is too static a concept. The forms of representation we learn to use themselves provide the basis for the invention of new forms. These in turn make it possible to achieve forms of thinking that previously were not possible. The mind is an achievement that evolves not simply in the genetic sense, but in the cultural sense as well. As educators we have the privilege of celebrating its possibilities and contributing to its achievements. The exercise of that art – the art of education – as Dewey himself said, 'is the most difficult and most important of all human arts.'[10]

Notes

1. *Vital Statistics of the United States*, Monthly Vital Statistics Report, June 1976.
2. *Yearbook of American and Canadian Churches*, Nashville, Abingdon Press.
3. As of 1978–79, since the Furman vs. Georgia Decision, 36 states have death penalty statutes. Council of State Governments (1978) *The State Book 1971–79*, Vol. 22, Kentucky.
4. *The Miami Herald*, 24 October, 1977.
5. KUFFLER, S.W. and NICOLLS, J.G. (1976) *From Neuron to Brain: A Cellular Approach to the Function of the Neuron Systems*, Cambridge, Mass. Sinavar Associates, (especially chapter 19).
6. HAYNES, S.G., McMICHALL, A.J. and TYROLEV, H.A. 'Survival After Early and Normal Retirement,' in *Journal of Gerontology*, Vol. 33, No. 2, pp. 269–278.
7. SCHAFF, A. (1973) *Language and Cognition* New York: McGraw Hill Book Co., p. 118.
8. CHOMSKY, N. Foreword to SCHAFF, A. *Language and Cognition*, ibid.
9. DEWEY, J. (1934) *Art as Experience* New York, Minton, Balch and Co.
10. DEWEY, J. 'Progressive Education and the Science of Education,' in ARCHAMBAULT, R.O. (Ed.) (1974) *John Dewey on Education* Chicago, University of Chicago Press, pp. 181.

11 The 'Methodology' of Qualitative Evaluation: The Case of Educational Connoisseurship and Educational Criticism

During the past decade there has been a rapidly growing interest in what is called 'qualitative evaluation'.[1] This interest is in part due to the realization that standardized achievement tests do not provide all of the information that educators want in order to know what teachers have taught and what students have learned. Partly as a result of the growing literature on the 'hidden curriculum', those in the field of education have recognized that students learn a great deal more than they are explicitly taught and that teachers and the school as an institution teach more than either teachers or school administrators realize. Many of the most important lessons that students learn in schools are not those embodied in the explicit curriculum.[3]

But even more, educators working in schools have become increasingly conscious of something that football coaches, teachers of violin, and voice coaches have known for a long time: if you want to improve the way people perform, paying attention to the final score or to the performance on opening night is insufficient; it is important to see how the game is played during practice sessions and how rehearsals go before the curtain rises. Qualitative methods of evaluation are in large measure designed to focus upon the processes of educational practice in order to provide practitioners and others with information that cannot be secured from the scores that standardized achievement tests and other forms of summative evaluation provide.

The work that my students and I have been doing at Stanford University over the past decade is a species of 'qualitative evaluation'. It goes by the rubric of *educational connoisseurship and educational criticism* and it takes its leading ideas from the work that critics of the arts do when they appraise the efforts of writers, painters, film-makers, producers, actors, dancers, and others who make, direct, or perform works of art.[4] In this brief chapter I will describe the major features of this approach to educational evaluation, I will identify some of the concerns and issues that are commonly raised about it, and I will describe some of the methods that can be used by those who wish to employ educational criticism in their own work in schools and in universities in California and elsewhere.

Educational connoisseurship and educational criticism rest upon several assumptions. First, it is assumed that if individuals are to be able to describe the characteristics of complex social situations such as classrooms they must be able to see the interactions among the characteristics that occur, Second, seeing such characteristics requires more than merely looking. It requires being able to discern what is significant given some frame of reference. In this sense seeing is regarded as an *achievement* that is cognitive in nature, it is not simply a task to be performed. [5] Third, it is assumed that such situations can be described in a variety of ways, for example, social situations can be described through the use of propositions, through number, through literary prose, by means of poetry, and through visual narratives on video, through cinematography, and by visual still photography. Fourth, it is assumed that each form of representation has unique utilities and limitations for revealing the significant qualities that one has seen. Fifth, it is assumed that the function of description through any of the forms in which it might occur is to help some person or group better understand the situation being described than he would without the benefit of the description. Thus, the function of critical narrative, regardless of the medium used, is to help people see, understand and appraise the character and quality of educational practice and its consequences.

What my students do is to observe classrooms for extended periods of time (from two to ten weeks), and write educational criticisms about what they have seen. Their ability to see what is subtle yet significant is a function of the level of educational connoisseurship that they possess and the presence of particular qualities of life and learning within the classrooms that they visit. For qualities to be seen two conditions must be present: the qualities must be in the situation in the first place and the individual observing must have the ability to note their presence.

The development of whatever levels of connoisseurship students achieve is fostered through several means. Students enrol on a course in educational connoisseurship and educational criticism that I teach in the School of Education at Stanford. In this course they read and discuss the criticism of professional arts critics and of students who have written educational criticism. They read and discuss doctoral dissertations that have used educational criticism as a dominant methodology, they observe, write and discuss the teaching practices of elementary and secondary school teachers they view on videotapes, and they visit classrooms and write educational criticisms directly. These educational criticisms are then duplicated and discussed in class. The major aim of these exercises is to heighten their awareness to the subtleties of teaching and learning. Discussion with peers about what each has seen is one way in which observations can be tested, refined, and modified. For those who wish to do doctoral dissertations using educational criticism this process might be extended over the course of the year, even before they visit the schools and classrooms they wish to study and write about.

Before discussing the structure of the writing used in educational criticism, it will be helpful to know something about the kinds of topics or problems that my students study. Thus far twelve doctoral dissertations have been completed at Stanford that use educational criticism as a dominant method. I shall briefly describe the focus of three such dissertations.

One study was designed to identify the differences in curriculum content that was taught by three elementary school teachers working with the same curriculum unit – the planetary system – within the same science curriculum.[6] The three teachers had about the same amount of classroom experience, they taught children of the same age and socio-economic status attending three schools within one school district. The major concern of the study was to determine the similarities and differences in the content provided to students by these teachers. Put another way, the study asked: Given the same curriculum unit, what differences in content do children have access to as a function of the concerns, methods of teaching, and characteristics of the teacher? Given the fact that elementary school students spend a great deal of time each day with a single teacher, knowing something about how different teachers interpret content and manage student learning is important. Examining what students have learned about the planetary system through a common achievement test will not reveal what they have learned that was due to the unique contributions of their particular teacher.

A second study focused on the covert consequences of the use of a token economy to motivate elementary school students to learn mathematics.[7] This study combined both quantitative methods and educational criticism to determine the effects of different reward structures on mathematical achievement and other forms of learning.

A third study now in process is using educational criticism to identify the differences and similarities among three primary school teachers, each of whom has been identified as being very successful, moderately successful and unsuccessful in the teaching of reading as measured by their students reading achievement scores over a three year period and by the principal of the school in which they teach. The study is aimed at identifying and describing what accounts for the substantial differences in student performance. For example, it *might* be that the most successful teacher of reading achieves high student performance by using methods that might not be in the long-term best interests of the students. It *might* be that methods that are used are positive, subtle, and that once identified and described can be replicated by other teachers with appropriate in-service education.

These studies are designed to provide information about teaching practices that neither summative evaluation procedures nor student observation schedules are likely to reveal. In all cases the students doing the studies have been elementary school teachers whose average tenure in the classroom is approximately eight years.

What is the character of writing in educational criticism? What is its structure? What are its salient features?

Educational criticism typically takes the form of a written document whose aim it is to help others see, understand, and appraise the quality of educational practice and its consequences. This document has three components. I describe these components separately for purposes of clarity, but in the course of the writing they may be integrated and difficult to separate into neat compartments.

The first aspect of educational criticism is descriptive. What the writer attempts to do is to provide a detailed and vivid description of the situation he or she wants to help others understand. The writing of descriptive criticism is both factual and artistic. The factual aspect of the writing might employ numbers, direct quotations of teachers' and students' discourse, or propositional descriptions of the physical characteristics of the situation about which the criticism is written. The artistic aspect of description is literary and metaphorical; indeed, it can even be poetic in places. The task of the writer is to communicate what is salient about the situation and what the teacher and the critic have agreed to focus upon. In order to optimize communication, the potential of language is exploited so that the literary and the factual complement each other. Much that needs to be said about classrooms, teachers, and the quality of life and learning can be conveyed best not by factual description, but by literary narrative, metaphorical description, analogy. The problem of the writer is to help the reader vicariously participate in events that the reader has not experienced directly. To achieve this end the critic knows that emotions play an important role in understanding and knows how to use language so that it can reveal through emotion as well as through the presentation of the facts. When an educational critic[8] describes Dizzy Gillespie as a 'middle-aged Tom Sawyer' when Gillespie performed for students at a San Francisco junior high school, the reader gets a sense of the man in a way that a factual description of his age, height, weight, race or behavior can never provide.

A second aspect of educational criticism is interpretive. What educational critics do is to account for the interactions they perceive in school situations. Why do these activities occur? What explains this particular episode? Why is it that this teacher is so effective? What is the nature of the 'game' being played in this classroom? The effort here is not simply to describe the situation, but to interpret its processes and for this theory in the social sciences is appealed to. A good journalist might have the skills to vividly describe the situation but would not have the background to explain in theoretical terms the events that occurred. Doctoral students who have taken courses in educational psychology, sociology, history of education, and philosophy of education, are expected to draw upon concepts and theories from these disciplines to account for the events they have perceived and vividly described. This is far from an easy task: We tend in schools of education not to make the connections between theory and practice. But the connections are crucial if theory is to be more than an academic rite of passage instrumental to the achievement of a higher degree. By attempting to make applications of theoretical ideas, both theory and practice may be improved. One might be able to see when theory falls short and where practice can be illuminated by theory that is appropriate to it.

A third aspect of educational criticism deals with the task of making value judgments about the educational merits of what has been described and interpreted. Evaluation is a valuative activity just as education itself is a normative one. What we want education as a process to accomplish is not merely to change students, but to improve the quality of their lives. We want schools to be *educational* institutions – rather than miseducational or non-educational ones. To determine the *educational* value of the events perceived the educational critic appraises or evaluates these events by using criteria that are appropriate to their character. By this I mean that there are multiple views of educational virtue; there is no single 'good' in education. The educational critic attempts to appraise the situation in its own terms. If the teacher is giving a lecture, the appropriate criteria to apply deal with the possibilities of the lecture as a medium of instruction, not the criteria appropriate to small group discussion, even if the critic himself prefers such an approach. Taking a leaf from the arts, if the play is a tragedy, we apply tragedic criteria to it, not comedic. If the school is a conventional 'back-to-basics' school those criteria are applied, not the criteria appropriate for open schools. In short, within the limits of what is regarded as educationally sound and the varieties in which such soundness may appear, the criteria to be applied to appraise a classroom or a school is to be suited to the 'species' of educational practice described, interpreted and appraised.

In the end a written document will be prepared and educational criticism that is descriptive, interpretative and evaluative will be provided to some audience. The particular way in which the criticism is written depends upon the audience for whom it is intended. Since different audiences have different needs and different aims, and since the goal of educational criticism is to contribute to the improvement of practice, the criticism's relation to the audience is a crucial consideration. If the audience is a board or funding agency that wants to know how the project that it funded for months is doing, the criticism is written in a way suitable for such a concern. If the criticism is for the teacher who wants to know about how he or she is relating to students, how he or she is presenting ideas or leading discussions in class, then the criticism can be written with these needs in mind. Not everything that might have been observed needs to be shared at one time. Some feedback might be in a verbal form, other feedback will be written. How much to provide, in what form, in what tone, depends upon the critic's assessment of the situation and what is likely to be constructive.

I mentioned that the nature of the message is related to the needs of the audience. This relates as well to the critic's focus. When an agency, foundation, or at times a teacher requests or agrees to having an educational criticism prepared, the focus of the criticism is often *prefigured*, that is, the focus is determined by the specific needs of those groups of individuals. But the focus of an educational criticism might also be *emergent*. A critic might be invited to a school or classroom without a prefigured focus and after several days or weeks perceive an aspect of the school or classroom that is of considerable significance but which could not have been anticipated. For example, one of my students received permission from a secondary school English teacher to observe and to write an educational criticism about her class. What emerged during my student's observation was the extraordinary way in which the teacher used satire in her teaching. It was not the case that the teacher was herself teaching satire; it was that she was satirical in her teaching.[9] Such a process or an approach could hardly have been prefigured. There is no research on teaching that deals with the use of satire, nothing on this topic in the *Handbook of Research on Teaching*, or in the *Education Index*. The point here is that the focus of criticism can be either prefigured as a part of the research bargain between the critic and the teacher, or it can be emergent or it can be both. Indeed, in general, the latter is more prevalent in my students' work than the former.

What are some of the issues and concerns that people raise about such an iconoclastic approach to educational evaluation? Those professionally socialized in the tradition of the social sciences are concerned with matters such as (i) the reliability of observations; (ii) validity; and (iii) the generalizability of the findings or conclusions. The most frequently raised concern deals with reliability. How does one know whether there is bias in perception and reporting? The question itself reflects naiveté concerning the inevitable 'bias' in any form of observation. Any observation schedule or test leaves as much or more out than it includes, regardless of the form. In this sense, any form of data collection is biased by the assumptions on which it was built and the methods that it employs. Pristine objectivity is an epistemological impossibility. The empty mind sees nothing.

Reliability, or perhaps a better term, believeability, is achieved through a process of structural corroboration, a process something like 'triangulation' in sociological methodology, or circumstantial evidence in law. The writer of criticism provides compelling conclusions by supporting those conclusions with evidence embodied within the criticism that relates to events which have transpired. This process is much like what all of us do in our daily lives. We put pieces together as they emerge and we form a whole that makes sense to us. We do not typically engage in a controlled experimentation or use blind judging procedures in order to make inferences about the future or to draw conclusions about the present.

A second manner in which reliability can be determined is by assessing what is called the *referential adequacy* of the criticism. Good criticism should illuminate what it addresses. An educational criticism that is reliable *and* valid will enable someone with less connoisseurship than the critic to see what otherwise would have gone unseen. Just as a good music critic can help us hear counterpoint unheard, melodic lines unrecognized, the test of the educational critic is to be able, through the critic's work, to perceive what is subtle and complex within classrooms and schools. The educational critic is something of a midwife to perception.

As for generalizability, this is not a major concern for those doing evaluation but it is a major concern for those who are engaged in educational research. According to conventional research canons, generalizations can occur only if the samples researched have been randomly selected from a universe whose parameters have been defined. One can generalize if one knows these parameters and if the process has been random. Putting aside the fact that such assumptions are honored more in the breach than in fact, the belief that random selection is the only valid way to generalize is itself questionable. In fact, it hardly squares with our ordinary experience; we seldom form the generalizations we hold through a process of random selection. Generalizations occur by a build-up of common general features recognized in particulars. What we learn from particular situations we use to form expectations for the future. We modify those expectations as a result of subsequent experience. Educational criticism, by helping us perceive, understand, and appraise particular situations also therefore helps us form generalizations about educational practice. If we were restricted to practice in education only what we had learned from studies in which random selection was employed, we would be compelled to close the school house door tomorrow. Thankfully, we learn a great deal from a wide variety of methods of inquiry and in forms that are far wider than can be stated in formal propositions or through number.

There are, of course, a variety of issues that could be addressed in the analysis and appraisal of educational criticism. Space does not permit a full treatment here and hence I refer the reader to the works on educational criticism listed in the references. There is, though, one point that I would like to make about the efficiency of educational connoisseurship and educational criticism as a method of educational evaluation. Educational criticism, compared with the use of standardized observation schedules is not an efficient method. It takes time. It takes subtlety of perception. It takes considerable skill in writing. It requires the ability to apply theory to practice. It requires one to make educational judgments. Further, there is no recipe – like procedure or 'method' comparable to computing a test for doing this work. It is, in short, a method that requires no small degree of artistry. To know what educational criticism provides one must read it. It is more complex than looking at a set of raw scores, T-Scores, percentiles, or means. In this sense, it not only takes time to write, it takes time to read as well. Yet I know of no better way to learn how the game has been played than to watch it with sensitivity and intelligence while it is in process. Without knowledge of this process I know of no credible way to improve what we do in the schools. Evaluation as a process can perform many different functions in education: it can reward, it can screen, it can select, it can at times help us determine if our objectives have been achieved. But perhaps the most important function of evaluation from a strictly educational point of view is to help educators improve the quality of educational life for students. There are no short-cuts that I know of to this end. Educational connoisseurship and educational criticism have a modest contribution to make to its realization.

Notes

1. The word qualitative evaluation, as distinct from quantitative evaluation, is the result of a conceptual mistake. All empirical research is rooted in the description of qualities. Number is one mode of description. See my article: (1981) 'On the Differences Between Artistic and Scientific Approaches to Educational Research,' in *The Educational Researcher* April.
2. For an interesting article on the hidden curriculum see VALLANCE, E. (1973–74) 'Hiding the Hidden Curriculum' in *Curriculum Theory Network* Vol. 4, No. 1, pp. 5–22.
3. In my book *The Educational Imagination* I distinguish between three types of curricular: the explicit, the implicit and the null curriculum. Although the explicit curriculum is the one that gets the most attention from educators, the other two may be equally – perhaps even more – important.
4. For a full discussion of these concepts see (1979) *The Educational Imagination: On the Design and Evaluation of Educational Programs*, New York, Macmillan and Co.
5. This distinction between an achievement verb and a task verb is made by GILBERT RYLE (1949) in *The Concept of Mind* New York, Barnes and Noble.
6. McCUTCHEON, G. (1976) 'The Disclosure of Classroom Life,' doctoral dissertation, Stanford University.
7. STERNBERG, B. (1977) 'What Do Tokens and Trophies Teach'. doctoral dissertation, Stanford University.
8. SCHLOSSER, R. 'A Musical Program', mimeo, Stanford University, School of Education.
9. SHERMAN, A. 'Humor and Satire,' mimeo, Stanford University, School of Education.

Some doctoral dissertations that have used educational criticism as a dominant methodology are as follows:

ALEXANDER, R.R. (1977) 'Educational Criticism of Three Art History Classes,' Stanford University.

BARONE, T. (1978) 'Inquiry Into Classroom Experience: A Qualitative, Holistic Approach' Stanford University.

FEILDERS, J.F. (1979) 'Action and Reaction: The Job of an Urban School Superintendent' Stanford University.

VALLANCE, E. (1975) 'Aesthetic Criticism and Curriculum Development' Stanford University.

Also see EISNER, E.W. (1980) 'The Use of Qualitative Forms of Evaluation for Improving Educational Practice,' in *Journal of Educational Evaluation and Policy Analysis*, Vol. 1, No. 6, November–December.

12 On the Differences Between Artistic and Scientific Approaches to Qualitative Research

My intention here is to identify ten dimensions in which artistic and scientific approaches to qualitative research differ.

The term qualitative research does not have a long history in the field of education and in many ways it not only hides the important distinctions which need to be made, but it is, itself, misleading. The major distinction we seek is *not* between qualitative and non-qualitative forms of research since *all* empirical research must of necessity pay attention to qualities, but between what is studied in a scientific mode and what is studied artistically. There can be no empirical research, that form of research that addresses problems in a material universe, that does not aim to describe, interpret, predict or control qualities. The major distinction to be made in the conduct of research is not located in the phenomenon of study but in the mode in which that study occurs. The difference that counts is between what is studied artistically and what is studied scientifically. These differences are the ones to which this paper is addressed.

At the outset it should be said that research flying under the flag of science is extremely wide. Indeed, it is so wide that some philosophers of science regard no form of research in the social sciences as scientific. For philosophers of science such as Nagel (1961) or Popper (1959), the so-called social sciences are not yet what they claim to be.

We need not, and I do not, embrace the strict conception of science that they advocate. I am willing to regard as scientific, those inquiries ranging from the testing of formal mathematical models of learning through controlled laboratory experiments to the kind of studies done in the field of cultural anthropology by people like Redfield (1941). For our purposes, scientific research may be regarded as inquiries that use formal instruments as the primary basis for data collection, that transform the data collected into numerical indices of one kind or another, and that attempt to generalize in a formal way to some universe beyond itself. Although I recognize that there are forms of scientific research that differ from the characteristics I have just described, I believe that these characteristics are by far the most salient ones and hence should be regarded as modal characteristics.

As for the concept 'artistic,' it similarly has no single, simple definition. 'Art' and 'artistic' are terms that have been the subject of aesthetic debate and analysis for over 2,000 years. Plato, for example, viewed art as the creation of harmonious form whose mathematical relationships participated in the true, the good and the beautiful. Aristotle regarded art as the production of mimesis; Clive Bell as the presence in a work of significant form; Suzanne Langer as the creation of a nondiscursive symbol expressive of human feeling; John Dewey as coherent and emotionally moving experience.[1] The point here is simply that neither the concept of science nor the concept of art are settled issues among those who have thought about them most deeply. I provide this caveat now because my remarks will of necessity be based on an arbitrary, but I hope not an unreasonable, conception of both art and science. To provide a philosophically adequate discussion of these concepts would exceed my competence and would, at the very least, require a manuscript of book length.

Following is a discussion of ten dimensions in which scientific and artistic approaches to research differ.

The Forms of Representation Employed

One significant difference between research participating in a scientific mode and that participating in an artistic mode is the kind of form that each uses to represent what has been learned.[2] Scientific work, of necessity, employs formal statements which express either empirically referenced quantitative relationships or communicate through discursive propositions. The language which is used is formal in the sense that it is literal. That is, the syntactical rules to which such statements abide allow little or no scope for the poetic or the metaphorical. This is not to say that the poetic and the metaphorical do not find their way into scientific research; they do in a multitude of covert ways. House (1979) provides some illuminating examples of how this occurs. It is to say that the meanings conveyed aspire to literal rather than figurative form. Perhaps a classic example of such work is to be found in Birdwhistle's micro-analytic schemes for the recording and scoring of human gesture, posture and movement.[3] His aim is to operationalize both the perception and recording of human behavior through codification. Once codified, the methods of data collection and analysis can be routinized and the results objectified.

Artistic forms of representation have no comparable codifications. They place a premium on the idiosyncratic use of form – visual and auditory form as well as discursive form – to convey in nonliteral as well as literal ways the meanings the investigator wishes to express. 'One Flew Over the Cuckoo's Nest' is a brilliant example of how visual, musical and verbal forms can be combined to convey significant insights into human and inhuman relationships. For the artistic, the literal is frequently pale and humdrum. What one seeks is not the creation of a code that abides by publicly codified rules, but the creation of an evocative form whose meaning is embodied in the shape of what is expressed.

The Criteria for Appraisal

Scientific approaches to research ask whether or not the conclusions are supported by the evidence, and further, whether the methods that were used to collect the evidence did not bias the conclusions. In other words, scientific research is always concerned with questions of validity. For a research study to be judged valid, a variety of criteria need to be applied to it. These range from appraising the character of sampling procedures and the magnitude of instrument reliability to the less tangible areas of interpretation.

In artistic approaches to research, the cannons of test reliability and sampling do not apply. While one might question a writer's or film producer's reliability, there is no formalized set of procedures to measure writer reliability; one doesn't really want the mean view of four writer's observations about the mental hospital in Oregon which served as the subject matter for Ken kesey's play. One simply wants Ken Kesey's view. Its validity, if that is the appropriate term, is to be determined by our view of its credibility, and not by reducing his work to some average by using only that portion that it shares with the views of others. Validity in the arts is the product of the persuasiveness of a personal vision; its utility is determined by the extent to which it informs. There is no test of statistical significance, no measure of construct validity in artistically rendered research. What one seeks is illumination and penetration. The proof of the pudding is the way in which it shapes our conception of the world or some aspect of it.

Points of Focus

Scientific approaches to research tend to focus on the manifest behavior of the individual or group studied to a greater degree than artistic approaches. By this I mean that manifest behavior provides the primary data for research in the social sciences in which scientifically oriented research participates. What one attends to is what people do, how they behave, what they say. Such phenomena are open to experience, they are observable; their incidence can be counted, and once counted, they can be treated in a multitude of ways. Although one might make inferences from the behavior one observes and records, the farther the inference is from the behavior, the less trustworthy it is regarded to be. The distinction between 'high inference' and 'low inference' conclusions underscores this point.

Artistic approaches to research focus less on behavior than on the experience the individuals are having and the meaning their actions have for others. Just how does one focus on experience and meaning. How does one make sense of what is nonobservable? One way is to make inferences from observables to what is not observable. Manifest behavior is treated primarily as a cue, a springboard to get someplace else. The other way is to 'indwell,' to empathize; that is, to imaginatively participate in the experience of another.[4] The difference between the two is subtle but important. In the former, observables are used in a kind of statistical fashion; one intuitively (or statistically) estimates the probability that *this* behavior means one particular thing or another. There is no real need for empathy. The latter banks on the observer's ability to imaginatively project himself into the life of another in order to know what that person is experiencing. It is the content provided by this form of knowing that serves as a major source of understanding for artistic approaches to research. Thus, a major focus in artistic approaches to research is the meanings and experiences of the people who function in the cultural web one studies. As Geertz puts it with respect to his work, 'Believing, with Max Weber, that man is an animal suspended in webs of significance he himself has spun, I take culture to be those webs, and the analysis of it to be therefore not an experimental science in search of law but an interpretive one in search of meaning'.[5]

The Nature of Generalization

In the social sciences, the methodology required for generalizing from a set of specific findings to a universe is well defined. In this process the selection of a sample must be random and the parameters of the universe clearly articulated. Inferences from sample to population are acceptable only insofar as they meet these requirements. There is comparatively little interest in findings that deal only with the sample itself; social science research methods are after bigger fish. This orientation to generalization, one which is statistical in nature, is what Windelband has called nomethetic.[6] Studies of single cases or the examination of the idiosyncratic are not considered good resources for generalizing. Indeed, in statistical studies 'outliers,' that is individual scores that do not conform to the distribution of a sample or population, are often disregarded; they are considered part of the error variance. What one seeks are trends, robust central tendencies, or stable and statistically significant differences in the variances between groups as a function of treatment. Research in the social sciences attempts to move from the particular to the general, and is interested in particulars only insofar as they represent the general. Random selection is the cornerstone of the process.

Artistic approaches to research have no comparable mechanism for generalization. But this should not be interpreted to mean that generalization is not possible. While it is sometimes said that ideographic research does not generalize, I think such a conclusion is incorrect. But if so, then how does one generalize from a nonrandomly selected single case? Generalization is possible because of the belief that the general resides in the particular and because what one learns from a particular one applies to other situations subsequently encountered.[7] Consider literature as an example. Is it the case that Saul Bellow's novel *Mr. Sammler's Planet* is simply a story about Artur Sammler and no one else? Is Shakespeare's portrayal of Lady Macbeth simply about a particular Scottish noblewoman who lived in the later part of the 11th century? Hardly. What these writers have done is to illustrate significant, common human attributes by the way they have written about particular individuals. Artistic approaches to research try to locate the general in the particular. They attempt to shed light on what is unique in time and space while at the same time conveying insights that exceed the limits of the situation in which they emerge. This is precisely what Aristotle meant when he said that 'Poetry was truer than history.'

Put into more contemporary psychological terms, the expectations we acquire from our examination of the particular become a part of our anticipatory schema; we shape our information pickup system by what we learn from individual cases.[8] The artistically oriented researcher is interested in making the particular vivid so that its qualities can be experienced and because he believes that the particular has a contribution to make to the comprehension of what is general. The ability to generalize from particulars is one of the ways whereby humans cope with the world. I know of no one who forms the generalizations that guide his or her actions through a technically rigorous process of random selection.

The Role of Form

In the sciences, the manner in which data are presented is interchangeable. For example, one can use numbers to display a pattern of scores which a population received or one can use a bar chart. The two methods are regarded as equivalent. Indeed, if one form designed to replicate the information provided in the other fails to do so, an error has occurred.

The matter of form in scientific work goes even farther. If the articles published in research journals are examined for style, it becomes quite apparent that the standardization of style is considered a virtue. One is supposed to identify the problem, review the literature, describe the instruments and population, report the treatment, present and discuss the results and, finally, project possible implications. If, in this format, any sense of the personality of the investigator shines through, it is to be neutralized. This is accomplished by requiring that writers use the third person singular or the first person plural instead of using the 'I' form. The people studied are referred to as 'subjects' or 'Ss' and whatever uniqueness particular individuals might have is to be disregarded.

Not all research in the social sciences emphasizes so strict a formula as I have just described. Nevertheless, this is the dominant tradition in which social science research participates. The date an editor receives a manuscript is sometimes published with the manuscript, this being a clear indication of the effort editors of social science journals make to emulate their colleagues in the physical sciences where 'who discovered what first' counts a great deal.

In artistic approaches to research, standardization of form is counterproductive. What artistic approaches seek is to exploit the power of form to inform. What those engaged in artistic work take as a given is the belief that form and content interact; some would say that form *is* content.[9] The opposite view is salient in scientifically oriented work. Standardization of form is sought so that it does not confound the content. Because of its rule-governed syntax, the same things can be said in several ways. Rules of equivalence are comparatively easy to apply. In artistic approaches the particular words chosen, the location of specific ideas within a report, the tone and tempo of the writing, the sense of voice which it possesses have no literal equivalent. The potential of form is not regarded as a liability but as an essential vehicle constituting a significant part of the content of the communication. In short, form is regarded as a part of the content of what is expressed and bears significantly on the kinds of meanings people are likely to secure from the work. Hence, being skilled at the making of artistically expressive form – being able to write – is a critically important skill for those doing artistically oriented research in education.

Degree of License Allowed

Perhaps one of the most generally held beliefs about the differences between science and art is that the former deals with fact while the latter deals with fiction. The former is regarded as objective, the latter as subjective. Putting aside the point that scientific work is an artifact, that it is a human construction subject to all the human vicissitudes and foibles, there is a correct sense to the expectation that what is said in the name of science is to be more factual, less subject to imaginative fancy than, say, what is said by those who work within an artistic mode. We expect inventiveness and personal interpretation in the arts. We expect the artist to take liberties in order to drive home the point he or she wishes to make. These liberties – what we refer to as artistic license – are not intended to distract from artistic validity but to render more incisively and more persuasively what has been learned. Does such "bias" have a place in artistic approaches to research? Are the straight facts unencumbered by modulation more truthful? Is the longstanding expectation for pristine objectivity – even if such an aspiration were possible to achieve, which I think it is not – the most noble ideal for educational research?

One of the strengths that artistically oriented research possesses is that liberties in portrayal are wider than they are in scientifically oriented studies. Making things vivid through selective reporting and special emphasis occurs inevitably in any form of reporting, including scientific reporting. Artistically oriented research acknowledges what already exists and instead of presenting a facade of objectivity, exploits the potential of selectivity and emphasis to say what needs saying as the investigator sees it. Indeed, this orientation to writing has developed to such a degree of sophistication among the 'new journalists' that a neologism has been created to designate the new genre: it is called *faction*, the marriage of fact and fiction. I regard this term as extremely illuminating. After all, what can be more biased than emotionally eviscerated fact describing conditions or situations that are emotionally significant to those in the situations being described. Distortion can result not only from what is put in, but also from what is left out.

Interest in Prediction and Control

Scientifically oriented research aims at the production of ideas that will enable us to anticipate the future, if not to control it. The most rigorous form of scientific work, physics for example, makes both prediction and control possible and through them, the technological achievements that have captured the public's imagination. Some fields such as astronomy do not lead to control, but they do make accurate prediction possible. Most social science fields neither control nor successfully predict, they explicate. Archaeology and psychoanalysis are prime examples. As movement proceeds from the former to the latter, the affinity of scientifically oriented research to research that is artistically oriented grows stronger. Aside from the production of naturalistic-like generalizations[10], artistically oriented research does not aim to control or to produce formal predictive statements. It is after explication. It is closer in character to a hermeneutic activity than a technological one. What it yields at its best are ineffable forms of understanding which can only be conveyed through the figurative or nondiscursive character of the artistic image which such research yields.[11] The working assumption is that with such understanding, both cognitive differentiation and the ability of individuals to grasp and deal with situations like those portrayed in the research will be increased. It is not an algorithm that artistically oriented research seeks as much as a heuristic.

The Sources of Data

In artistic approaches to research, the major instrument is the investigator himself. By this I mean that although the investigator might use some formal instruments to collect data, the major source of data emanates from how the investigator experiences what it is he or she attends to. There are several utilities of such an approach. In the first place, many things that might be significant might not find a place on a formal observation schedule. One might now know in advance what is significant. Second, the meaning of an incident within a social situation might only be revealed by putting it in its historical context. No instrument which I know of can do this. Third, the expressive character of action and speech – their muted messages – are often so subtle that only a perceptive eye and an informed mind are likely to recognize their significance. Balance, tradeoff, context, and other features of social life must be considered if the interpretation of socially shared meanings is to have validity. These are precisely what are so difficult to standardize on test instruments or interview and observation schedules. The ideal of the hermetically sealed test, which is administered according to a standardized procedure and whose ticks are optically recorded and computer-scored and then mailed with standardized interpretations to anxious students, is very far from the ideal in artistically oriented research.

Not only are standardized methods of data collection marginal rather than central, but the way in which what has been learned is shared with others is also non-standardized. Reporting is guided by considerations of how the message is likely to be interpreted by those who receive it. In short, not only is there no standardized way of getting information, there is no standardized acontextual way of communicating what has been learned. What and how one says something depends on whom the message is for. Each report is, in this sense, a custom job.

The Basis of Knowing

In artistic approaches to research, the role that emotion plays in knowing is central. Far from the ideal of emotional neutrality which is sought in much of social science research, the artistically oriented researcher recognizes that knowing is not simply a unidimensional phenomena, but it takes a variety of forms. The researcher knows also that the forms one uses to represent what one knows affects what can be said. Thus, when the content to be conveyed requires that the reader vicariously participates in a social situation context, the writer or filmmaker attempts to create a form that makes such participation possible.

This orientation to knowledge embraces an epistemology that

rejects the positivistic view which holds that only formal propositions can, in principal, provide knowledge.[12] It rejects the view that affect and cognition are independent spheres of human experience. Instead, it gives to Rome what is Rome's; when you want to know how many students dropped out of a high school class you don't want a set of sonnets, you want a set of numbers. And it gives to others what they need to have in order to understand. Methodological pluralism rather than methodological monism is the ideal to which artistic approaches to research subscribe. To know a rose by its Latin name and yet to miss its fragrance is to miss much of the rose's meaning. Artistic approaches to research are very much interested in helping people experience the fragrance.

Ultimate Aims

This brings me to the last dimension I wish to discuss regarding the differences between scientific and artistic approaches to research: the question of differences in ultimate aim. Historically, one of the traditional aims of science is the discovery of truth. The Greeks had a word for it: *episteme*, the discovery of true and certain knowledge. Although many modern philosophers and historians of science such as Thomas Kuhn take a softer, more nominal view of science, not all philosophers of science do, and for a great many researchers in the social sciences, the correspondence theory of truth still holds sway. Propositions about reality are believed to be true to the extent to which those propositions correspond to the reality that they attempt to describe or explain. Given this view, science aims at making true statements about the world.

Artistic approaches to research are less concerned with the discovery of truth than with the creation of meaning. What art seeks is not the discovery of the laws of nature about which true statements or explanations can be given, but rather the creation of images that people will find meaningful and from which their fallible and tentative views of the world can be altered, rejected, or made more secure. Truth implies singularity and monopoly. Meaning implies relativism and diversity. Truth is more closely wedded to consistency and logic, meaning to diverse interpretation and coherence. Each approach to the study of educational situations has its own unique perspective to provide. Each sheds its own unique light on the situations that humans seek to understand. The field of education in particular needs to avoid methodological monism. Our problems need to be addressed in as many ways as will bear fruit. Interest in 'qualitative research' is symptomatic of the uneasiness that many in the research community have felt with the methods of enquiry promulgated by conventional research tradition. I have suggested in this paper that looking to qualitative methods to reduce this uneasiness will prove inadequate. The issue is not qualitative as contrasted with nonqualitative or quantitative, but how one approaches the educational world. It is to the artistic that we must turn, *not* as a rejection of the scientific, but because with both we can achieve binocular vision. Looking through one eye never did provide much depth of field.

Notes

1. See WEITZ, M. (1959) *Problems in Aesthetics* New York, Macmillan.
2. See EISNER, E. *A Basis for Deciding What to Teach* New York, Longmans, Green and Co.
3. See Part IV of BURDWHISTELL, R.L. (1970) *Kinesics and Context* New York, Ballantine Books, pp. 183–216.
4. For a vivid example at indwelling as a technique for describing the experience of others see BARONE, T. (1978) *Inquiry into Classroom Experiences: A qualitative, holistic approach* unpublished PhD dissertation Stanford University.
5. GEERTZ, C. (1973) *The Interpretation of Cultures* New York, Basic Books, p. 5.
6. See Von WRIGHT, H. (1971) *Explanation and Understanding* Ithaca, Cornell University Press.
7. See DONMOYER, R. (1980) *Alternative Conceptions of Generalization and Verification for Educational Research* unpublished PhD dissertation, Stanford University.
8. See NEISSER, U. (1976) *Cognition and Reality* San Francisco, W.H. Freeman.
9. SHAHN, B. (1957) *The Shape of Content* Cambridge, Mass., Harvard University Press.
10. See STAKE, R. (1978) 'The case study method in social enquiry' in *Educational Researcher* 7 (7), pp. 5–8.
11. See LANGER S.K. (1957) *Problems of Art* New York, Scribner and Sons.
12. AYER, A.J. (n.d.) *Language, Truth and Logic* New York, Dover Publications.

References

KUHN, T.S. (1962) *The Structure of Scientific Revolution* Chicago, University of Chicago Press.

NAGEL, E. (1961) *The Structure of Science: Problems in the Logic of Scientific Explanation.* New York, Harcourt, Brace and World.
POPPER, K. (1959) *The Logic of Scientific Discovery* London, Hutchinson.
REDFIELD, R. (1941) *The Folk Culture of Yucatan.* Chicago, University of Chicago Press.

13   *The Role of the Arts in Cognition and Curriculum*

My thesis is straightforward but not widely accepted. It is that the arts are cognitive activities, guided by human intelligence, that make unique forms of meaning possible. I shall argue further that the meanings secured through the arts require what might best be described as forms of artistic literacy, without which artistic meaning is impeded and the ability to use more conventional forms of expression is hampered.

To talk about the cognitive character of the arts or about the kind of meaning that they convey is not particularly common. The models of mind that have typified U.S. educational psychology (particularly that aspect of psychology concerned with learning and knowing) have made tidy separations between thinking and feeling, feeling and acting, and acting and thinking.[1] The view of thinking that has been most common is rooted in the Platonic belief that mind and body are distinct, and, of the two, body is base while mind is lofty.[2] Feeling is located in *soma*, idea in *psyche*. The literature distinguishes between cognition and effect, and we tend to regard as cognitive those activities of mind that mediate ideas through words and numbers. We consider words more abstract than images, icons less flexible than propositions. We regard words as high in that hierarchy of cognitive achievement we use to describe cognitive growth. Jean Piaget, for example, regarded formal operations, those mental operations that deal with logical relationships, as the apotheosis of cognitive achievement.[3] For some cognitive psychologists, thinking is a kind of inner speech that allows one to reason.[4] Since reason is a condition of rationality and since reasoning is believed to require the logical treatment of works, operations of the mind that do not employ logic are placed on the margins of rationality.

In this view the arts, if not considered irrational, are thought of as *a-rational*. As for meaning, it is most commonly regarded as an attribute of propositions, the property of assertions for which scientific warrant can be secured. The arts are considered emotive forms that might provide satisfaction – but not understanding.

The consequences of this view of mind have, in my opinion, been disastrous for education. First, this view has created a dubious status hierarchy among subjects taught in schools. Mathematics is the queen of the hill; other subjects, especially those in which students 'work with their hands,' are assigned lower intellectual status. Simply recall the standard whipping boy of school activities, basket weaving. Basket weaving epitomizes low status and mindlessness. Let me state quickly that I reject mindless forms of basket weaving in school. But let me add just as quickly that I also reject mindless forms of algebra and that I find nothing inherently more intellectually complex in algebra than in basket weaving; it depends upon the nature of the algebra and the nature of the baskets we choose to weave.

Besides making some subjects the targets of verbal abuse, the status hierarchy among subjects that emanates from such an indefensible conception of mind has practical day-to-day consequences in schools. Consider how time is allocated in school programs. Time is surely one of the most precious of school resources. As researchers of time on task have told us,[5] the relationship between the amount of time allocated and learning is a significant one. Partly because of our view of intellect, however, some subjects – the fine arts, for example – receive very little attention in school programs. On the average, elementary school teachers devote about 4% of school time each week to instruction in the fine arts.[6] And this time is not prime time, such as the so-called cognitive subjects command. For the fine arts, Friday afternoons are very popular.

Space does not permit a lengthy recital of sins that have been committed by schools in the name of cognitive development. Yet it is important to remember that the conception of giftedness used in many states excludes ability in the fine arts, that tax dollars support programs whose criteria discriminate against students whose gifts are in the fine arts, and that colleges and universities do not consider high school grades in the fine arts when making admissions decisions.[7] We legitimate such practices by distinguishing between intelligence and talent, assigning the former to verbal and mathematical forms of reasoning and the latter to performance in activities we deem more concrete: playing a musical instrument, dancing, painting.

I could elaborate at length on each of these points. But I mention them simply to highlight the model of mind that has been so widely accepted and to provide a context for my remarks concerning the role of the arts in cognition and curriculum.

If you were to consult the *Dictionary of Psychology* regarding the meaning of cognition, you would find that cognition is 'the process through which the organism becomes aware of the environment.'[8] Thus cognition is a process that makes awareness possible. It is, in this sense, a matter of becoming conscious, of noticing, of recognizing, of perceiving. It is a matter of distinguishing one thing from another: a figure from its ground, the various subtleties and nuances that, when perceived, become a part of one's consciousness.

In this process, the functions of the senses are crucial. They bring to awareness the qualitative world we inhabit. To become aware of the world, two conditions must be satisfied. First, the qualities must be available for experiencing by a sentient human being. Second, the individual must be able to 'read' their presence. When both of these conditions are met, the human being is capable of forming concepts of the world. These concepts take shape in the information that the senses have provided.

The process of forming concepts is one of construing *general* features from qualitative particulars. The perception of the qualitative world is always fragmented: we never see a particular immediately, in an instant. Time is always involved.[9] General configurations are formed – that is, built up from parts to wholes. Through time they yield structured patterns that constitute a set. The patterns formed in this way are concepts. They are root forms of experience that we are able to recall and to manipulate imaginatively.

The importance of the senses in concept formation is that: (i) no concepts can be formed without sensory information;[10] (ii) the degree to which the particular senses are differentiated has a large effect on the kind and subtlety of the concepts that are formed; and (iii) without concepts formed as images (whether these images are visual, auditory, or in some other sensory form), image surrogates – words, for example – are meaningless.[11]

It is easy to see how such concrete concepts as dog or chair, red or blue, depend upon sensory information. But what about such abstract concepts as justice, category, nation, infinity? I would argue that these words are nothing more than meaningless noises or marks on paper unless their referents can be imagined. Unless we have a conception of justice, the word is empty. Unless we can imagine infinity, the term is nothing more than a few decibels of sound moving through space. I do not mean to imply that we conjure up an image every time we hear a word. Our automatic response mechanisms make this unnecessary. But when I say, 'The man was a feckless mountebank,' the statement will have meaning only if you have referents for 'feckless' and 'mountebank.' If you do not, then you turn to a friend or a dictionary for other words whose images allow you to create an analogy. It is through such analogies or through illustrative examples that so-called abstract concepts take on meaning. Concepts, in this view, are not linguistic at base; instead, they are sensory. The forms concepts take are as diverse as our sensory capacities and the abilities we have developed to use them.

The process of concept formation is of particular importance in the development of scientific theory. In the social sciences, for example, theoreticians form concepts by construing social situations in ways that others have not noticed. Terms such as class, social structure, adaptation, role, status, and reinforcement are meaningful because they bracket aspects of the social world for us to experience.[12] They call to our attention qualities of the world that otherwise would have gone unseen. But the reality is in the flesh and blood of experience, not simply in the words. Put another way, there is an icon – a stylized image of reality – underlying any term that is meaningful. The makers of such icons are people we regard as perceptive or insightful. Indeed, the Latin root of 'intuition' is *intueri*, meaning to look upon, to see. In the beginning there was the image, not the word.

One important characteristic of concepts is that they can be not only recalled but imaginatively manipulated. We can combine qualities we have encountered to form entities that never were but that might become: hence unicorns, helixes, ideals of perfection toward which we strive, and new tunes to whistle. We can construct models of the world from which we can derive verbal or numerical propositions or from which we can create visual or auditory images. The point is that, while the sensory system provides us with information about the world in sensory form, our imaginative capacities – when coupled with an inclination toward play – allow us to examine and explore the possibilities of this information.[13] Although our imaginative lives might be played out in solitary fantasy or daydreaming, imagination often provides the springboard for expression. How is experience expressed? What vehicles are used? What skills are employed? And what do the arts have to do with it? It is to that side of the cognitive coin that I now turn.

Thus far I have emphasized the cognitive function of the sensory systems, and I have pointed out that concepts formed from sensory information can be recalled and manipulated through imagination. But thus far, this manipulation of concepts has been private, something occurring within the personal experience of individuals. The other side of the coin deals with the problem of externalization. In some way an individual must acquire and employ a form that can represent to self and to others what has been conceptualized. This task requires what I call a *form of representation*.[14] The problem of representing conceptions is a problem of finding or inventing equivalents for those conceptions. In this task, the form or forms to be employed must themselves appeal to one or more of the senses. A visual concept, for example, might be externalized in a form that is visual, or the form might instead be auditory, verbal, or both. Thus, for example, we could represent an imaginary stream of rolling and flowing blue amoebic shapes either visually or through sound. The stream might be described through words, or it might be represented through movement – perhaps dance. Regardless of the form we select, it must be one that the sensory systems can pick up. Put another way, the form must be empirical.

The kind of information that we are able to convey about what we have conceptualized is both constrained and made possible by the forms of representation that we have access to and are able to use. Some of the things an individual knows are better represented by some forms than others. What one can convey about a river that slowly wends its way to the sea will be significantly influenced by the form of representation one chooses to use. The same holds true for portrayals of classrooms, teaching, love affairs, and memorable cities one has visited.

Consider suspense. Almost all of us are able to invent a way of conveying suspense through music. From old cowboy movies and mystery dramas on radio and television, we already have a repertoire of models to draw upon. But think about how suspense would be represented through painting or sculpture. Here the problem becomes much more difficult. Why? Because suspense is a temporal experience, and painting and sculpture are largely spatial. It is more difficult to use the latter to represent the former than to use music, which itself is temporal.

Some forms of representation can illuminate some aspects of the world that others cannot. What a person can learn about the world through visual form is not likely to be provided through auditory form. What an individual knows takes shape in the empirical world only through a vehicle or vehicles that make knowing public. The vehicles we use for this purpose are the forms of representation.

Although I have described the externalization of concepts as one-directional – that is, as moving from inside out – the process is actually reciprocal. For example, what a person knows how to do affects what he or she conceptualizes. If you walk around the world with black and white film in your camera, you look for contrasts of light and dark, for texture, for patterns of shadow against buildings and walls. As Ernst Gombrich put it, 'Artists don't paint what they can see, they see what they can paint.' The ability to use a form of representation skilfully guides our perception. The process flows, as it were, from representation to conception as well as from conception to representation.

Dialectical relationships between conception and representation occur in other ways as well. For example, the externalization of a conception through a form of representation allows the editing process to occur. By stabilizing what is evanescent, the conception can be modified, abbreviated, sharpened, revised, or discarded altogether. Further, in the process of representation new concepts are formed. Indeed, the act of discovery through expression is so important that R.G. Collingwood describes its presence as the difference between art and craft.[15] The craftsman knows how to do a job well, but produces nothing essentially new. The artist not only has the skills of the craftsman but discovers new possibilities as work progresses. The *work* of art is to make expressive form become a source of surprise, a discovery, a form that embodies a conception not held at the outset.

The selection of a form of representation does not adequately resolve the question of how that form, once selected, becomes 'equivalent' to the conception. I suggest that we secure equivalence by treating forms of representation in one of three ways. The first of these modes of treatment is *mimetic*, the second is *expressive*, and the third is *conventional*.

Mimetic modes of treatment are efforts to imitate the surface features of perceived or conceptualized forms, within the constraints of some material. Early examples of mimesis are the running animals found on the walls of the Lascaux Caves. According to Gombrich, the history of art is replete with efforts to create illusions that imitate the visual features of the environment as it was or as it was imagined.[16] But mimesis as a way of treating a form of representation is not limited to what is visual. Mimesis occurs in auditory forms of representation, such as music and voice, and in movement through dance. Mimesis is possible in any of the forms used to provide information that the senses can pick up.

As I have already said, the creation of an equivalent for a conception is always both constrained and made possible by the medium a person employs. Different media appeal to different sensory systems. Thus, when a person transforms visual conceptions into sound or movement, he or she must find what Rudolf Arnheim calls the 'structural equivalent' of the conception within the medium he or she elects to use.[17] Such transformation requires the invention of analogies.

In language, analogic functions are performed by metaphor. When we move from the auditory to the visual, however, we must create a structural equivalent between the auditory and the visual. For example, the sounds 'ooo loo loo' and 'eee pee pee' are represented best by two very different kinds of graphic lines – one waving, the other pointed or jagged. Humans have the capacity to perceive and grasp these structural equivalences even when they take shape in different forms of representation – one visual, the other auditory. Thus mimesis, the business of imitating the surface features of a conceptualization within the limits of some medium, is one way to secure equivalence between a conception and its forms of representation.

The second way to do this is by treating the forms expressively. By expressively, I mean that what is conveyed is what the object, event, or conception expresses – not what it looks like. Thus 'sorrow' can be represented mimetically, but it can also be represented expressively. In the arts, this expressive mode of treatment is of particular interest: the tense nervousness of Velasquez's Pope Innocent X, the celebration of color in a Sam Francis, the asceticism of a late Barnett Newman, the ethereal quality of Helen Frankenthaler's work, the symbolic undertones of an Edward Hopper, the crisp architecture of Bach's fugues, the romantic expansiveness of Beethoven's Seventh Symphony, the lighthearted whimsy of the poetry of e e cummings. What these artists have created are expressive images. In general, mimesis is a minor element in their works, used only to complement the dominant intent. Pablo Picasso succinctly stated the importance of the expressive mode of treatment in art when he said, 'A painter takes the sun and makes it into a yellow spot, an artist takes a yellow spot and makes it into the sun.'

By contrast, the conventional model of treatment uses an arbitrary sign, on whose meaning society has agreed, to convey that meaning. Thus words and numbers are meaningful, not because they look like their referents but because we have agreed that they shall stand for them. The use of convention is, of course, not limited to words and numbers. Swastikas, crosses, six-pointed stars, the iconography of cultures past and present are all examples of visual conventions. Conventions in music take such forms as anthems, wedding marches, and graduation processionals.

In much of art the three modes of treatment are combined. Erwin Panofsky made his major contribution to the history of art – to the study of iconography – by describing these relationships.[18] The works of Jasper Johns, Marc Chagall, Joseph Cornell, Jack Levine, Robert Rauschenberg, and Andy Warhol demonstrate the ingenious ways in which visual artists have exploited all three modes of treatment in their effect to convey meaning.

I hope that I have made my point clear: any form of representation one chooses to use – visual, auditory, or discursive – must also be treated in some way. Some forms tend to call forth one particular mode of treatment. The treatment of mathematics, for example, is essentially conventional, even though we may recognize its aesthetic qualities. The visual arts, by contrast, tend to emphasize the mimetic and the expressive. Language tends to be treated conventionally and expressively (save for occasional instances of onomatopoeia, which are obviously mimetic). The forms we choose provide potential options. The options we choose give us opportunities to convey what we know and what we are likely to experience.

Just as any form of representation we elect to use must be treated in a particular way, the elements within that form must also be related to each other. This relationship constitutes a syntax, an arrangement of parts used to construct a whole. Some forms of representation, such as mathematics and propositional discourse, are governed rather rigorously by publicly codified rules, through which the operations applied to such forms are to be performed. To be able to add, one must be able to apply correctly a set of prescribed operations to a set of numerical elements. To be able to punctuate, one must follow certain publicly articulated rules so that the marks placed within a sentence or paragraph are correct. Similarly, in spelling, rules govern the arrangements of elements (letters) that constitute words. There are only two ways to spell most words in English: correctly or incorrectly. Forms of representation that are treated through convention tend to emphasize the rule-governed end of the syntactical continuum. When forms are treated in this way, the scoring of performance can be handled by machines, because the need for judgment is small.

Forms of representation that are treated expressively have no comparable rules. There are, of course, rules of a sort to guide one in making a painting of a particular style or designing a building of a particular architectural period. But the quality of performance in such forms is not determined by measuring the extent to which the rules were followed (as is done for spelling and arithmetic). Instead, quality is judged by other criteria – in some cases, criteria that don't even exist prior to the creation of the work. Syntactical forms that are open rather than closed, that allow for the idiosyncratic creation of relationships without being regarded as incorrect, are figurative in character. Thus it is possible to array forms of representation not only with respect to their modes of treatment but in relation to the ends of the syntactical continuum toward which they lean. In general, the arts lean toward the figurative. That is why, given the same task, 30 students in music, poetry, or visual art will create 30 different solutions, all of which can be 'right,' while 30 students in arithmetic will – if the teacher has taught effectively – come up with identical solutions. That is also why the arts are regarded as subjective: one cannot apply a conventionally defined set of rules to determine whether the meanings that are conveyed are accurate. Idiosyncratic arrangements are encouraged when figurative syntaxes are employed.

The importance of this distinction between rule-governed and figurative syntactical emphases becomes apparent when we consider the kinds of cognitive processes that each type of syntax elicits. Learning of rules fosters acquiescence: one learns to *obey* a rule or to *follow* it. Figurative syntaxes, by contrast, encourage invention, personal choice, exploratory activity, and judgment. The use of forms whose syntax is figurative is an uncertain enterprise, since there are no formally codified rules to guide judgments. The student, like the artist, is thrown on his or her own resources. How does one know when the painting is finished, the poem completed, the story ended? There is no predefined standard by which to check a solution. There is no correct answer given in the back of the book, no procedure for determining proof. The necessary cognitive operations are what were known, in earlier psychological jargon, as 'higher mental processes.' At the least, tasks that emphasize the figurative give people opportunities to form new structures, to make speculative decisions, and to act upon them. Such tasks also enable people to learn to judge – not by applying clear-cut standards, but by appealing to a form of rationality that focuses on the rightness of a form to a function.

It would be well at this point to recall the theme of this article, the role of the arts in cognition and curriculum. I began by describing a commonly held view: cognition requires that ideas be linguistically mediated, whereas the arts are expressive and affective activities depending more upon talent than intelligence or cognition. I next analyzed the role of the senses in concept formation, arguing that all concepts are basically sensory in character and that concept formation requires the ability to perceive qualitative nuances in the qualitative world and to abstract their structural features for purposes of recall or imaginative manipulation. From there I moved to a discussion of the task of representation. An individual who wishes to externalize a concept must find some way of constructing an equivalent for it in the empirical world. To do this, people invent new forms of representation or borrow from those already available in the culture. Because these forms can be treated in different ways and because they appeal to different sensory systems, the kind of meanings each yields is unique. What we can convey in one form of representation has no literal equivalent in another. I have labeled the modes of treating these forms as mimetic, expressive, and conventional. Because the elements within forms of representation can be ordered according to different rules, I have identified a syntactical continuum, highly rule-governed at one end and figurative at the other. The rule-governed end of the continuum prescribes the rules of operations that must, by convention, be followed in ordering those elements. The figurative end allows maximum degrees of latitude for idiosyncratic arrangement. The former is more of a code; the latter, more of a metaphor.

But what is the significance of such analysis for education? What bearing does it have on what we do in school? What might it mean for what we teach? There are four implications, I believe, for the conduct of education and for education theory.

First, the view that I have advanced makes it impossible to regard as cognitive any mental activity that is not itself rooted in sensory forms of life. This expands our conceptions of intelligence and literacy. Any conception of intelligence that omits the ordering of qualities through direct experience is neglecting a central feature of intellectual functioning. But no intelligence test that is published today includes such tasks. The models of mind that underlie current tests assign only marginal intellectual status to what is an intellectual activity. One no more plays the violin with one's fingers than one counts with one's toes. In each case, mind must operate, and the kind and number of opportunities a person is given to learn will significantly affect the degree to which his or her ability develops. The concepts of talent and lack of talent have been used too long to cover up weak or non-existent programs in the arts. To be sure, individual aptitudes in the arts vary, but such differences also exist in other content areas. So-called lack of talent is too often nothing more than an excuse for absent opportunity. It also serves as a self-fulfilling prophecy.

Second, the view that I have advanced recognizes that the realm of meaning has many mansions. Science, for example, despite its enormous usefulness, can never have a monopoly on meaning because the form of representation it employs is only one among the several that are available. It is not possible to represent or to know everything in one form. The way Willy Loman conveys his inability to cope with a sinking career can only be represented through the expressive treatment of form that Arthur Miller employed in *Death of a Salesman*. The quality of space in the paintings of Georgio De Chirico or Hans Hoffman depends on the artists' arrangements of visual images; it cannot be rendered through number. When Dylan Thomas wrote, 'Do not go gentle into that good night,/old age should burn and rage at close of day;/rage, rage against the dying of the light,'[19] he conveyed a message about being in the anteroom of death that cannot be translated fully, even in propositional prose.

What this means for education is that – insofar as we in schools, colleges, and universities are interested in providing the conditions that enable students to secure deep and diverse forms of meaning in their lives – we cannot in good conscience omit the fine arts. Insofar as we seek to develop the skills for securing such meanings, we must develop multiple forms of literacy. Such meanings do not accrue to the unprepared mind. The task of the schools is to provide the conditions that foster the development of such literacy. At present, for the vast majority of students, the schools fail in this task.

Third, educational equity is one consequence for students of the change in education policy that my arguments suggest. As I have already pointed out, the benefits derived from excellence in differing forms of representation are not equal. Students who perform at outstanding levels in the fine arts do not have these grades taken into account when they apply for admission to colleges and universities. The beneficiaries of the funds allocated to education for the gifted often do not include students whose gifts are in the fine arts.[20] The amount of school time devoted to cultivating abilities in the arts is extremely limited; hence, students with abilities and interests in the arts are denied the opportunities that students in science, mathematics, or English receive.

Such policies and practices amount to a form of educational inequity. This inequity would cease if the arguments I have presented were used as grounds for decisions about the allocation of school time, about the criteria used to identify gifted students, and about the aptitudes suitable for college and university study. It is an anomaly of the first order that a university should confer credit in the fine arts for courses taken on its own campus and deny credit to students who have taken such courses in high schools. At present, that's the way it is.

Finally, the view I have presented implies that the cultivation of literacy in, for example, visual and auditory forms of representation can significantly improve a student's ability to use propositional forms of representation. The ability to create or understand sociology, psychology, or economics depends on the ability to perceive qualitative nuances in the social world, the ability to conceptualize patterns from which to share what has been experienced, and the ability to write about them in a form that is compelling. Without such perceptivity, the content of writing will be shallow. Without the ability to manipulate conceptions of the world imaginatively, the work is likely to be uninspired. Without an ear for the melody, cadence, and tempo of language, the tale is likely to be unconvincing. Education in the arts cultivates sensitive perception, develops insight, fosters imagination, and places a premium on well-crafted form.

These skills and dispositions are of central importance in both writing and reading. Without them, children are unlikely to write – not because they cannot spell but because they have nothing to say. The writer starts with vision and ends with words. The reader begins with these words but ends with vision. The reader uses the writer's words in order to see.

The interaction of the senses enriches meaning. The arts are not mere diversions from the important business of education; they are essential resources.

Notes

1. These distinctions are reified most clearly in the customary separation between the cognitive and the affective domains, which are typically discussed as if they were independent entities or processes.
2. See especially (1951) *The Republic* (trans CORNFORD, F.M.) New York, Oxford University Press.
3. INHELDER, B. and PIAGET, J. (1958) *The Growth of Cognitive Thinking from Childhood to Adolescence*, (trans PARSONS, A. and MILGRAM, S.) New York, Basic Books.

4. See, for example, SCHAFF, A. (1973) *Language and Cognition*, New York, McGraw-Hill.
5. ROSENSHEIN, B. 'Classroom Instruction,' in GAGE, N.L. (Ed.) (1976) *Psychology of Teaching*, 75th Yearbook of the National Society for the Study of Education, Part 1, Chicago, University of Chicago Press, pp. 335–71.
6. If an elementary teacher provides one hour of instruction in art and one hour of instruction in music each week, the percentage of instructional time devoted to both is about 7%. Many teachers provide less time than this.
7. The University of California System, like many other state universities, provides no credit for grades received in the fine arts when computing grade-point averages for students seeking admission.
8. *The Dictionary of Psychology* Cambridge, Riverside Press, 1934.
9. The acquisition of visual information over time is a function of micro-movements of the eye and brain called saccades.
10. Insofar as something is conceivable, it must, by definition, be a part of human experience. Experience without sensory content is an impossibility.
11. This view argues that the reception and organization of sensory material require the use of intelligence. Intelligence is not something that one applies after experiencing the empirical world. Rather, it is a central factor in the process of experience.
12. See WEITZ, M. (1956) 'The Role of Theory in Aesthetics,' *Journal of Aesthetics and Art Criticism*, September, pp. 27–35.
13. In a sense, play is the ability to suspend rules in order to explore new arrangements. See SUTTON-SMITH, B. (Ed.), (1979) *Play and Learning* New York: Halsted Press.
14. This concept is elaborated in greater detail in my 1982 book, *Cognition and Curriculum. A Basic for Deciding What to Teach.* New York, Longman Inc.
15. COLLINGWOOD, R.G. (1958) *Principles of Art* New York, Oxford University Press.
16. GOMBRICH, E.H. 'Visual Discovery Through Art,' in HOGG, J. (Ed.) (1969) *Psychology and the Visual Arts* Middlesex, England Penguin Books.
17. ARNHEIM, R. (1954) *Art and Visual Perception* Berkeley, University of California Press.
18. PANOFSKY, E. (1955) *Meaning in the Visual Arts: Papers in and on Art History* Garden City, N.Y., Doubleday.
19. THOMAS, D. 'Do Not Go Gentle into That Good Night' in *The Collected Poems of Dylan Thomas* New York, New Directions, 1953, p. 128.
20. Until a couple of years ago the Mentally Gifted Minor Program (MGM) in California – now Gifted and Talented Education (GTE) – did not include students who were gifted in the fine arts.

14 Conceiving and Representing: Their Implications for Educational Evaluation

The Current Context in Education

The nature of knowing and the character of the forms through which what is known is made public have not been salient themes in the training of educational evaluators. This chapter constitutes an effort to identify and discuss the processes of conception and representation, and to exemplify, at least partially, the implications of such ideas for practice and theory in evaluation. But to put this discussion into a context that will be meaningful we must start with a detour. We must start not with the nature of cognition, but with the context in which the schools find themselves today. Theory, or if a more modest term is more appropriate, perspectives, should in some way relate – as Dewey suggested – to the problems of men. They should relate to the problems with which people now cope, or should illuminate problems that through present perspectives go unseen. My aspiration here is to contribute to the realization of both goals: to provide some leads that can be used by those in the schools who must evaluate the processes and consequences of classroom life; and to identify issues and to describe problems that practitioners and theorists alike never knew they had. In no way does this chapter pretend to provide answers or blueprints for the solution of educational problems. We regard our work more in the spirit of heuristics than algorythmics. Its value is to be tested in what it suggests rather than what it resolves.

Anyone familiar with American education c.1980 cannot help but conclude that whether warranted or not, there is a feeling on the part of the American public that the schools of the nation are no longer as educationally effective as they once were. From various quarters one hears that high school students can no longer read, that 'bonehead

English' is oversubscribed, even for those admitted to universities, that the recruits to the armed forces cannot use the manuals necessary for operating even simple military equipment because their reading skills are so poor, and that test performance has been on a steady decline for over a decade.

One finds the covers of major magazines such as *Time* exclaiming that teachers can no longer teach because student discipline is so poor, and that many teachers, even if they could teach, cannot spell well enough to make what they teach worthwhile.[1] One hears on CBS Walter Cronkite, one of America's most respected commentators, hosting programs titled 'Is Anyone Out There Learning?' The mere fact that the question is raised in the first place is tacit condemnation of the educational quality of the schools.

What are the facts of the case? Has the quality of education declined? Are schools no longer as educationally effective as they once were? To those steeped in educational theory, answers of a definitive nature are very difficult to provide. What constitutes quality in education? Whose educational values should prevail? How adequate must the data be to make such judgments? In which communities is there a decline in educational quality, regardless of the particular way in which quality is conceptualized? Such queries are not hedges to protect professional status but efforts to avoid simplistic answers to complex questions. The quick, cocky answer in matters such as these can lead to solutions that create greater problems than the ones they were originally intended to resolve.

Yet, for all that, test scores *have* been dropping, and not in one indicator but in many. Harnischfleger and Wiley (1975) report that the drop in performance indicators has occurred not only in the much publicized Scholastic Aptitude Test, but in measures designed specifically to assess achievement in the so-called 'basic skills'. The drop in test scores has been one source of concern for that great mass called the American public, and it is by no means the only source of concern. America since the 1960s has undergone a period of enormous social change. The young of the sixties made it quite clear that conventional values and lifestyles were not necessarily sacrosanct, that a great many were not willing to participate in what they regarded as an immoral war, that they and other minorities wanted to have more than a token voice in shaping social policies. It was in the sixties that the civil rights movement was tested, it was in the sixties that the innovative federally funded programs of the Great Society came into being, and it was in the sixties that the American family, as the hub of American life, was brought into question, first by the young and then later by Margaret Mead (1980) who, as an anthropologist, reconceptualized the way in which 'family life' could be led.

Such developments are not, I believe, unrelated to the current drift of American education. The challenge to conventional values has been to a great many people a source of puzzlement and difficulty. The student whose school gives him an opportunity to design his own secondary school program presents something of an anomaly to parents who fully believe that the school authorities know best *and* that they should, therefore, prescribe what students should study. Schools without walls, flexible scheduling, open education, team teaching, schools within schools are regarded by many as forms of educational exotica that are in part responsible for what they believe to be a decline in the quality of education. When these forms of educational innovation are combined with the social upheavals that pervaded so much of the Sixties – the challenge to accepted conventional values, the redefinition of social aims, the emergence of a strong civil rights movement, the exploration of new forms of communal life – it becomes understandable that a return to a more conventional life in and out of schools should seem attractive.

America seems to want to go 'Back to the Basics'. 'Back to the Basics' is significant as a slogan in at least two senses. First, it calls for a return to the past rather than for an expedition into the future. What is needed is a retreat to older values, a return to what has been lost. One moves ahead by going backward. Second, the 'back to the basics' slogan calls attention to something that is basic in education, and for most people what is basic is no mystery: the ability to read, the skills of arithmetic, and the competencies needed to write clear prose, in a word, the three Rs. What the 'back to the basics' signifies is, I am suggesting, not simply an educational prescription designed to raise test scores, but a symptom of a larger social malaise that is seeking the stability of the familiar in the context of the present and a return to the past as a way of stabilizing what appears to many a destabilized social life in America. The manifestations of this movement backwards to recapture older, more enduring, values emerge in the politics of the day, in the rise of evangelical religious fundamentalism,[2] a fundamentalism that is increasingly active in the political arena, in the reinstitution of capital punishment,[3] in the fiscal conservatism that is so general in the nation, in the failure of the Equal Rights Amendment, and in the ubiquitous nostalgia for the 1920s on the one hand and the growing interest in nature, natural foods, health care, and the like on the other. We seem, as a nation, to be yearning to recapture a life that never was for most of us, while at the same time we are captivated by the dazzling possibilities and accomplishments of scientific technology. We are a nation that seems to want once again to sit with good friends close to a warm fire, drinking our favorite brand of beer, while our meal is being cooked in a microwave oven in the next room.

The combination of these factors, both historical and technological, has set the tone for the schools of America in the 1980s. I say tone because the practices and prescriptions that have emerged in American schools during the past decade are an offshoot of a more general *weltanschung*; there is a basic compatibility between the way the nation goes as a whole and what it expects of its schools. When conventional values are threatened, when the divorce rate approximates the rate of marriage, when the adolescent suicide rate increases tenfold over the decade, when the nuclear family is no longer for many the accepted model of family life, people seek a rock on which to stand, something to stabilize them in the flux and flow of social change; and they look to the schools as one such rock, as a bastion of stability, a kind of haven in which the young can be socialized in the older, more familiar ways. The consequences for schools are predictable. Consider its impact on curriculum.

When the public demand is for a return to the basics, when the basics are defined as the three Rs, when public schools are judged by their performance on the three Rs, it is not likely that significant amounts of time and attention will be devoted in elementary schools, in particular, to subjects that are not directly related to student performance in reading, writing, and arithmetic. Teachers who once operated on the assumption that children needed a balanced curriculum – even though the concept of balance itself was not well defined – would with good conscience plan field trips, encourage projects in science, plan group activities in the social studies, develop art and music programs in their classes, pay significant attention to the social and emotional well-being of their students. Many teachers still do. However, such programs swim upstream. Teachers who once devoted as little as ten per cent of their formal classroom instructional time to art or music in the elementary school curriculum do so at the risk of being regarded as frivolous in the utilization of one of the school's most precious resources: time. Such a use of time would not be positively sanctioned by a great many school principals who know, as do teachers, that student growth in the fine arts, even if it should develop by spectacular leaps and bounds, would not show up on the tests that are now used to assess the quality of education. And what principal can endure the enmity that would flow from a community that believed his/her school was wasting their children's time and jeopardizing their chances for educational mobility by paying so much attention to what is 'nice but not necessary', to quote Harry Broudy's (1979) telling phrase. The answer is all too clear: only a few. Time cannot be devoted to support programs that are consistent with one's philosophic commitments when one knows that one is to be evaluated on other criteria.

Support for a restricted array of curriculum content comes also from researchers who have focused on what is called 'time on task'. During the past decade a great deal of educational research has focused on the use of time in school.[4] Researchers have asked questions about the ratio of time devoted to formal instruction and time devoted to problems of management and discipline, to questions dealing with the amount of time devoted to each of the subjects taught in school, and to questions dealing with time allocated by the teacher in relation to the time in which students are engaged in the time that has been allocated. Perhaps the major single general conclusion that can be drawn from such studies is that the amount of time allocated to particular content areas within the curriculum has a significant bearing on the level of achievement students attain. Put more prosaically, children who are given an opportunity to learn something are more likely to learn it than those who are not.

What the results of such research have suggested for some researchers is summed up by Barak Rosenshein[5] as follows:

> The message in this section seems clear. The stronger the academic emphasis, the stronger the academic results. Time spent on reading and numbers is associated with growth in those areas, whereas time spent in other areas appears to detract from growth in reading and mathematics. Furthermore, there are *no* non-academic activities that yielded positive correlations with reading and mathematics achievement. This finding is somewhat surprising, since it has frequently been argued that some of these other activities contribute to reading achievement by motivating students or by providing additional stimulation or practice. Such indirect enhancement was not evident in this study.

Neither in this quotation nor in the article in which it appears is there any discussion of the implications of such research conclusions for a more generous conception of education than is implied in the quotation. No discussion is provided of the possible benefits of exposure to other curricular areas, no analyses of the possible trade-offs among the things learned in different content areas, and no examination of the ways in which skills acquired in some fields emerge in others. The conclusion, to the contrary, is straightforward. 'The stronger the academic emphasis, the stronger the academic results'. What occurs here is the legitimation from the research literature of curriculum practices that they themselves limit what children have access to in school. Without adequate interpretation of the educational implications of the research, it is easy to continue to move toward a restrictive view of curriculum content, and this in the name of improved educational quality.

The impact of the current cultural ethos on schools is in no way limited to what schools emphasize. While the character of curriculum content is a fundamental influence on what students learn (the surest way to reduce the probability of learning something is to eliminate opportunities to learn it), the manner in which students are taught also significantly influences what they will learn. In artistic terms, form is content, *how* one teaches has a significant bearing upon *what* one learns. Or in Dewey's words, 'It is one of the major educational fallacies that a student learns only what he is being taught at the time'.[6]

In what sense have teaching practices changed, and what is their impact on what students learn in school? How do changes in practice relate to the context or social ethos in which the schools function? It is to these questions that we now turn.

One aspect of the conservative ethos that has emerged in America during the past decade takes the form of educational accountability. Not only are goals to be defined with precision, but methods must also be employed that will provide evidence of their accomplishment. To be accountable in this sense is to give an account of what has been attempted and what has been accomplished. Not an unreasonable expectation. Teachers and school administrators should have aims, they should know where they are headed, and they should be able to provide evidence regarding what the students have learned. Yet the spirit of the move toward educational accountability does not stop with general goals or with informal evidence regarding the consequences of teaching. Goals need to be precise, they need to specify the behaviors the student is to display, according to some they need to identify criterion levels to be achieved, and the means through which they are assessed need to be objective and replicable. More of those matters will be addressed later, but here let us focus upon the consequences of this view upon teaching.

Teachers come to believe that in order for precision to occur in goal formation, small units of behavior are more appropriate than configurations of behavior at general levels of abstraction. The more global a goal is, the more complex its assessment. Teachers also come to believe that if they are to be held accountable for the achievement of goals that they formulate, it would be prudent not to formulate goals that might be difficult to achieve. The payoff for the teacher who functions within this system is the achievement of the goals they select, not the achievement of complex or difficult ones. Teachers also come to realize that the achievement of goals that are related to small units of material to be learned makes it possible to keep an account record for each child regarding their achievement on these units. For some teachers such accounting takes the form of contracts between student and teacher, for others it is handled through workbooks. Programs are laid out in advance. They are individualized for each child and the teacher-cum-accountant records achievement on small units of material, behaviorally defined and criterion referenced. The assumption is that these small units eventually aggregate into complex wholes.

The practical consequences of this approach to teaching and learning for students and teachers are several. First, prediction and control of student behavior looms as a prime virtue. The goals specified in advance become a contract between teacher and school district and between student and teacher. The exploration of educational opportunities that emerge during the course of the school year are given short shrift; they are not a part of the original scheme of things. Second, pupil-teacher planning diminishes, since to give students a meaningful role in the formulation of curriculum activities and educational goals is to risk taking directions that do not coincide with the goals originally formulated. Third, individualization means in a great many classrooms that the benefits of group deliberation and class planning also go by the boards. In most classrooms individualization means that virtually all students proceed down the same paths toward the same ends but at different rates of speed. Fourth, because students do not participate in the conceptualization of ends, their role is limited to the execution of means instrumental to the achievement of ends defined by others. Conception is separated from execution, means are severed from ends, and meaning in the intrinsic sense is relinquished by the use of artificial incentives designed to motivate the student's activity.

But in such a system standardization is possible, and with standardization uniform achievement standards can be formulated and their attainment assessed. Surprise, ingenuity, discovery, the sense of play and exploration have little place in such a scheme. Put another way, schools become increasingly academic and decreasingly intellectual.

Seldom in the consideration of educational innovations, whether to the left or to the right, is the question asked: 'But what is in it for the teacher?' For many teachers the accountability movement and the consequences I have identified have dissipated the satisfactions they sought and once had from teaching. The same constraints that limit students to prespecified goals and preformulated workbooks also constrain the teacher. The elementary school teacher whose major source of pedagogical satisfaction was in developing with children projects in the social studies, projects that would take on a life and momentum that might pervade the classroom for a week or two, now feels unable to allow this to occur. The teacher hears from *Time* and from Walter Cronkite, from the Gallup and the Harris polls, from businessmen and from Navy recruiters, that students cannot read, write, or cipher. The teacher knows that he/she will be held account-able for the scores his/her students receive. In such a climate personal joys in teaching must be set aside for the 'real' business of the schools. In the meantime, school truancy becomes a national problem and school teachers – the best of them – leave teaching to take positions where the pay is larger and the criticism smaller.

The reduction of the scope of the curriculum and the fragmenta-tion of what is taught are two general consequences of the effort to rationalize educational practice within the scope of the educational accountability paradigm. These consequences are not trivial; they constitute an educational way of life. Yet as important as they are, it is the assumptions about evaluation and objectivity that constitute the heart of the movement. The logic of the movement looks something like this.

Student performance as measured by a variety of achievement tests has been falling, thus providing prima facie evidence that schools are not as educationally effective as they once were. To make them more effective, greater attention must be paid to the teaching of basic skills. But attention in terms of more time, while laudatory, is not enough; goals for each grade level in the basic skill areas must be specified. Furthermore, they must be specified in a way that makes them amenable to objective evaluation. To be objectively evaluated they must be stated in a form that makes measurement possible, since through measurement objectivity is maximized. Once statements of goals are translated into testable items of performance, criteria defining acceptable standards for performance must be defined. Once defined and tests constructed that measure the achievement of behaviorally stated goals, students are to be tested to provide evidence of the effectiveness of the instruction they have received. Once such data are secured, information can be provided to the relevant publics so that they may know how effective the schools have been, which schools and which teachers should be rewarded, which need assistance, and which need a change in personnel. Through the monitoring of student performance the educational productivity of the school and of teachers can be appraised and the public informed about what it is receiving for its investment in education.

At first glance the logic seems impeccable. Objectivity, if one means by that term the replicability of observations, can be increased when conventions are defined and specifications for the use of those conventions provided. What then are the problems? What makes the evaluation practices used to assess competency less than satisfactory, and what makes a less than satisfactory process so widely used in the schools?

One reason the process of evaluation, as defined through what is essentially a testing approach to evaluation, is so significant in shaping practice is because evaluation results have a public status that neither curriculum nor teaching have. The results of evaluation practices are public results, they can be inspected and appraised by principals, by other teachers, by parents, and by the community at large. Goals formulated for the curriculum and even what is taught are by comparison vague and general. They are statements having to do more with intentions than with results. Furthermore, the criteria through which their adequacy can be appraised are not well known. Few parents, and unfortunately even many school administrators, do not know what questions to ask when appraising educational goals or curriculum content. Evaluation results can be rank ordered, schools and classrooms can be compared, and when the data are reported on a quantitative scale an aura of precision exists that facilitates comparison and that easily leads to the conclusion that the higher the students or schools score, the higher the quality of educational practice, a conclusion that simply cannot by itself be defended.[7] Thus, one reason why evaluation is at the heart of the accountability movement is because evaluation procedures yield consequences that are substantially more significant in affecting the status of the school or the teacher than are other aspects of educational practice shaped by the movement. It is not the goals that drive the system as much as it is the way in which the system is to be evaluated: the form of the evaluation and the content to which it attends *become* the operational goals of the system.

A second source of difficulty with evaluation procedures used to measure competencies deals with the limits of measurement and the assumptions that are held about the nature of objectivity. These limitations are several. First, the use of a measure applied to a group consisting of individual events, say the performance of thirty students on some task, results in a description of those events on a common scale applied to dimensions that cut across the individuals in that group. For example, in evaluating writing skills, say in the area of composition, the features that constitute excellence in composition are treated as common across all compositions evaluated. The scores that are assigned derive from a common scale and are applied to dimensions of composition believed to be common to all compositions. The results of procedures based on such assumptions is that (i) characteristics not included in the dimensions are neglected; and (ii) the qualities that uniquely constitute excellence in one composition as compared to another might be entirely different, but because the score assigned is derived from a common scale, unique features of particular compositions are obfuscated. It is erroneously implied by such procedures that two or more compositions are of high, medium, or low quality for the same reasons, on the same dimensions, when in fact the reasons and the dimensions may be radically different.

A third problem deals with the fact that numbers simply cannot convey all that can and often needs to be said about the qualities that constitute educational objects or events of interest. Numbers are reporting devices. Their meaning derives from two sources, the scale of which they are a part and the referents they are used to represent. To know what a number means one needs to know its position on a scale and the qualities it is selected to represent. It is in the latter area that number is severely limited. No number looks like its referent; numbers are conventions, and the transformation of qualities experienced into such conventions *never*, without the ability to imagine the qualities of its referent, can 'contain' those qualities. This means that numerical indices as surrogates are not self-explanatory. They fail to portray even though by convention the operations that lead to certain scores are replicable and, hence, regarded as objective. Perhaps an example will make this point clear. A person's height is measured as five-foot-eleven-and-a-half inches. Individuals competent in measuring height will, time after time with small errors of measurement, conclude that this individual's height is five-foot-eleven-and-a-half inches. Insofar as replication occurs, we regard the numerical conclusion as an objective datum. But the number five-foot-eleven-and-a-half inches is not the same as the experience of five-foot-eleven-and-a-half inches; two individuals both five-foot-eleven-and-a-half inches can provide two very different experiences to an observer. One is slender and imperious, the other fat and slovenly. The experience of each, due to the pattern of qualities that constitutes each, is not represented by the measurement even though the same numerical conclusion can be reached on independent trials time after time. Thus, while we have an objective representation of a set of qualities, the objectivity is a function of the process of replication rather than a function of the re-presentation of the qualities the number stands for. It is only when one can imagine the referent to the numbers that we can know the meaning behind the numbers. For educationally relevant qualities this is extremely difficult to do. Indeed, even the same scores on sub-tests may be the result of different patterns of performance on those sub-tests, not to mention the comparability of total test scores or means among groups.

Furthermore, because objectivity is seen as such a prime virtue in evaluation, qualities that are difficult to measure reliably are often altogether neglected in evaluation. The so-called affective areas of learning are familiar examples. Because a rationalistic orientation to procedure provides the baseline criterion that method must meet, those aspects of educational life that are more easily susceptible to measurement command the attention of evaluators. What occurs is that methodological commitments influence the character of evaluation procedures and evaluation procedures influence the character of curriculum priorities. Curriculum priorities, in turn, influence the opportunities students will have access to, which in turn shapes the kind of mental skills they are able to develop. Put another way, the ethos of this historical period embraces a systematic and objectified approach to knowledge and necessitates the use of methods that yield conclusions that are replicable. Because quantification is a paradigm for conventionalized description, it is regarded as a necessary condition for achieving objectivity. The ethos of the time supports an epistemology that tends to neglect the idiosyncratic and those aspects of educational life that are difficult to objectify through measurement. What results is a biased assessment of the very life we are trying to understand and improve.

At the beginning of this section I said we would need to get into questions about the nature of conception and the forms humans use to make their conceptions public by way of a detour. That detour has moved through some of the terrain that constitutes the context for current practices in American education. I have taken this detour because I believe that the methods we employ and the aims we seek are a part of a larger social ideology. To understand what we do we need not only to know what goes on in schools, but we need also to peer below the surface of those practices in order to uncover the tacit assumptions on which they rest and to see how those assumptions connect with the social ideology of the time in which we live. In the course of my reading I have come across the work of a German sociologist, Ferdinand Toennies,[8] who has provided a pair of concepts that elegantly differentiates two major modes of social life, one of which seems to characterize quite nicely our current situation in America and in American schools. The distinctions that Toennies makes are between what he calls *Gemeinschaft* and what he refers to as *Gesselschaft*. According to Toennies, social arrangements can be characterized by the extent to which they emphasize two different styles of life. *Gesselschaft* is that style that emphasizes objectivity in human relations, moral detachment, order defined by rationally articulated rules. It is a social order in which explicitly developed criteria for defining status, role and function are the guide to proper action, and in which order, regularity, and a disposition towards abstract values are salient.

Gemeinschaft is characterized by organic rather than formal or mechanical relationships, where status emerges from the context in which individuals function and which varies with context. It characterizes a social order whose prime value is in the establishment of community and group identity as contrasted to *Gesselschaft*, which emphasizes society and individuality. Accordingly to Toennies, modern industrialization has led to personal anonymity, to, as Robert Nisbet[9] puts it, 'deprivation of the sense of organic relatedness to others'. Writing of Toennies' work, Nisbet says

> The kind of society that had for Adam Smith, David Ricardo, and other prophets of the industrial system, carried the promise of a higher freedom for modern man, carried something quite different for Toennies: not freedom, but increasing anonymity, displacement and deprivation of the sense of organic relatedness to others... The important point here, however, is the image that Toennies' classic acquired almost from the day of its publication and retained thereafter, of being profoundly negative in its representation of modern society as *Gesselschaft*,

which where Toennies meant the whole complex of impersonal, abstract, and anonymous relationships which characterized capitalism, nationalism, and all the forces of individual-
ism, bureaucratization, and secularism, which he could see
eating away at the social fabric.

Conversely, no reader can remain blind to Toennies extremely positive treatment of *Gemeinschaft* and of the social
structures and forms of human mentality associated with it. In
kinship, religion, village, and social class, overwhelming in
their medieval forms, Toennies found that kind of society
which he thought organic and vital and which had been largely
destroyed or greatly diminished under the impact of modernity.

Summarizing his views on the distinction he has made, Toennies writes

'*Gesselschaft* deals with the artificial construction of an aggregate
of human beings which superficially resembles *Gemeinschaft*
insofar as the individuals live and dwell together peacefully.
However, in *Gemeinschaft* they remain essentially united in spite
of all separating factors, whereas in *Gesselschaft* they are essentially separated in spite of all uniting factors.'

What strikes me as I think about the two modes of social life that
Toennies has described is the fit of *Gesselschaft* to our present condition
in the schools and in the society, while at the same time there emerge
groups intent on establishing communities within the Great Society
that can lead the kind of life that Toennies describes as *Gemeinschaft*.

The formalization of goals, the bureaucratization of evaluation
procedures, the stress on individualization, the need for objectified
evidence, the faith in hyper-rationalization of activity, the use of
contracts between teachers and students and teachers and school boards
as a way of defining responsibility, the preoccupation with hierarchical
relationships, the prescription of status, all fit the image of *Gesselschaft*
that Toennies has described. And at the same time, we see television
commercials portraying the warmth of communal life in order to sell
Macdonald's hamburgers, of male camaraderie in order to sell Bud-
weiser beer, of the recall of tradition in order to sell Mazola oil. There
seems to be a deprivation that the ad agencies have recognized, and like
the astute merchants that they are, they have exploited our sense of
deprivation to sell their wares.

Lest there be doubt about the relationship between the context I
have described and theory and practice in educational evaluation, I shall

make these relationships explicit here. Conceptions of educational practice, including practices in evaluation, are not natural entities; they are constructions of mind. Such constructions are influenced by the leading values of the society in which practitioners function. In our society we have developed a faith in the power of scientific rationality to help us resolve problems that we confront and to enable us to realize the values we aspire towards. At present our society appears to have an especially acute need to find stability; the world has changed in ways that are unsettling, the young appear to question older values, the schools do not appear to be effective. Stabilization is to be achieved by going back to older values, recapturing them as it were, and by instituting standardized methods of assessment that address themselves to publicly stated goals and which can be objectively appraised to determine the extent to which the goals have been attained. The character of the assessment procedures are such as to place great reliance upon quantification, thus increasing the probability of the replicability of the results. What is distrusted are processes that are exploratory in nature, that value surprise, that cultivate idiosyncrasy and ingenuity, that depend for their assessment on the sensibilities of individuals and that use reporting procedures that require interpretation and judgment. In a word, *Gesselschaft* dominates our approach to the improvement of educational practice and to the ways in which we believe we should assess its consequences. The burden of this book is to provide the grounds for using other modes of evaluation, not as a replacement for conventional ones, but in order to secure a rounder, more balanced understanding of what goes on in schools and what we reap as a result. The burden here is both theoretical and practical. The theoretical is not yet complete – and never will be – and the examples provided are simply that, examples of leads that need refinement. Let us, therefore, first turn to the basis for seeking new modes of evaluation in the first place, and then later to some of the efforts that have been made to develop these modes in the practical order.

Conception, Representation, and the Evaluation of Educational Practice

The previous section attempted to describe the context for educational practice in America and to link the ethos of the nation at this particular period in its history to beliefs that are held about the curriculum, about teaching, and about educational evaluation. Its mission was to make clear the fact that these aspects of practice are not immune to ideologies, and that any ideology or social way of life neglects some ways in which people can live and in which reality can be conceptualized. I have argued that *Gesselschaft* characterizes quite well the style in which America functions at present and that our efforts to rationalize practice and to ensure the effectiveness of schools has led to a neglect of content areas that do not lend themselves to rationalized methods. I have argued that such methods neglect the cultivation of certain modes of thought, and limit in significant ways the data we believe we can use to understand schools, classrooms, and the kind of life that students and teachers lead within them.

In this section I turn to evaluation in particular; as I have indicated, it constitutes the heartbeat of the accountability movement, it drives the priorities of the school, and it embodies the view of mind and the conception of knowing that is socially dominant. To secure a foothold on that terrain on which a wider and more adequate view of evaluation must be built we must start not with extant theories of evaluation but with an examination of the nature of mind and of the forms it uses to represent what it has come to know.

The fundamental question that any adequate theory of evaluation must address is not what can be evaluated, or how, or whether or not objectives have been achieved, but how it is that humans come to know in the first place. And in the second, how it is that they represent what they know to others. Without a conception of the ways in which knowing occurs and the forms through which it is represented the assumptions about cognition that now hold sway are likely to continue and the possibilities of broadening the dominant view of knowing, and thereby extending the grounds and methods of evaluation, are diminished. New conceptions of evaluation I am arguing need to be grounded in new views of mind.

The starting point of my discussion is the starting point for experience, the consequences of the sentient beings' interaction with the qualities of the environment. It is this interaction that generates what in educational and psychological circles is referred to as cognition. Although cognition is often regarded, indeed defined by some, as thinking that is mediated by language – as a kind of inner speech – cognition is a process far wider in scope. Cognition is a process through which the organisms achieve awareness. To engage in cognitive activity, to be cognizant of, to cognize, is not simply to think about the world through words or number, but in the first instance to be aware of the qualities of which it is constituted. This awareness is what we mean by cognition. In fact if the *Dictionary of Psychology* is any guide, it is the way in which cognition is defined. Cognition depends upon experience, and experience depends upon our ability to discern qualities, either those that emanate from the world or those that we generate as images in the privacy of our psychological life. What we cannot experience, we cannot know.

Why is it that in our educational and psychological discourse cognition has been identified with speech and number? Several reasons commend themselves. First, in the literature in these fields distinctions have been made between cognition and effect. The former refers to thinking while the latter refers to feeling. Thinking is associated with symbolic mediation, not with direct experience. Hence, language and number are regarded as the chief mediators of thought, and cognition and words and number are seen as being reciprocal in nature. Like buying and selling, one cannot do one without the other. For example, one writer on cognition describes the situation this way:

> When we adopt the monistic standpoint, we reject the claim that language and thinking can exist separately and independently of one another. Of course, we are talking about specifically *human* thinking, in other words about *conceptual* thinking. Thus we assert that in the process of cognition and communication, thinking and using a language are inseparable elements of one and the same whole. Integration is so perfect and interdependence is so precise that neither element can ever occur independently, in a 'pure' form. That is precisely why the functions of thinking and language may not be treated separately, let alone contrasted with one another.[10]

What we see here is a view that conceives of cognition – human cognition at least – as requiring discursive mediation, a view which incidently even one so steeped in the role of language in mentation as Noam Chomsky rejects.

A second reason for conceiving of cognition in terms of linguistically mediated thought is because of our conception of abstraction. We believe that concepts are general (which they are), and that to be general they must be abstract (which they must), and to be abstract they must be linguistic (which they do not). Thus, what is not linguistic is not cognitive and what is not cognitive must belong to lower realms of human functioning, the realm of the senses, of feeling, of the subjective, in other words to the non-cognitive aspects of human life. Indeed, it is not for nothing that mathematics, the subject considered most abstract and least dependent upon sense data, is also regarded as the apotheosis of human cognition.

A third reason is that in language there are rules of procedure, there is among formal languages such as those used in science and mathematics a logic and a grammar that increase the degree to which common meanings can be secured among the community of readers. Contrasted with expressive forms that have no comparable rules or criteria, meanings are personalized, they are less amenable to consensual validation, and they appear to be related in greater degree to the subjective, personal and imaginative life of individuals. Activities using such forms make verification tasks difficult, and since cognition is identified with knowing, and since knowing is wedded to 'truth tests', 'warranted assertion', and other forms of verification, processes that do not use language as a mediator or vehicle for expression are not regarded as cognitive.[11]

These views of cognition have a long history, one going back at least as far as Plato.[12] It is a tradition that has separated mind from body, thought from emotion, feeling from knowing, cognition from perception. Cognitive activity is widely regarded as a process so abstract that sense data are never considered a part of it. Sense data are considered particular, whereas thinking requires concepts and concepts are general. Sensory awareness is believed to be immediate, whereas cognition requires mediation. I find such views naive and wish to argue a wholly different case. I wish to argue that thinking always requires a content – we must think about something – and that at base that content is sensory. Put another way, I wish to argue that the senses play a crucial role in thinking, that we cannot think without the content that they provide, and that the senses are biologically given information pick-up systems through which that content is made available.

To say as I have that the senses play a crucial role in picking up information about the environment is not to suggest that the individual is merely a block of moist clay upon which the qualitative world impresses itself. The individual *construes* the world, his prior history, the frames of reference he can use; his needs and purposes perform a selective function in his interactions with the world. But without a fully functioning sensory system the qualities of the world are mute, and in silence the content for reflection is unavailable.

If we examine how the senses function, it becomes clear that they are qualitatively specific. That is, the senses are so designed that they are responsive to some but not all of the qualities that constitute the environment. The world is made up of qualities and the extent to which those qualities can be experienced depends upon the acuteness with which each of the sensory systems can function. Thus, with vision we are able to see those aspects of the environment that are visual, but we cannot with our eyes hear the sounds of the world. Through audition we are able to hear, but we cannot see. Through our ability to taste, the gustatory qualities of the world can be experienced, but not heard. And so it goes. We are biological creatures designed to be able to pick up information about the features of the world in which we live. What we know about those features depends initially on what our sensory systems pick up.

The significance of the senses in our developing awareness of the world might be illuminated by imagining for a moment that a red filter was placed over our eyes. What would we be able to see? Under such conditions the visual features of the world would not be eliminated from our experience, but the variety of qualities we could experience would be radically curtailed. We would experience no colors other than red and its value gradations. Whatever we would be able to see would fall within a highly restrictive color range. If we were congenitally blind, even the limited range of color would not be available. Thus it is with all of the senses; if any are impaired or not functioning the kind of information we receive from our contact with the world is reduced. In this sense the kind of consciousness we can achieve is dependent upon (i) the acuteness with which our sensory systems can function; and (ii) the variety in the qualities that constitute the environment we inhabit. When certain qualities are absent or restricted, the possibility of achieving certain levels of consciousness is also curtailed, as much as if the sensory systems were impaired. The ability to achieve any form of consciousness depends upon the interaction of the sentient being with a qualitative universe.[13] If sentiency is diminished, or if the qualities of the world are restricted, the character of consciousness is affected. When this occurs, the basis for knowing is also restricted.

Human experience is not limited to what the organism can experience directly. Human organisms have the capacity to recall and to imagine. Recall may be regarded as the retrieval of experience secured when the organism was in direct contact with the qualitative environment. We can remember what we ate for breakfast because we experienced breakfast only a few hours ago. Imagination is the creative reconstruction of recalled images so that experience is created that never was secured directly. We are able to picture ourselves eating a hearty breakfast consisting of foods we have seen but never tasted in a setting in which we have never been. Through imaginative processes we can construct events that are made up of elements of more prosaic experiences. The difference between recall and imagination is one of degree; in all recall there is alteration, no recalled experience – even so-called eidetic images – are identical with the experience from which they were derived.

The utilities of recall and imagination are considerable. When we are not in the presence of one of Bach's Brandenberg concerti we can hear it for ourselves as we walk to our office; when we are far from home we can recall our family and imagine sitting with them in the comfort of our living room. Our imagination – the central term of which is image – allows us to create experiences, to achieve modes of consciousness that are built upon the information that the senses provided in the first place.

To talk about the role of the senses in knowing and to relate sensory information to cognition may appear to some as incongruous. Sensory data has for decades been separated from cognition through the differentiation of sensation, perception, and cognition. My effort here is to bring the message to those in educational evaluation who embrace such distinctions that among the most sophisticated work in cognitive psychology, perception and cognition are no longer separated or regarded as independent processes. For example, Ulric Neisser states, 'Perception is a cognitive event'. And forty years earlier Dewey himself pointed out the intellectual aspects of perceptual activity.[14] Piaget underscores the transactional relationships among the processes he calls adaptation, relationships that depend upon the use of schema for purposes of accommodation and assimilation. To disregard the selective and adaptive character of the individual's interaction with the environment and to regard sensory information a function of some mindless process is to dismiss the organic relationships occurring with a living system. It is to reinstitute the separation between body and mind. The senses provide, I am arguing, the 'stuff' from which experience is secured; and experience is what is required for consciousness to arise. I am arguing further that because the nature of experience is directly related to the kind of information the particular senses pick up, when the senses are impaired or underdeveloped, or when the qualities to which they can react are unavailable, the form of consciousness that would otherwise have been secured will be absent. Further, that when such content is absent, the imagination will have little, *in that mode at least*, with which to work.

Given that the senses always interact with particular qualities of the environment, how is it that concepts which are general are formed from such particular interactions? The process of concept formation that Aristotle described moved from sensation, to experience, to memory, to generalization; it was a process that was inductive in character.[15] Other philosophers, most notably Mill, argued that concepts were mental constructions that were then tested in the empirical world. The argument offered by Mill, Locke, and most recently by Popper is deductive rather than inductive in character. The separation of mind from body, whether through a deductive or an inductive view of mind, does not appear to be satisfactory. The organism to be sure has genetically defined intellectual capacities, but these capacities require commerce with specific qualities in order to function. Kittens, for example, deprived of light from two to twelve weeks of age will be blind even after being put in an environment in which light is available after twelve weeks.[16] In the case of the kittens, what is latent cannot become manifest without certain forms of stimulation, in this case light. In humans the capacity to form general concepts is latent, indeed, it is necessary for survival. But to form concepts the qualities of the world must be available to the organism. In the transaction between particular events, the individual forms patterns which allow transfer of what has been experienced in one context to be applied to the next. Thus, a face seen from one angle, in one light, in one context will be recognized in another context; the individual child does not have to learn to cope with each situation as if it were entirely new. In this sense *every* concept formed, insofar as it is the grasping of the structural features of a particular, is a vehicle through which generalization occurs. That is why in the vernacular we say we learn through experience, not because we structure our lives to yield generalizations or because we randomly sample events from a universe through a table of random numbers, but because we recognize that the significance and meaning of particulars are not limited to the experiences secured from the particular at the moment. Particular events leave a residue that forms structures that are necessary for anticipating the future. Concepts that are formed through the images that the senses make possible provide the forms that are later named first through metaphor and still later through vernacular language and later still through the formal language of science. These initial concepts are the schema to which other experiences are assimilated: The universe is likened to a great machine and later to a cloud; the heart is first seen as a furnace and later as a pump. It is the basic structures or principles within particular machines, clouds, furnaces, and pumps that we use to make our world comprehensible, and it is our experience of them – how they look, sound, feel and taste that provides the basis for the primary conceptual image.

The argument presented thus far aimed at calling attention to the role that the senses perform in providing contact with the qualities of the world. But even more, I have argued that conception itself depends upon the information provided by the senses. We form our concepts, the images that organize or structure our conception of the world, through the information that each of the senses makes available. Because the content the senses provide is qualitatively specific, that is, because each of the senses provides information limited to different qualities of the world and because these qualities as experienced create different forms of consciousness, the character of our experience is directly related to what our senses make possible. Once available we can both recall and treat imaginatively these qualities, qualities that take shape as images. Thus conception depends upon sensory information but is not limited to the specific information that arises from particular contacts the individual has with the qualitative world. Through imagination we can recombine, extend, vivify, delete, and create images that insofar as the world is concerned never were – hence, unicorns, twenty-first century spaceships, models of mind, theories of motivation, and tunes you can whistle. Even more, conventional conceptions such as 'infinity', 'truth', 'virtue', and 'the double helix', are the fruits of the imagination. The content it provides constitutes much of the subject matter of our reflective life.

Thus far I have tried to sketch a picture that re-establishes the unity of sensation and cognition. Perhaps it would be useful to list the major points of the argument here.

1   The senses provide the means through which the qualities of the environment are experienced.
2   Each sensory system is sensitive to some, but not all environmental qualities.
3   The information picked up through the senses provides the basis for concept formation.
4   Once concepts are formed they can be recalled and treated imaginatively.
5   Conception, born of sense material, provides the basis for knowing.
6   The kind of knowing that is achieved depends upon the kinds of concepts formed which in turn depend upon (i) the sensory system employed; and (ii) the qualities available to the individual in the environment in which he/she functions.

These six points are important ones regarding the relationship of the sensory systems to conception, but concept formation is a private affair. It resides as an experience in the possession of an individual. If humans did not have a need to express and communicate what they have conceptualized, we would need go no farther than to pursue in greater depth the nature of conception. But humans fortunately do have a need to make public what they have conceptualized. Through the public articulation of conceptions our environment itself is enriched and the sources for our own concepts are broadened. Through the process of communication we are able to share what we have come to know. This public sharing constitutes a significant aspect of culture. Our problem now is to identify the means through which such sharing takes place, and for this task we must turn to what I have called the *forms of representation* that humans have invented to make public privately experienced conceptions.

Forms of Representation

Human conception is a private affair; it occurs within the experience of an individual. Because of the human's social nature, he has a need to express and to communicate what has been conceptualized to himself and to others. I say 'to himself' because, as we shall see, the process of expression occurs not simply through an empty tube through which conceptualizations are brought forward, but it is a process that itself shapes conception and provides the conditions that make its modification possible. To make public what is private some vehicle must be employed; these vehicles are forms that are used to represent the conceptions that have been achieved or that are formulated through the process of expression. Because conceptions are related to the information provided by the senses that are used in conceptualization (we can recall visually or kinesthetically, audially or tactilely, for example), the problem of expression is one of transformation. How shall experience, that is, say, tactile, be conveyed or made public in a way that does not vitiate its content? How does one move from the qualities of a particular experience into the public realm without destroying the meaning that the experience provided in the first place? Humans have historically had to cope with such a task, the task of inventing vehicles that made such transformation possible. One way to achieve this transformation is to employ a form that, itself, shares features of the initiating conception. If the conception is visual, one may employ a visual analogue in the public realm. But the use of public qualities that are veridical with the visual conception are not the only means through which such transformation and communication occur. Forms can be used that are not themselves visual, but which suggest visual features or convey the feeling that those features possessed. Music is one example. Program music often suggests visually through sound, while romantic music sounds like the feeling that the composer wishes to convey. Distinctions among *modes* of treatment will be discussed momentarily, but for now the point is that forms of representation must be invented to make public what is private, and these forms, if we examine the culture at large, are designed to present patterned qualities that are picked up by the sensory systems. Although forms of representation often combine information so that several senses are appealed to – cooking, film, drama, for example – in general, forms of representation are constructed that appeal dominantly to one or two of the senses at one time. Thus painting is, in general, more visual than auditory or kinesthetic; music more auditory than visual; dance more visual than auditory, gustatory or olfactory. These forms exist – including poetic, literary, and propositional language – because if what has been conceptualized is to have a public status, the use of such forms is necessary. Musical conceptions cannot be conveyed without a musical form of representation.

What is it that shall count as a form of representation? The examination of the culture will be instructive here. I make no attempt in this essay to provide a definitive or exhaustive list of the forms of representation. There can be no definitive or exhaustive list because forms of representation are human inventions and the inventions through which expression and communication occur have not been, nor are they likely to be, exhausted. Yet, some forms of representation have special social significance and have had a very long history. For example, speech and writing in its several forms, poetic, literary, and formal, visual art, music, dance, cooking, mathematics, and comparatively recently, film and holography. Such forms serve as crucially important means through which conceptions are publicly articulated, and because they appeal to different sensory systems, the kind of experience they are able to provide differs. There is every reason to believe that as technological developments occur, the forms of representation that individuals will have access to will also expand. The development of new devices for combining sound with tactile experience, of integrating words with color, and the use of devices that are now not even imaginable will surely broaden the repertoire of such forms. Even new developments within existing forms of representation, the invention of day-glow-color, for example, adds new possibilities in the use of visual art for conveying conceptions that previously could only be dimly suggested.

Once again the point here is that experience is sense specific. The senses are the vehicles through which information about the world is picked up. Forms of representation are devices that appeal to the senses; they capitalize on their sensory specificity and exploit their potential to bring to consciousness the conceptions held by others. Through their use communication is expanded.

Consider the converse. Suppose it was the case that the government placed a moratorium on the use of all forms of representation except the formal use of discursive language. All that we wish to communicate, say for a period of a year, must by law be conveyed through this form and this form alone. What fetters would fall upon us? What would we want to say that we could not express? What frustrations would we experience? What kind of conceptions would remain buried in our cortex? And what would eventually happen to the capacities of our brain?

Speculation such as this highlights the utilities of the forms we have access to and use with varying degrees of skills. Prose is not translated poetry, a visual image is not a substitute for a sonata, a mathematical proposition cannot be translated to poetry. Forms of representation are non-redundant, and their non-redundancy is what has commended them to us over the years. They make different kinds of experience possible, and from different kinds of experience flows different kinds of meaning. Indeed, the character of our consciousness is affected largely by the kinds of forms of representation with which we interact: a musical consciousness requires music, a mathematical consciousness, mathematics – although if Einstein is any example, a visual and a kinesthetic one.[17]

For the field of evaluation the implications of this thesis, I hope, are clear. We do not need to have a government moratorium on the use of forms of representation to have restrictions on how we communicate. Tradition, entrenched professional groups with vested interests to protect, ignorance of alternatives, and sloth can be almost as restrictive. Yet, with a restricted range of expressive vehicles the content of our conceptual life is also restrained. This restraint impedes not only what we are able to express, but what we seek when we enquire in the first place. In the end, our conventional expectations in educational evaluation provide us with comforts that diminish our ability to understand.

I indicated above that the forms of representation that we have become accustomed to not only influence what we can convey, but also shape the questions we ask and the information we seek. The formative functions forms of representation need at least some further explanation.

It was E.H. Gombrich, the noted art historian, who observed that artists did not paint what they could see, they saw what they were able to paint. The skills they had acquired within the form of representation called visual art became, in a way, templates through which they perceived the world. Thus the interest of a Monet in qualities of light reflecting off haystacks, church facades, and lily ponds were fundamentally different from those of a Constable or a Wyeth, whose interests were directed to matters of texture and atmosphere. The artist who comes to a small fishing town looks for the scenic, the quality of the fog as it surrounds the houses and trees and seems to rise, slowly from the ground. He looks for color and value, for compositional arrangements that are interesting, and seeks complementary fields of color that can be transformed into visual images on canvas or paper. The sociologist, with his tools, looks for the social structures within the town, how groups are formed, what statuses exist, in which context, the role of the local tavern and filling station as a source of information and social contact for the town's people. He tries to bring the particulars of his data within the power of social science theory. He is after propositional explanation.

Each inquirer, the artist and the sociologist, have different backgrounds, they have acquired different skills, they use different media, they raise different questions, they seek different data and have different things to tell us about the 'same' place. Their training in the use of the tools of their respective trades becomes for each a salient frame of reference for construing a small piece of the world, and it is because the vividness that the images each creates are telling ones, that we learn to experience the town in its several dimensions vicariously. When these images are particularly compelling, as they are when made by people of genius, the images become a paradigm or structure to which other experiences are assimilated. By creating the compelling images of ego, superego, id, and the mechanisms of defense, or of surplus value and the alienation of labor, Freud and Marx have provided the world with images of wide scope that do much more than simply convey the ideas they had; they shape our very conception of man and society. The same is true of dance, visual art, music, and theater. Those skilled in these realms look at the world through the terms the forms they use

239

command. In turn, the work they produce within these forms compels our attention to the dimensions of the reality that those forms have portrayed. Through a multiplicity of forms we begin to appreciate the multi-dimensionality of experience and the complexity of the qualities through which that experience is secured. Evaluators have much to learn by studying the uses people make of the forms of representation employed within the culture. The very existence of such varieties should be clue enough that they perform important functions in helping us grasp aspects of the culture in which we live.

Modes of Treating Forms of Representation

The conceptualization of forms of representation as vehicles through which conceptions are externalized does not, by itself, describe the particular ways in which such forms can be treated. Given a form of representation, say visual art or discursive language, how might such forms be treated to allow them to represent what one has come to know? To describe these treatments the term *modes of treatment* has been formulated. Any form of representation can be treated in one or more of three ways. These modes of treatment are *mimetic*, *expressive*, and *conventional*.

The mimetic conveys through imitation, that is, it represents by replicating within the limits of the medium employed the surface features of some aspect of the qualitative world. There are throughout human history numerous examples of how mimetic modes of treatment function, from the use of hieroglyphics and pictographs that were employed to imitate the basic structural features of the visual world to the most advanced forms of pictographs and holography. Just what is it that mimetic modes of treatment do? Simply stated, they extract the salient features of some aspect of the world and represent them as an image within some medium. Thus, the images of animals drawn on the walls of the Lascaux Caves were a result of early man's interest in representing his observations of the world. It seems reasonable to assume that members of his community knew when they looked at these drawn images that they were representative, that they were intended to describe through their visual correspondence to their referents. In the use of hieroglyphics we have not only the abstracted visual representation of human figures, animals, furniture, and so forth, but we have them in a time sequence, a visual narrative that individuals are able to read. Hieroglyphics exemplify man's ability to combine both his spatial experience (the visual image) and his temporal experience by sequencing visual images in a form that not only parallel his visual experience at a particular point in time, but over time as well.

If we look at a more modern example of the ways in which mimetic modes of treatment occur, it is vividly apparent in the use of highway signs. Particularly in Europe, one will find signs that tell the driver what he/she can expect to encounter as the car moves down the highway; a curve in the road, a dip, animals crossing, zigzags, castles nearby, turnoffs, and the like. In each case the image created shares some structural similarity with the object or situation it is designed to represent. Even though the form of representation is highly abstracted, it presents the driver with as much information as he/she needs – and probably as much as can be handled at 70 miles per hour.

Consider also paintings and photographs. Suppose you wanted to know what the south of France looked like, or the Chartres Cathedral, or your long-lost cousin Beatrice. You could, of course, read descriptions of such places and people and perhaps, if the writer were very skilled, it might be possible to gain a fairly good idea of their features. But a photograph or a painting will usually do the job much better. Special features of these places and people are more likely to be represented in a form that displays their characteristics through a medium and form of representation that is, itself, spatial than a form that is not. If we are trying to find someone disembarking from an airplane we have never met before, we would probably do better if we had a photograph than if we had a verbal description or a set of numbers describing the person's height and weight.

Perhaps the most telling example of mimetic modes of treatment are to be found in the use of fingerprints. Here what one has is a direct visual imprint of a textured surface. The prints duplicate virtually exactly the configurations of the surface of the fingers. Indeed, the correspondence is so close that among several million examples of prints on file in the FBI offices in Washington, no two are identical. One print is structurally isomorphic with the finger or fingers of a particular individual.

Now it is curious to me to encounter Nelson Goodman's assertion[18] that 'A Constable painting of Marlboro Castle is more like any other picture than it is like the castle . . .' or that 'None of the automobiles off an assembly line is a picture of the rest'. These statements I find curious because we do, in fact, expect a portrait to represent, that is to say, to look like the sitter. If it does not, we are disappointed. And if we go into an automobile showroom, select a car and ask the salesman to order the same car except in a different color, we are in fact using the car on the showroom floor as a model that we expect our car, when delivered, to duplicate. If we find that another model has arrived instead, or that the grill has been altered, or that another motor has been installed or different tires affixed, we would not only have cause for complaint, but for canceling our order as well.

Or consider still another example, the use of a prototype in the production of automobiles. It is standard practice to build a prototype automobile which in every respect is to be reproduced on the assembly line. Cars coming off the line are models of these prototypes, which themselves are representations of the designers' and engineers' conceptions. When a car coming off the line does not possess the features of the prototype, there is or should be a call-back: something has gone amiss.

What such practices exemplify is our efforts at mimesis, the prototypical model being the standard against which other cars coming off the line are to be appraised. In this way, as well as through the pictures and specifications provided in sales brochures, a mimetic function is performed. Like the highway signs, the prototype automobile describes what is to be found when the journey is completed. It 'pictures' in detail, ideally as a perfect replica, what the efforts of the workers, the buyers, and the management are to find when the work has been completed. In this sense one car does indeed stand for another.

Now it is true that in some respects a painting of a car is more like *any* other painting or car than it is like a person or like some other thing. But that is true only if we shift context and disregard the function of representation. A scientific formula H_2O is more like any other formula CO_2 than it is like water. We can always, I suppose, choose to disregard the central function of a form if we are intent on doing so, and for some purposes such disregard is functional. But Goodman's argument that imitation is largely irrelevant to representation is, I believe, wrong-headed. Man has for thousands of years represented through efforts of mimesis. Indeed techniques such as perspective were invented to make more credible the representations attempted. This is not to say that paintings and even photographs are simply copies, in the way in which fingerprints or death masks are copies. Idiosyncratic expression and interpretation are always to some degree present. It is to say that we have learned how to read abstracted and interpreted images, and that for a great many kinds of information we do not require the degree of mimesis that fingerprints provide.

Most of the examples I have used thus far are visual, but mimesis occurs not only in the visual but in other forms of representation as well. Music can be composed to imitate the sound of thunder, running brooks, riders on horseback, and the like. Words can be onomatopoetic. Smells can be created to imitate a wide range of other smells, and so forth. The point here is that the imitation of selected features of experience within an empirically available material has been and is one of the major means through which representation occurs.

There is another point about the mimetic mode of treatment that is so obvious that it is often neglected. That is, for the purposes of mimesis the closer the form is to the content represented, the closer the mimesis is likely to be. Thus, to represent what is visual, forms of representation that appeal to the visual sensory system are likely to be more revealing than forms that emphasize the use of other systems. To know how something sounds, forms of representation that emphasize the auditory are more appropriate than forms that emphasize the visual. To know what someone said, a duplication of the words is more appropriate than a picture. This is not to suggest that transformations of experience from one sense modality to representation in forms that emphasize another should not occur. To do so would be the demise of literature. It is to suggest that mimetic functions operate most successfully when the sense modality emphasized in the form of representation is like that which it aims to represent.

One other observation. In many situations the meaning of an experience is not simply the function of the experience secured through one of the senses, but due to the interaction among the 'data' of the several senses. Consider discourse. When people talk, the meanings conveyed are simply not due to 'what is said' but how they say what they say, that is, the intonation and emphasis they give to the words they use, the gestures they make while speaking, their expression, the context in which what they have to say is said, what is preceded in the conversation, and so forth. The absence of these features in transcripts of discourse can radically alter the meanings that, in fact, were conveyed when the discourse took place. To pick the varieties of information that accompany the discourse itself – if indeed one can talk about the 'discourse itself', since it is never by itself – a variety of sensory systems must operate and one must know how to read the meanings that the content they make possible provides. The ability to reconstruct varieties of information through sound and sight, tempo and context, is one of the virtues of film. Perhaps that is one of the reasons why film is so captivating and compelling. The absence of such contextual information in so much research on teaching might be one of the reasons why it has been so uninformative: more information is left out of most research reports on teaching than in fact is included within it.

A second mode of treatment that is used to shape the character of forms of representation is called expressive. By expressive I mean that what is represented is not the surface features of the object or event, but rather its deep structure. Consider the movement of a jet plane speeding down a runway about to take off. The plane moves along very slowly and gradually increases its speed, its speed continues to increase and about three-quarters down the runway its nose rises and, like a duck leaving a lake, it lifts off the surface of the earth. Such an experience, if we were standing on the bridge of an airport building, would be auditory as well as visual. We would experience a stark white form accelerating and gradually becoming nothing more than a small speck against the vast expansive blue sky. It is this movement, this graceful takeoff, the sound of the jet engines gradually diminishing in volume, the gradual reduction and size as the plane moves into the sky that a dancer or a graphic artist might create. Such creations have very little to do with mimesis, but more to do with the experience of acceleration, with the gradual increase in speed and with the experience of a slow rise into the atmosphere. How these expressive qualities might be represented is precisely what the artist has to create: There are no codified formula for producing such expressive forms. What the artist wants to do is not to imitate the surface features of a moving plane, but to capture its essential properties, that is to say, its expressive character. Here a kind of imitation is also at work, but it is not imitation of things seen, but rather of things felt. The form of representation is treated expressively rather than mimetically. The analogic relationship is not through the imitation of appearance, but through the creation of a form that generates the expressiveness of slowly accelerating movement.

Why have artists been interested in such a task? Why should such efforts occupy such a central place in the history of the arts? At least a part of the reason is because much of what is most important in human experrience is not what is apparent, but rather what is felt about what is apparent. Things are not always what they appear to be on the surface, but in the kind of emotional life that they generate; the sense of curiosity displayed by a very young child exploring a new toy or the fear of an old man anticipating his imminent death are not simply physical movements, but configurations that possess a pervasive quality that conveys to the sensitive perceiver the character of curiosity and fear. The behavior is read by looking below its surface features. Just how forms, whether human or not, convey such qualities of life is not altogether clear. Gestalt and associationist theory hold competing views, and it is not particularly necessary for explanations of these theoretical views to be given here. What is important is that the expressive treatment of forms of representation do occur and do function to shape our experience.

If to know about the character of life in a school or classroom, suburb or ghetto, requires one to know not only about their surface appearance, but also about the character of life within them, then it is imperative that those who wish to make such knowledge public must use means that embody the qualities they seek to express. It is here that expressive modes of treatment are crucial. In literature and in poetry the artistic achievement is realized in the expressive character of the forms created, not because such forms are necessarily beautiful or pleasant, but because without them the very content that the artist wishes to convey could not be expressed. The expressive mode of treatment is, therefore, not simply a pleasant affectation, a dressing up of content to make it more palatable, but is itself part and parcel of the content of the form of representation. When descriptions of situations that are emotionally loaded for individuals are presented that do not possess the emotionality that they hold for those who live in those situations, a significant form of bias and distortion results. To use a form of representation of Buchenwald or Dachau that leaves out of its content the character of life as experienced by the inmates, is to render less than a partial view of those camps: it is to mislead.

A third mode of treatment is conventional. By conventional, I mean simply that as individuals are socialized within a culture they learn that certain conventions such as discursive language, traffic signs, bells and alarms of one kind or another, stand in the place of something else. A red light, the word 'table', the flag, the almost wholly arbitrary vocabulary of our discursive language are examples of the conventional mode of treating forms of representation. Words and colors are neither mimetic (although at one time they might have been) nor are they expressive (although they might be used expressively as words are used in literature and in poetry). The relationship between the form and referent is arbitrary. 'Pain' in English means something like a sharp, uncomfortable feeling, while in French it means bread. There is nothing in the word per se to commend it to one rather than to the other referent. What matters is that within a culture there is an agreement among those who use its conventions that the referent for each is so and so. This is not to suggest that meanings, even those related to convention, do not have variability in interpretation by different individuals. However, the range of the variance is far narrower than in either of the other two modes of treatment.

There is, of course, an important and interesting difference between the mimetic and the expressive modes of treatment and the conventional mode. In both the mimetic and the conventional analogical relationships operate. In each case what is created parallels some aspect of the form being represented. In conventional modes of treatment this is not the case. A table does not look like how it sounds. For the word or the sentence to have meaning, the individual must be able to imagine the referent for the term or terms employed. This does not mean that for every word used there is a corresponding image. We have so mastered discourse that we do not need to create a representational form in order to speak or write. However, if we are unable to imagine the referent for a discursive term that we encounter, even terms whose referent can only be imagined through induction or extrapolation – terms like nation, category, infinity – we cannot have a conception of what it means. Thus language in the ordinary sense of the term functions as a surrogate for an image. If the surrogate is to have meaning, we must be able to imagine the referent to which the term refers. This is why when children do not understand a word, we try to help them by providing examples.

The distinctions I have made between the mimetic, the expressive, and the conventional should not be taken to mean that a form of representation uses only one mode of treatment. The three are often combined. For example, much visual art, particularly painting, uses mimetic, expressive, and conventional elements within the same work. Literature and poetry exemplify the mimetic in the way in which the sound of events is emulated, the expressive in the way in which the structure of the prose penetrates the surface features of the events portrayed, and the conventional through the standardized use of language and symbol.

But perhaps the most vivid example of a form of representation that combines modes of treatment is to be found in film. The modern film not only lets us see how something looks or sounds, but when artistically successful, also enables us to experience the underlying structure of the event and places portrayed. Films such as 'Breaking Away' give us not only a glimpse of middle America, its streets, people, and the stone-cutting plant in which Indiana limestone is cut, but is also makes it possible for us to participate vicariously in the race between the 'Cutters' and the campus cycle team. Furthermore, the conventional and unconventional use of language serve as vehicles through which we understand the interaction among the characters. Indeed, it is the 'Italianization' of the English language from which so much of the film's comic quality emerges. In addition, the use of camera angle, the character of the film's music, and the skilful editing all combine to convey through all three modes of treatment the meanings that constitute the film itself. We not only acquire some sense of what Bloomington, Indiana looks like, we also get some sense of the tension between 'town' and 'gown'. We not only encounter five adolescent males discussing their ambitions and fantasies but we are helped to identify with them and to experience their triumphs and defeats. The film is an extremely potent vehicle through which a form of representation can employ different modes of treatment. And it is the awareness of this potentiality that directors, writers, and actors exploit to inform us about the events of the people that they portray.

The Syntactical Structure of Forms of Representation

Forms of representation are forms whose elements are arranged in a pattern. This arrangement is what is here called a syntax. The term syntax is most typically used in dealing with spoken and written language, but the term is not restricted to these forms of representation. The term syntax emanates from the Latin *sintaxis* which means 'to arrange'. A syntax is an arrangement of parts within a whole, thus, in visual art there is an arrangement called a composition, in music compositions are arranged by composers or arrangers. There are arrangements made in dance, architecture, cooking, in any sphere of human activity in which patterns must be produced.

The design of these patterns in different forms of representation are guided or controlled by different criteria. If the basis for arrangements are examined, it becomes clear that some rest upon clearly defined conventions whose violation yields expressions that are either wrong or without meaning. Consider arithmetic. To be able to create an arrangement that is correct within arithmetic an individual must know how to combine elements within the canons of arithmetic procedure. If these canons are erroneously employed, the answer to arithmetic problems will be wrong. Consensual validation of the correctness or incorrectness of the conclusion can be determined without difficulty and with virtual unanimity. Indeed, the criteria are so clear that human judgment is not necessary, a machine can perform the same functions.

Spelling and punctuation are similar, but are not quite as rule-governed in character. Nevertheless, in American English words misspelled can be identified without difficulty by matching them to conventionally accepted standards. Punctuation also, in somewhat lesser degree, is highly rule-governed and can be determined correct or incorrect by appraising the use of punctuation according to accepted rules of punctuation. The point here is that some forms of representation are highly rule-governed in nature, and the results that are achieved by the use of such forms can be appraised with little difficulty by comparing them with standardized expectations.

At the other end of the continuum are those forms of representation whose elements are arranged not by obeying codified rules of procedure but by trying to approximate a figurative coherence or by juxtaposing elements within a whole so that productive novelty and meaning result. This end of the continuum we shall call *figurative*. The use of a figurative syntax is, of course, epitomized in the arts. There is no such thing as an incorrect or correct poem, painting, musical composition, because there are no codified standards or rules that such forms much meet. A poem might be more or less coherent and cohesive, but that judgment is made by appraising the relationships among the qualities it possesses, not by looking for isomorphism between the arrangement and an acceptable standard. The task requires judgment and uses criteria, not standards, it is a deliberative activity, not a calculative one.[19] Thus, when one selects a form of representation, one also selects the kind of criteria that will be used to appraise the results of one's work. An objectivity and precision can be secured in mathematics and spelling that is simply impossible to achieve in film or music.

To suggest as I have that forms of representation can be distributed on a continuum from the rule-governed to the figurative, and to say as I have that the arts move toward the figurative end of the continuum, is not to suggest that in using artistic forms rules of a kind do not apply or do not influence what artists create. Clearly in the arts and in forms that use a figurative syntax there are expectations that are already embedded within the forms previously created. Thus, a novelist who wishes to write a romantic novel functions within the criteria called 'the novel' and within the form called 'the romantic'. A painter who wishes to create a painting that participates in an impressionist genre works within the historical exemplars of impressionism: the work of Monet, Vuillard, and Bonnard. These painters have established some of the parameters within which the work must fit. The images these and other works have generated are defined by terms called style, and establish the grounds that artists, composers, writers, architects, and others must work within or depart from. In this sense there are 'rules' in the arts, and in this sense artistic forms of representation are rule-governed.

But the rules I have identified are fundamentally different from those used in forms whose syntax is at the rule-governed end of the continuum. As I said, arithmetic, and mathematics more generally, are paradigm cases. Here the canons of procedure are publicly articulated and codified, they can be explicitly taught. A machine can be programmed to produce correct arrangements and to identify incorrect ones, truth and falsity can be determined unambiguously and finally, rules of equivalence can be applied, and translation – in the literal sense – is possible without loss of information: five plus three times two means exactly what fifteen plus one means, no more, no less. There is no comparable translatability in those syntaxes which are figurative. Their meaning emanates from the *particular* configuration among the elements the form possesses. When that configuration is altered, there is an alteration in meaning.

It is both interesting and significant to note that during the primary years of schooling, and even beyond, the use of forms of representation that emphasize rule-governed syntaxes are quite dominant. The three Rs are classic examples. There are probably several reasons for this. The use of forms of representation that are rule-governed does increase the precision of communication. By emphasizing conformity and obedience to convention, children will come to develop skills for simple decoding, writing, and basic computation. Such skills are of undoubtable importance in dealing with many of the messages received within the culture. Furthermore, because school curriculum to a very large degree requires the use of such skills, a self-fulfilling prophecy occurs; the needs of the future in school define the skills to be acquired in the present. If the skills needed in the future were those that made the imaginative treatment of music important, the skills of the present in school would be quite different.

It is also noteworthy that performance in rule-governed forms of representation are simple to evaluate compared to those which require the use of judgment. Teachers need to have skills that are far more complex and subtle in order to assess the quality of a poem than to determine whether the words that the student has used were spelled correctly. Even factually oriented material in the social studies and in science can be used to evaluate student responses on a matching basis that is not possible in evaluating student work and performance in music and in art. There is after all a back of the book to which teachers can turn for correct answers that are simply unavailable in the fine arts.

One cannot help but wonder about the meta lessons children, especially young children, learn when forms of representation that emphasize rule-governed syntaxes are used so overwhelmingly in school.[20] One lesson which it seems to me is unavoidable is that problems – at least the kind they encounter in school – have correct and incorrect answers, that the teachers know what the answers are, and that their task is to work in a way that will lead them to the correct answers. Ambiguities, matters of judgment, trade-offs among competing alternatives, holding conclusions in abeyance until more evidence comes in, these are not significant features of classroom life. We emphasize by both what we teach and how we evaluate that there is a right and a wrong answer to virtually everything. The student's task is to arrive at the correct destination. In school, as in the movies, we are a nation of happy endings.

Such an emphasis, albeit covert, is curiously incongruous with a school concerned about helping the young prepare for the future. The future, and indeed the present for most people, is riddled with ambiguities, trade-offs, dilemmas, competing alternatives and conflicting answers. It is far from clearcut. There are very few problems the solutions to which can be determined once and for all by adding up the columns of pluses and minuses. Yet we seem to prepare the young, in school at least, in a way that provides little practice in dealing with such problems and we reinforce the significance of right answers that hint of no ambiguity by the ways in which we evaluate. The multiple-choice test leaves no room for doubt. Again, not only our evaluation practices but the forms of representation and syntaxes they employ support and reflect a social ethos where rule, prediction, control, and standardization appear to be pressing social needs.

Some Practical Implications for an Impractical World

Do discussions of the relationship of the senses to conception and of the forms used to represent them have any bearing upon the practical problems of educational evaluation? It seems to me that the implications are several and significant. In the first place, if concept formation is, as I have argued, based upon information provided by the sensory systems, then it follows that any representation of those concepts into public form requires, depending upon the forms used, various degrees of translation. Words and sentences, for example, are surrogates for what is known in non-verbal ways. In translation there is always a loss or change of information. Second, the extent to which the qualities of the environment are known in the first place depend upon the extent to which the sensibilities are able to pick them up. When those sensibilities are dulled, ill-developed, disregarded, or in other ways diminished in importance, the qualities of the environment to which those neglected sensibilities are related are not likely to be experienced. To the extent that those qualities go unexperienced, to that extent is our information partial and incomplete. Third, the traditional restriction to particular forms of representing information that has been conceptualized leads to two egregious faults. First, it restricts attention to aspects of the environment most amenable to the forms of representation that are permitted. Second, it limits severely what can be rendered even about those qualities to which the forms themselves may be related.

Given such limitations, why is it that certain conventional forms, namely language and number, have received so much attention in the social sciences, and more particularly in educational research and evaluation? Part of the reason is due to what I have described earlier. Conventionalized criteria and a conception of objectivity rooted in replicability breed confidence in the conclusions that methods that meet such criteria yield. Replicability and rule-governed procedures fit quite well with our need to stabilize a rapidly changing world. With such procedures we believe we are more likely to be able to predict and control our environment. Finally, an entire professional constituency exists consisting of individuals who have spent a great deal of time and effort in developing the skills needed to use such methods. This group does not play an insignificant political role in maintaining the status quo.

To bring change in the evaluation field is an epistemological problem, a political problem, and an educational one. It is an epistemological problem because the philosophical grounds for claims that forms other than discursive ones can provide knowledge needs to be justified. Such justification requires work of the kind presented here. It is a political problem because, as I have already indicated, vested interests exist. People do what they know how to do. Few professionals are eager to be displaced by others having different skills and working with different assumptions. The politics of university life and of professional associations, of journals and of schools, tend to support the status quo, although it is reassuring to see some change occurring in all four arenas. It is an educational problem because the development of the sensibilities upon which consciousness depends is not an automatic consequence of maturation. To be able to pick up what is qualitatively specific and subtle requires training. Universities can play an important role here. To be able to represent with skill in non-discursive forms of representation what has been conceptualized requires even greater skill. Each form of representation is a kind of language. Its structure needs to be learned. One must know how, for example, to take and read photographs or to speak poetically about classrooms, schools, or the qualities of an individual student's work. Such skills are difficult ones to acquire, but they can be acquired. We now train doctoral students interested in educational research and evaluation by requiring that they take courses in statistics, measurement, research design, and evaluation theory. These courses neglect the use of forms of representation that are neither quantitative nor propositional. Indeed, the *idea* of their use, with the exception of only a few evaluation courses that I know of in the nation, simply never become a part of the conversation, let alone the training.

In attempting to lay the groundwork for a wider approach to educational evaluation, I have risked overstating the case for non-quantitative and non-discursive forms of representation. I have taken this risk because quantitative and propositional forms are presently very strong and highly refined. Let me say explicitly that what I have tried to convey is not the need for a replacement of existing methods, but the need for an expansion of methods. The use of propositional discourse and number cannot be substituted. They, like other forms of representation, make unique contributions to our understanding. But they do not tell the whole story. In restaurants in Japan examples of the variety of food being served is placed in the window outside the restaurant. Passers-by can look at these plates and get a very good idea what the food is like. The Japanese recognize that words on a menu provide limited information about what will be served, and so they represent what they serve with a mimetic visual form of representation. We can take a leaf from the Japanese. There is much to be learned about classrooms, teaching, and the quality of student work by seeing what it looks like, by hearing what it sounds like, by reading literary prose that illuminates its subtleties as well as by reading the scores the students received on standardized tests or the teacher secured on observation schedules ticked off by impartial observers. No single form of representation will do justice to everything.

The particular ways in which forms of representation can be used in educational evaluation constitute a field of work that needs yet to be done. If this chapter and other beginnings take root, as I hope they will, the next quarter century should see a much richer array of tools available to educational evaluators for the evaluation of educational practice.

Notes

1. *Time* 16 June 1980, p. 54.
2. The membership of churches that can be described as fundamentalist and evangelical in their orientation is documented in the *Yearbook of American and Canadian Churches* Nashville, Abingdon Press.
3. At the present time, thirty-six states have statutes that provide for capital punishment, Council of State Governments *The State Book* 1971–79, Vol. 22, Kentucky, 1978.
4. For a discussion of research that has been conducted on 'time on task', see ROSENSHEIN, B.V. (1978) 'Academic Engaged Time, Content Covered, and Direct Instruction', *Journal of Education*, 160, August, pp. 38–66.
5. ROSENHEIN, B.V. (1976) 'Classroom Instruction' in *The Psychology of Teaching Methods Part 1* 75th Yearbook of the National Society for the Study of Education, Chicago, University of Chicago Press, p. 345.
6. DEWEY, J. (1938) *Experience and Education* New York, Macmillan.
7. Higher scores can be achieved in some subjects by neglecting other equally important subjects, thus lowering the overall quality of education.
8. FREDERICK TOENNIES. For a discussion of Toennies' work, see NISBET, R. (1976) *Sociology As An Art Form* New York Oxford University Press.
9. NISBET, R. (1976) *ibid.*
10. SCHAFF, A. (1973) *Language and Cognition* New York, McGraw Hill Book Co.
11. Perhaps the classic example of this view is provided by Alfred Jules Ayer in (n.d.) *Language, Truth and Logic*, New York, Dover Publications.
12. See for example, Plato's *Republic*, especially Books Six and Seven, translated by CORNFORD, F.M. (1951) New York, Oxford University Press.
13. For a brilliant discussion of the role of the senses in the achievement of consciousness see READ, H. (1955) *Icon and Idea* Cambridge, Mass., Harvard University Press.
14. DEWEY, J. (1934) *Art as Experience* New York, Minton, Balch and Company. see especially chapters 3 and 4.
15. Rudolph Arnheim reviews Aristotle's thoughts on sensation, perception, and cognition, in *Visual Thinking* Berkeley, University of California Press, 1969, pp. 8–12.
16. KUFFLER, S.W. and NICOLLS, J.G. (1976) *From Neuron to Brain: A Cellular Approach to the Function of the Neuron Systems* Cambridge, Mass., Sinovar Associates, see especially chapter 19.

17. Albert Einstein is quoted as follows: 'The words or the langue, as they are written or spoken, do not seem to play any role in my mechanism of thought. The psychical entities which seem to serve as elements in thought are certain signs and more or less clear images which can be 'voluntarily' reproduced or combined... But taken from a psychological viewpoint, this combinatory play seems to be the essential feature in productive thought – before there is any connection with logical construction in words or other kinds of signs which can be communicated to others. The above-mentioned elements are, in my case, of visual and some of muscular type. Conventional words or other signs have to be sought for laboriously only in a secondary stage, when the mentioned associative play is sufficiently established and can be reproduced at will. HOLTON, G. (1967–68) 'Influences on Einstein's Early Work in Relativity Theory' in *The American Scholar*, 37 (1), Winter.
18. For a very full treatment of the concept of symbol systems, see Nelson Goodman's book (1968) *The Languages of Art* Indianapolis, Bobbs-Merrill.
19. The distinction between the deliberative and the calculative is Aristotle's. See, for example, ACRILL, J.L. (Ed.) (1973) *Aristotle's Ethics* London, Faber and Faber, pp. 114–122.
20. The concept 'meta lesson' is related to notions concerning the hidden curriculum. It is also related to the older notion of concomitant learning. Stated more simply, it underscores the idea that students learn more than one thing at a time, and that the syntactical structure of the forms that are used in school curricula instruct in many unexpected ways.

References

BROUDY, H. (1979) 'Arts Education: Necessary or just nice?' in *Phi Delta Kappan*, January, *60*, pp. 347–350.
CHOMSKY, N. (1973) Forward in SCHAFF, A. *Language and Cognition* New York, McGraw Hill Book Co.
COUNCIL OF STATE GOVERNMENTS (1978) *The State Book* 1971–79, Vol. 22, Kentucky.
GOODMAN, N. (1968) *The Languages of Art* Indianapolis, Bobbs-Merrill.
HARNISCHFLEGER, A. and WILEY, D. (1975) *Achievement Test Score Decline: Do we need to worry?* Chicago, CEMREL.
MEAD, M. (1980) *Aspects of the Present* New York, Morrow.
NEISSER, U. (1976) *Cognition and Reality: Principles and implications of cognitive psychology* San Francisco, W.H. FREEMAN.
PIAGET, J. (1971) *Biology and Knowledge* Edinburgh, Edinburgh University Press.
POPPER, K. (1980) *The Logic of Scientific Discovery* New York, Harper and Row.

15 Can Educational Research Inform Educational Practice?

That enterprise known as educational research is predicated on the supposition that research is vital to the improvement of educational practice. As a former vice president of one of the divisions of the American Educational Research Association (AERA), I suppose I should endorse that supposition. As a member of the faculty of a school of education committed to the belief that educational research informs educational practice. I might be expected to embrace that belief as a matter of institutional loyalty. Yet I have worked in the field of education for 26 years, 23 of them in universities – Ohio State for one year, the University of Chicago for five years, and Stanford for 17 years – and, despite efforts to socialize me to the prevailing norms, I still have questions about the relationship of research to practice. I would be less than honest to accept as a matter of faith a belief about which I have serious doubts. Hence I write this article not to proclaim that educational research informs educational practice, but to ask whether it *can* inform educational practice.

By *educational research* I mean correlational and experimental studies of the type typically published in the *American Educational Research Journal*. And by *educational practice* I mean the things that teachers and administrators do when they formulate educational aims, plan curricula, manage a class or a school, teach a lesson, motivate a group of students or staff, and attempt to discern what progress they have made.

I raise this question of the relationship of research to practice in good will. I have no intention of harping on the gap between what we know and what we do, on the reluctance of teachers to use the information that researchers provide, or on the fact that educational research is only 80 years old and that the breakthrough on teaching and learning is right around the corner. My aim is to seriously inquire about the relationship of what we do as educational researchers and what practitioners do in schools. Since I assume that the conduct of educational research is intended to do more than to advance the careers of educational researchers, asking about the relationship of research to practice is not altogether irrelevant.

Let me confess that I have long been intrigued about the relationship of theory to practice in education, but was motivated to write about this topic because of my experience as a faculty member at three research-oriented universities. This experience made it increasingly clear to me that research findings, and even the theories from which they are derived, seldom – indeed, hardly ever – enter into the deliberations of faculties, regardless of the area of education about which these faculties deliberate. Of course, this experience might be unique to my tenure at Ohio State, Chicago, and Stanford. Other institutions might be different.

At the institutions where I have worked, questions having to do with curriculum planning, the evaluation of teaching, or the identification of institutional strengths and weaknesses are hardly ever answered in light of educational research. Thus those who are best informed about educational research seldom use the fruits of their labors either to make practical decisions or to shape institutional policy within the institutions where they work. If educational researchers do not use research findings to guide their own professional decisions, why should we expect those less well informed to use research findings to guide theirs? This anomaly and others like it moved me to raise the question that is the title of this article: Can educational research inform educational practice?

Some readers may justifiably wonder if I could really know whether or not my colleagues use educational research in their own activities as teachers or as planners of curricula. Even if the fruits of educational research do not emerge in faculty deliberations, perhaps they are used by individual faculty members as they plan and teach their courses.

To get answers to these questions, I asked one of my research assistants to interview faculty members in the School of Education at Stanford.★ The interviewees were guaranteed anonymity, and I do not know who provided which response. What I do know is that,

★ I wish to acknowledge the assistance I received from David Flinders, who conducted the interviews with the Stanford faculty members and with the teachers and school administrators.

although my colleagues in the School of Education say that they 'use' research in their planning and teaching, they find it extremely difficult to give any examples of how they use it. The typical response is that research findings function in the background, as a sort of frame of reference.

I suspect that my colleagues are correct, but I wonder what they mean by educational research. Altogether, I find their remarks – as reported verbatim by my research assistant – vague and unconvincing. I would hate to have to make a case for the utility of educational research in educational practice to a school board or a congressional committee if it had to be based on statements of the kind that they provided. In addition, I collected from each faculty member who responded to my request a copy of the reading lists and introductory course materials for the course or courses that the faculty member offered in the autumn of 1982. I examined these materials to determine whether they contained any features that might have been influenced by educational research. Did these materials contain educational objectives, for example? Alas, only the materials from one professor contained anything resembling educational objectives. Perhaps this omission is a function of the other faculty members' having read the research on behavioral objectives, but I doubt it. I use this example simply to provide what I regard as further evidence that, although we prescribe to teachers and school administrators one thing, we do another thing for ourselves.

In commenting about the behavior of my colleagues, I in no way mean to depreciate them. My behavior is no different from theirs. Furthermore, I do not believe that our behavior is exceptional. On the contrary, I believe it to be typical of research-oriented professors of education.

Thirty elementary and secondary school administrators were also interviewed by my research assistant. Perhaps they use educational research in ways of which I was unaware. Perhaps they use what university professors of education appear to neglect. The story for teachers and school administrators is largely the same as it is for professors. Not one of the 30 people interviewed provided any examples of how they actually used research to make a decision or to shape a practice – although several assured my research assistant that research is useful. Some simply said that research has little to do with their work.

Readers might not be surprised by these findings. After all, research in education does not provide the kind of prescriptions that are employed, say, in medical practice as a result of research in medicine. The use of research in education is more heuristic; it provides a framework that we can use to make decisions, not a set of rules to be followed slavishly. Hence, to expect even my research-wise colleagues to use research in a prescriptive way is to expect too much. Had I expected less – or something other than a prescriptive use of research – I would not have been as disappointed.

This is a plausible view. It is one that I have advanced myself in a number of papers and books.[1] But in some ways this view is a bit too comforting. There are two problems with it that I wish to identify.

The first problem has to do with what it means to use research as a framework for making practical decisions. Does this mean knowing how to think about a problem, or does it mean having a research-supported theory to guide decision making? Does it mean that we have examined a body of research studies, extracted generalizations, determined that the theory is supported by the evidence, and then used the theory as a tool for shaping decisions? If this is what 'using research to inform practice' means, then I think that it seldom occurs. Practitioners seldom read the research literature. Even when they do, this literature contains little that is not so qualified or so compromised by competing findings, rival hypotheses, or faulty design that the framework could scarcely be said to be supported in some reasonable way by research.

Or does 'using research to inform practice' mean simply that practitioners have read the distillations found in reviews of research, in order to garner conclusions that they can then act upon? Can it be legitimately claimed that a teacher or a school administrator who seeks to increase students' time on task is using research to justify this decision? I suppose one might claim that popularized research conclusions that are employed by practitioners are a use of research. Yet, in popularization the findings are not only popularized, they are vulgarized as well. By *vulgarization* I mean that the qualifications that researchers specify in stating their conclusions are often absent in the versions used by practitioners. The specific limits within which these conclusions hold are seldom enumerated or described. What one then has is a vague apparition of the work that was done in the first place. Indeed, the conclusions of the practitioner are likely to look nothing like the conclusions of the researcher. Is this what we mean by using research to inform educational practice? Although such use of research might *influence* practice, whether it *informs* practice is quite another matter.

A second problem with the less strict (but more comforting) view of the uses of research in education is that, in principle, such uses should improve practice. Those practitioners who rely on decision-making frameworks that are supported by solid research findings should be better at their jobs. But here too the available evidence is altogether unconvincing. Those who are informed about educational research – i.e., professors of education who do research – are, in my view, in no way better at teaching or course planning than liberal arts professors who have never seen the inside of the *American Educational Research Journal* or the *Review of Educational Research*.

What shall we make of this? I recognize that teaching is complex and course planning difficult and that strong effects on tasks so demanding are not likely. But does educational research have *any* noticeable effects? I must confess that I believe the variance in teaching abilities to be as wide in schools of education as it is in history departments – and the mean no higher.

Despite these observations, it still does not seem intuitively correct to say that educational research does not inform educational practice. What researcher among us wants to entertain the idea, let alone conclude, that the research in education that we do or have done has no impact on the education of the young? Such thoughts are disquieting. Perhaps we can take some consolation in the idea that *some* educational practices have changed as a result of educational research – programs using operant conditioning to shape the behavior of autistic children, programs in the teaching of reading using, for example, the DISTAR materials. Surely there are dozens of others. Yet even these programs need to be intelligently interpreted and employed. Teachers have no algorithm to which to appeal. These programs are not easily generalized in prescriptive ways to large populations of students in a variety of schools and school districts. In addition, their benefits are far from clear.

But what about the impact of research on our image of the child, our conception of thinking, and our view of perception? Our images of the child, thinking, and perception are certainly different today from those held at the turn of the century. Research must surely have had something to do with shaping those images, and surely new images of the learner and of learning affect practice.

As plausible as these observations seem, we should not become too comfortable. In the first place, many – perhaps most – changes in practice emanating from new views of the learner *preceded* rather than followed the findings of educational research. We built architecturally open schools *before*, not after, we studied their effects. We unscrewed desks from the classroom floor *before*, not after, we researched the effects of small-group instruction. We embraced a problem-centered curriculum *before*, not after, we investigated the effects of problem-centered tasks on cognitive development. In short, I believe our propensity to change practice is a function of the attractiveness of a set of ideas, rather than of the rigor of a body of data-based conclusions.

Beliefs about how children should be taught, views of what knowledge is of most worth, positions on the use of rewards in schooling need not emanate from those in the research community, nor must they be based on empirical evidence to be found attractive. Much of what we do in the schools is influenced in some way by such beliefs, models, images, metaphors. But when it is, can we legitimately claim that it is educational research that is informing educational practice? Rhetoric might be informing practice – but research? I wonder. Thus you can see that when I think of educational practice – not only in the public schools but in my own School of Education – and of educational research, I find it difficult to articulate the way in which the latter informs the former.

Despite what some may think, I am not a nay-sayer for educational research. My motive is not to argue that research can have no place in educational practice. I have not chosen this theme to hound those who have committed their professional lives to the conduct of research in education.

I write with different motives. I am professionally committed to the improvement of education, and I would like educational research to be useful to those engaged in educational practice. If research is to inform both educational practice in the schools as well as our own teaching, I believe that researchers will need to do something quite different from what we have been doing over the past 80 years. I am not sanguine about forthcoming breakthroughs from cognitive science; I have enough gray hairs to have a sense of déjà vu when I hear such forecasts. I am not optimistic about the putative benefits of tightly controlled experiments; classrooms are complex places, and well-controlled experiments have little ecological validity. I am not optimistic about achieving effects so robust as to vitiate interactions within classrooms.[2] Children have an enormous capacity to learn how to cope with treatments that they wish to manage for their own purposes.

Where does this leave us with regard to the place and function of research in education? Can we develop an approach to research that will be more useful for improving educational practice than what we have at present? What would such an approach look like? I believe that educational research ought to take its lead from the practices that pervade school programs. That is, those engaged in educational research should have an intimate acquaintance with life in classrooms. I say this because the tack that has been taken in educational research by educational researchers has, in the main, distanced itself from practice. We have imported concepts and theories from fields other than education and mapped them onto classroom phenomena. Thus, what has been learned from rat maze learning, the use of memory drums, and operant conditioning we have applied to teachers and students to explain how the former might go about shaping the behavior of the latter; teachers were to be guided in their work by what experimental psychologists have learned about the ways in which pigeons learned to play ping pong and rats learned to run mazes.

If one invokes the Sapir-Whorf hypothesis concerning the impact of language on perception, it seems reasonable to expect that educational researchers employing theories that were suitable for rats and pigeons – or for prisons and asylums, small communities and monasteries, the armed services and factories – are able to see those things that schools and classrooms have in common with pigeons, rats, prisons, asylums, small communities, monasteries, the armed services, and factories. To be sure, some relationships exist – even, I suspect, between pigeons and adolescents. Yet classrooms and schools are also distinctive places that use distinctive processes.

To see what is common to such settings and practices and other institutions is not necessarily to see what is unique or special about schools. To miss what is special about schools and classrooms is to diminish the probability that what will be learned will be useful to those who work in such settings. Like language, theory is both an asset and a liability. It is an asset because it provides guidelines for perception: it points us in directions that enable us to see. But it is also a liability because, while it provides the windows through which we obtain focus, it creates walls that hamper our perception of those qualities and processes that are not addressed by the concepts we have chosen to use. Our theoretical frameworks function as templates for perception – every template conceals some parts of the landscape just as it brings other parts to our attention.

To develop more relevant windows is, of course, a very difficult task. It is the task of theory construction. Theory construction, I am arguing, is more likely to be fruitful for educational practice when educational researchers become well acquainted with the life of schooling. Contact with such phenomena is more likely to yield useful concepts from which educational investigators can proceed than by extrapolating from frameworks that were designed for situations having other than educational missions.

Consider research on teaching. Most such research regards excellent teaching as a generic set of skills. The aims of most researchers are to identify the moves that effective teachers make in their classrooms, to understand the nature of their verbal behavior, and, through such analyses, to identify the factors that make for effectiveness. Often, the model of excellence is the recitation – one teacher talking, explaining something, or lecturing to students.[3] The dependent variables are frequently achievement in the three R's and satisfaction with school – typically elementary schools, where most studies of teaching occur.[4]

Is it really the case that excellent teaching of mathematics to 7-year-olds requires the same sorts of pedagogical skills as excellent teaching of history to 17-year-olds? Are kindergarten teachers excellent on the same criteria as teachers of algebra or English? What might we learn about the extent to which teaching skills are domain-specific, if we were to study excellent teachers within different disciplines and at different grade levels? What might we learn about the components of excellent teaching, if we were to carefully study artistic teachers in action? And to complicate matters further, what do different educational orientations held by teachers of different subject matters mean for what we regard as important to appraise in the study of teaching? There are a dozen ways to read a novel, eight major orientations to social studies education, over half a dozen rationales and teaching practices within art education. What might we learn by studying teachers in each of these ways, not to speak of the special conditions that different levels of schooling require?

Yet, in research on teaching, we tend to ignore the unique requirements that particular subject matters exact, the ages and developmental levels of the children being taught, and the aims to which a teacher is committed. Instead, we define our dependent variables – often using scores on standardized, norm-referenced tests of basic skills – and then try to find relationships between generic teaching skills and these outcomes. Thus we arrive at the astounding conclusion that the more time a student is engaged in studying a subject, the more likely he or she is to achieve high test scores in that subject.

What I am suggesting is that we have distanced ourselves from the phenomena that should be central to our studies, that we employ models that have been designed to deal with other than educational phenomena, and that we reduce what is a rich source of data into a pale reflection of the reality we seek to study. We do this by proscribing language that has the capacity to do justice to life as it is lived in classrooms and to teaching as it is practiced by excellent teachers.[5] For example, how can a typescript of classroom discourse that is dissected into units in order to locate patterns of speech provide robust generalizations that inform educational practitioners? Such material is radically eviscerated of most of the content of classroom life. Language exists in context; it is accompanied by gesture, expression, tempo, cadence, melody, silence, emphasis, and energy. A tape-recorded version of such activity already distorts by omission the reality it seeks to describe; it contains no visual content. When that tape is reduced even further by having it put into typescript, melody, cadence, tempo, emphasis, and energy are further obliterated. Then one more reduction into small speech units administers the coup de grâce.

Why do we use such procedures? Our absence from classrooms and our inveterate reliance on such methods as I have described are, I believe, a legacy of our own uneasiness with our status as social scientists. A great many in the educational research community wish to be known not as educators who research educational practice, but as psychologists, sociologists, or political scientists who happen to work in schools of education. As they see it, the better their work is, the more indistinguishable it will be from the work of their colleagues in the parent disciplines. Indeed, many educational researchers claim that education is not and can never be a discipline; it is an applied field – and what is applied is psychology, sociology, and so on.

If we continue the way we have been going the past 80 years, education will remain an applied field with, I fear, as much impact on educational practice in 2020 as it had on educational practice in 1980. I believe that this model and the assumptions on which it rests are inadequate. They are inadequate for dealing with the problems of practice, and they are inadequate for building a secure intellectual place for education as a field of study. As long as schools of education are nothing more than geographical conveniences for those whose work is indistinguishable from the work of specialists in the social sciences, schools of education will never have a secure place within the university. If the best work in education is indistinguishable from the work that is done in the social sciences, the best place to train educational researchers is not in schools of education but in the social science disciplines. If the social sciences define the criteria for excellence in educational research, the promotion and tenure of untenured professors of education who look like educationists is going to be very difficult indeed.[6]

To collect some information on this matter, I wrote to the deans of six research-oriented schools of education: those at the University of California-Los Angeles, Harvard University, Stanford University, the University of Chicago, the University of Illinois, and Teachers College, Columbia University. I asked the deans of these schools how many individuals were appointed as full-time members of the faculty during the Seventies, in what fields these individuals held doctorates, and of this group how many were promoted to tenure and in what fields those who attained tenure secured their doctorates. I indicated to the deans that the information that I received would be pooled and presented anonymously, as part of my vice-presidential address to the AERA. Only one institution responded – UCLA. When I mentioned to William Cooley, then president of the AERA, that I was not able to collect the data that I wanted, he sagely replied, 'I think you have.'

What I believe we need if educational research is truly to inform educational practice is the construction of our own unique conceptual apparatus and research methods. The best way I know of for doing this is to become familiar with the richness and uniqueness of educational life. If we are sufficiently imaginative, out of such familiarity can come ideas, concepts, and theories of educational practice. Out of these theories can come methods of inquiry that do not try to achieve levels of precision better suited to fields other than our own.

Consider, for example, our proclivity to avoid confounding in the experiments we conduct in the schools. What we do is to abbreviate experimental treatment time in order to maximize control and thus to increase our ability to interpret. Superficially, this does not seem to be an unreasonable goal. Yet its consequences are often unfortunate. Consider the length of treatment in educational experiments. I reviewed all of the 15 experimental studies published during 1981 in the *American Educational Research Journal*. Of the 10 studies out of the 15 that reported experimental treatment time per student, the median treatment time was one hour and 12 minutes. Seventy-two minutes to make a difference. We conduct educational commando raids to get the data and to get out. Yet 72 minutes is almost a 60% increase over the average amount of treatment time per student that educational researchers reported in 1978. The studies published that year in the *American Educational Research Journal* reported an average experimental treatment time of 45 minutes. How can we hope to achieve *educationally* significant results when the models of inquiry we employ virtually preclude achieving them?

As you can see, I am skeptical about the current impact of educational research on educational practice, and I am not sanguine about its future impact, if we continue to do what we have been doing in the past. If educational research is to inform educational practice, researchers will have to go back to the schools for a fresh look at what is going on there. We will have to develop a language that is relevant to educational practice, one that does justice to teaching and learning in educational settings, and we will need to develop methods of inquiry that do not squeeze the educational life out of what we study in such settings.

The achievement of these aims – and they are enormously difficult ones – will do much to contribute a sense of intellectual integrity to the field of education. It will do much to create the kind of knowledge that practitioners will find useful. But even with the development of the field's own language and with its own array of appropriate research methods, educational research will, in my view, always – in principle – fall short of what practitioners need. Let me explain why.

As it is now conceptualized, educational research is a species of scientific inquiry, and scientific inquiry couches its conclusions and its theories in a language of propositions. Science makes assertions, it provides explanations, and it specifies the means or criteria by which propositions about the world can be refuted or verified. Because in science it is propositions that must carry forward meanings about empirical matters and because propositions can never (in principle) exhaust the meanings of the qualities for which they stand, propositions are de facto reductions of the realities we hope to know.[7]

Because the realities of the classroom and of social life in general are, at base, an array of qualities for which meanings are construed, they will always present more to the perceptive teacher than propositional language can ever capture. The particularity of a set of conditions, the uniqueness of an individual child, the emotional tone of something said in love or in anger, the sense of engagement when a class is attentive will always elude the language of propositions. Yet it is precisely these qualities that the teacher must address in his or her own work. The language of propositions is a gross indicator of such qualities: it cannot capture nuance – and in teaching as in human relationships nuance is everything. It is nuance that converts repetition to repetitiousness, assertiveness to boorishness, diffidence to shyness, inquisitiveness to prying, dignity to aloofness. Theory in science cannot, I suggest, even in principle, replicate the qualities of life as it is lived. And yet it is these qualities upon which subtle pedagogical decisions must be made. The teacher who cannot see such qualities in his or her classroom cannot know what needs to be known to function effectively. Theory and generalizations from educational research can provide a guide – but never a substitute – for the teacher's ability to read the meanings that are found in the qualities of classroom life.[8]

Propositions and theory fall short for another reason as well. The rationality of action and the logic of exposition may very well appeal to different psychological bases. Exposition is sequential; action requires the perception of configurations in space. The simultaneity found in the patterns of context is lost in the sequence of propositions. Grasping these patterns of context and modifying one's decisions almost cybernetically, as patterns change, might depend on a kind of intelligence and a form of knowing that differ in kind from the kind of intelligence and form of knowing carried by words. To be sure, the two modes of grasping the world must overlap, but the extent of the overlap, particularly in situations that one cannot completely control, may be smaller than we imagine.

If this view makes sense to you, what might it suggest for our work as researchers in education? To me it suggests that, while we can increase the relevance of educational research to educational practice by becoming intimate with practice and by developing theories that are unique to what we see, such theories, because they are propositional, will always fall short of the mark in guiding practitioners who must deal not only with the qualitative, but with the qualitative *as a particular*.

To increase the capacity of educational research to capture the qualitative, a language capable of conveying qualities must be permitted to develop. Such a language needs permission because such a language is often regarded as impressionistic and nonscientific – and therefore unworthy of our respect or admiration. Such a language *is* both impressionistic and nonscientific, but it is nonetheless worthy of our respect and admiration when its instrumental utility is high. The language of criticism is such a language.

By a *language of criticism*, I mean a language rooted in the humanities. This is a language that does not shrink from metaphor, that does not make mute the voice of the writer, that recognizes that form is an inescapable part of meaning. By a *language of criticism*, I mean a language perceptive to what is subtle, yet significant, in classrooms and schools – a language that uses the artistic, when it must, to render the subtleties of classrooms vivid to the less discerning. When well crafted, such a language provides insight and the kind of guidance that the emotionally drained language of propositions cannot provide. A language of criticism will not provide prescriptions, but it can illuminate precisely those aspects of classroom life that propositional discourse cannot locate. It enables the teacher to see and therefore to have a basis on which his or her intelligence can operate.

In the past decade we have already moved forward to a wider view of research methodology in education. Anthropological inquiry is perhaps the most prominent step that has thus far been taken in that direction. But anthropological inquiry is still a species of social science; it is a useful but still too timid step. A full complement to the social sciences will be found when humanistic sources are drawn upon for describing, interpreting, and appraising educational life. It is the humanities to which we must turn to make the particulars of the life of schooling vivid.

I sincerely hope that readers will not regard this article as pessimistic. Education is an optimistic enterprise, and I write with a sense of optimism. What is pessimistic is a failure or unwillingness to recognize our condition – to look at our professional world through glasses that allow us to see only what we wish. *That* would be pessimistic. The identification of our problems is the important first step toward their resolution. My aim here is to suggest what some of the other steps might be.

I wish to emphasize that in identifying the need to create a critical language for describing educational practice, I do so not as a replacement for the equally important need for an *educationally relevant* scientific language. We need not one but two eyes through which to see and understand what concerns us. Both achievements, if they are to be realized, are iconoclastic in character. For the kind of educational science we need, we will have to design our own ship and sail it into the waters we seek to map. For the language of criticism we need, the philosophical and political space must be provided for new forms of disclosure to be developed. Educational research will come of age when we muster the courage to move ahead in both domains so that we can, without qualification, doubt, or hesitation, say with confidence that educational research truly does inform educational practice.

Notes

1. See, for example, ELLIOT W. EISNER, (1979) *The Educational Imagination: On the Design and Evaluation of School Programs* (New York: macmillan); and idem, 'The Art and Craft of Teaching,' *Educational Leadership*, January 1983, pp. 4–13.
2. LEE J. CRONBACH, (1975) 'Beyond the Two Disciplines of Scientific Psychology,' *American Psychologist*, February, pp. 116–27.

3. See, for example, NATHANIEL GAGE, (1978) *The Scientific Basis of the Art of Teaching* (New York: Teachers College Press).

4. For an extremely lucid and intelligent review of research on teaching, see KAREN KEPLER ZUMWALT, (1982) 'Research on Teaching: Policy Implications for Teacher Education,' *Policy Making in Education: 81st Yearbook of the National Society for the Study of Education* (Chicago: University of Chicago Press), pp. 215–48.

5. It is not insignificant that, in reporting results of educational research, writers are encouraged to write in the third person, singular or plural, rather than in the first person and that students and teachers are regarded as 'subjects', rather than as students or teachers.

6. For a lucid analysis of the state of graduate education in the U.S., see HARRY JUDGE, (1982) *American Graduate Schools of Education: A View from Abroad*, a report to the Ford Foundation.

7. For a discussion of these and related matters, see ELLIOT W. EISNER, (1982) *Cognition and Curriculum: A Basis for Deciding What to Teach* (New York: Longman).

8. ELLIOT W. EISNER, Toward an Artistic Approach to Supervision,' *1983 Yearbook of the Association for Supervision and Curriculum Development*; and idem, 'On the Use of Educational Connoisseurship and Educational Criticism for Evaluating Classroom Life,' *Teachers College Record*, February 1977, pp. 345–58.

Index

accountability, 110, 220–4, 229
Acrill, J.L., 254
Adelman, C.
  see Walker and Adelman
Air Force (U.S.), 50
Alexander, R.R., 133, 148, 160, 188
Alpha and Beta tests, 3
American Educational Research
  Association, 40, 255
American Educational Research Journal,
  74, 76, 107–8, 145, 255, 259, 264
Ammons, Margaret, 49–50, 68
Anderson, Robert H., 28
anthropology, 6
'anticipatory schemata', 151–2
aptitude-treatment-interaction work,
  76
Archambault, R.O., 177
Aristotle, 149, 190, 193, 234, 253, 254
Army (U.S.), 3
Arnheim, Rudolph, 132, 207, 213,
  253
art
  and criticism, 112–16, 138, 179–80
  and curriculum development, 36–7
  and education, 47–9, 104–5
  and educational evaluation, 9–10,
    87–9, 91–2, 102, 147, 158–9
  and expression, 9
  and intelligence, 171–5
  and perception, 8–9, 34–5, 81–4,
    92–3, 154–5
  and qualitative research, 189–200
  and visual images, 7–8

  see also arts; representation;
    symbols
arts, the
  and cognition, 201–13
  and connoisseurship, 105–7,
    112–16, 130
  and the curriculum, 201–13
  and educational evaluation, 87–9
  see also art
Ashton-Warner, Sylvia, 84, 85
Assessment of Performance Unit
  (APU), 144
Ayer, Alfred Jules, 199, 253

Bach, J.S., 207, 233
'back to basics' movement, 135–6,
  184, 217–18
Bacon, Francis, 106
Baker, E.L.
  see Popham and Baker
Barone, Tom, 7, 11, 188, 199
Barton, George E., Jr, 31, 37
Beethoven, Ludwig van, 207
behaviorism, 31, 33–4, 41, 43–4, 47,
  48, 50–1, 60, 65–7, 89–90, 111–12
Belford, E.
  see Jackson and Belford
Bell, Clive, 190
Bellack analysis, 140
Bellini, G., 105
Bellow, Saul, 159, 193
Berenson, Bernard, 107
Bergman, Ingmar, 105
Berk, L.M., 133, 148, 160